Bad Choices Make Good Stories

The Heroin Scene in Fort Myers

How The Great American Opioid Epidemic of The 21st Century Began – Volume 2

ISBN: 9781947258082

Published by
Becker and Malloy
www.BeckerandMalloy.com

A raw, uncensored and brutally honest glimpse into the crazy lives of drug addicts. Shocking, heartbreaking and mesmerizing. Once you start reading, you won't be able to stop.

Oliver moves from New York to Florida. Battling with depression, he gets sucked into the seedy underworld of Fort Myers, where he encounters a number of female drug addicts. He empathizes with them because of his own traumatic past. Oliver feels compelled to try to help them escape the addict lifestyle, but he soon finds out that he is in way over his head.

Table of Contents

Dear Reader,

what you're about to read is the bizarre true story of my life. This is the second book in a trilogy.

The first book, **Going To New York***, is about growing up in Europe as a teenage hacker, and my life as a comic artist and self-made Internet millionaire in New York.*

This second book, **The Heroin Scene in Fort Myers,** *is about my years in Florida, during the Great American Opioid Epidemic. It was the lowest point of my life. After my divorce, I was struggling with severe depression and was trapped in a self-destructive cycle of codependence with not one but several drug addicts.*

The third and final book, **Finding Happiness in Los Angeles***, is about my new life as a writer in California.*

But first: the Florida years. This book is not for the faint of heart. It's not a pretty story. It involves lots of sex, drugs, and really bad choices. We Europeans are not fans of censorship. We don't have a habit of bleeping words on TV, like Americans do, or blanking out words because someone might be offended. So there is no flowery language. No harmless euphemisms. It's the unvarnished truth in all its brutal ugliness.

The first book ended, when my drug-addicted girlfriend Alice ran away from rehab, and I decided to move to Fort Myers without her. And this book continues exactly where we left off.

Oliver

WELCOME TO FORT MISERY

*"You come to Fort Myers on vacation, leave on
probation, and come back on a violation."*
Local Saying

Alice and I had planned to renovate the condo in Bonita
Springs together. She loved the way I had decorated the
mansion in the Poconos, so we planned to recreate the
interior of that big house in the condo in Florida, only
on a smaller scale.

But when I arrived in Florida, I was so heartbroken,
miserable and depressed, the last thing I wanted to do
was start some big renovation project. Especially not all
alone. I didn't feel like doing anything. Nothing seemed
to bring me any kind of joy. I tried cheering myself up
by going to the beach. But when I got there, I couldn't
wait to go home and wallow in misery in the privacy of
my own home. Movies couldn't hold my attention, and
video games seemed boring and pointless. Nothing I
used to enjoy could cheer me up.

I spent hours lying on the floor or on the bed, just
staring at the ceiling. I wasn't even thinking about
anything. My mind was blank, and I just stared at
nothing. And before I knew it, the day was over. This
went on day after day. Life was painful. I felt like I was
never going to be happy again. Like there was no point
to even go on living. I wasn't really suicidal. I wasn't
thinking about killing myself. But continuing to live
and be this miserable seemed so pointless.

As a child, when all that stuff with my alcoholic father was going on, I often felt trapped by my problems, like a bird in a cage. When things were really bad, I thought about killing myself, and ending all my problems. I began to look at suicide as an emergency exit from my cage. I told myself that if I really couldn't take it anymore, I could leave the cage at any time. Suddenly I didn't feel so powerless anymore. Now I had a choice.

Every time I faced another situation that made me miserable, I asked myself if it was so unbearable that I should just leave my problems behind by escaping through my emergency exit. But now that I had a choice, and I no longer felt like the powerless victim of circumstances that were beyond my control, my problems really didn't seem all that bad anymore.

Was a bad grade on my math test really worth killing myself over? No, of course not. In a few weeks or months from now, this math test would be long forgotten. The thought that I could commit suicide if I really wanted to, was actually comforting to me. It helped me put trivial little problems into perspective. Don't sweat the small stuff. And it's all small stuff. In the grand scheme of things, almost nothing that happens ever really matters in the long run. I still have the same laid back attitude today. I guess once your own dad tries to kill you, nothing else seems all that scary anymore.

So I didn't really want to kill myself after losing Alice. But I didn't really want to go on living either. I didn't eat for 8 days. Not because I wanted to starve myself to death, but because I just wasn't hungry, and I had no interest in food. My world was not ok without Alice.

Have you ever played Silent Hill? Your game character explores a haunted village, cut off from the rest of a world by a mysterious fog. Every now and then your character falls into a different dimension, where the same village now looks grotesque and evil. Like the whole world has cancer. That's how I felt without Alice. It was still the same world, but somehow everything was different.

When I had been hanging out with Liz the yoga pothead about a year or two earlier, she was very self-conscious about her body. She was so short that even just a few extra pounds made her look like a chubby garden gnome in her head. As a teenager she had been anorexic, and even when she was in her 20s, she still struggled with her body image.

One day she told me that she was going to go on some kind of new age three day cleansing fast. She was going to eat nothing for three whole days. She claimed it was good for the body and the soul. Plus it's a great way to lose a few extra pounds. She asked me if I wanted to go on the three day fast with her. Well, she had already talked me into smoking pot for the first time, so why the hell not go on some silly three day hunger strike, too? Who knows, maybe I'd like it. (Yeah, right.)

I was fucking STARVING by the end of the first day. I thought each day the hunger pains would get worse and worse. But they didn't. Once your hunger reaches a certain level, it maxes out. It doesn't get worse. You're just really hungry all the time.

After completing the three day fast, I was proud of myself. I had accomplished my goal and resisted temptation. I had cleansed myself. And I had not given into the urge to shove some food in my mouth, no matter how strong that urge was. And when you haven't eaten in three days, a chocolate donut starts to look an awful lot like crack, believe you me.

When Liz and I met at the Sushi restaurant in New Paltz, to celebrate our victory over food, I proudly told her how I had kept telling myself, "food is an addiction, food is an addiction," every time I felt tempted to grab some food and break my promise to myself.

She was suspiciously quiet. Finally she fessed up and admitted that she had relapsed after just one day of staying off food. She hadn't told me, because she felt stupid, and because she didn't want to discourage me. So, like an idiot, I had starved myself for three damn days for no good reason.

Now I was so hungry that I ordered 2 full meals at the Sushi restaurant. When I weighed myself the next morning, I weighed more than before I had started the fast. So starving myself for three days had actually made me gain weight. Go figure.

Anyway, back to my deep dark vortex of depression, after I moved to Florida without Alice. I didn't eat for eight days in a row. And it didn't even bother me. My depression was so intense, it was even stronger than extreme hunger.

And I had nobody. No support network. No close friends who could come over and pat me on the back while I whine about how much I miss Alice. For several weeks, I was a shut in. I didn't want to go outside, because there was nothing out there that interested me. The only two people I talked to on the phone every day were Alice's friend Becky, and Linda the con artist turned hooker. Both were 1200 miles away, in New York. Both of them listened to me whine on the phone for hours every day. That couldn't have been easy. But they called me back every day to comfort me. (And to get their foot in the door.)

After a few weeks, I told myself it couldn't go on like this. If I ever wanted to be happy again, I needed to go out there and meet some new people. Make some friends in Florida.

But I had no ambition to go out on a blind date with some stranger and try to force myself to make small talk. I didn't have the strength to be witty, charming or amusing. And who would want to go out on a date with a sullen, bitter, dull, totally depressed sad sack? Nobody.

It was a vicious cycle. I didn't want to go out and meet someone new, because I was depressed. And as long as I didn't meet someone new, I was going to continue to be depressed.

Finally I had an idea. It seemed like the perfect solution at the time. I was going to approach this like any other problem I had tackled in the past, and take the path of least resistance. I was going to take the easiest shortcut to reach my goal. At this point, my goal was simply to get laid. (Shut up. Don't judge me.)

I figured that having sex would make me forget about how miserable I felt. At least for a little while. And who knows, maybe I'd meet a nice girl, have sex with her a bunch of times, and we'd actually get to know each other, like each other, and we'd end up in a real long term relationship.

In hindsight, that was obviously the dumbest plan ever. But at the time it seemed like a valid approach to ending my depression. (Obviously my cognitive abilities were a little impaired at the time.) So I was going to try to meet a girl that's wife-material by posting an online ad looking for a hoe. What could possibly go wrong?

HUSSY

"Don't trust a hoe, never trust a hoe..."
3OH!3

I posted an online ad, looking for a girl who might be interested in a mutually beneficial relationship. Rrright to the good stuff! She'd get what she really wants, and I'd get what I was looking for, without the tedious hassle of getting to know each other on awkward dates first.

Several girls responded to my ad. Hussy was one of them. Of course her name wasn't really Hussy. But it's my book, so I'm going to call her whatever I want.

Hussy was a short, petite 27-year-old with blonde hair. She wasn't exactly the most beautiful girl in the world, but she wasn't all that bad looking either. She had been in a bad car accident as a teenager, and she was self-concious about the big, noticeable scars on her pale forehead. About a year or two later, after we had gotten so close we had planned on moving in together, she revealed that she had lost all her teeth in the accident as well and was wearing dentures. She said only 3 people had ever seen her without her false teeth in: her mother, her baby daddy, and me. Apparently I really did have a way of making girls feel comfortable around me.

Anyway, let's start at the beginning: I had finally mustered enough energy to hire a handyman to renovate my condo. When Hussy came over for the first time, my place looked like a war zone.

We went straight into the bedroom, sat on the bed and talked for a few minutes. She told me she was taking care of 4 small children all by herself and needed to make money. Then we had sex. She had no boobs at all, except for dark nipples that poked out of her flat chest like two large peas. After seeing Hussy's nonexistent boobs, I realized how spoiled I had been with my ex-wife Donna's boobs. She had really nice 36 Ds, and during all our years of marriage, I had just taken them for granted.

Hussy was very shy and soft-spoken. We felt comfortable around each other and we started hanging out every day. At first she only stayed for a few minutes of chatting and then sex. But after a few days she stayed longer, and we often ended up having sex a second time, after taking a break for about an hour and talking, or getting something to eat at Bice, my favorite restaurant at the Coconut Point Mall.

Hussy opened up to me about her sad life and told me that her father had raped her for years when she was just a little girl. Then she ended up in several abusive relationships with guys who beat her regularly. It was a familiar story that I had heard many times before by now, and would hear many more times from other girls I met after Hussy. It was pretty obvious that it's really true: people who grow up in abusive households often end up in abusive relationships.

She told me she was trying to get away from her abusive ex, Dick, so she had recently moved back in with her parents. But she was afraid her father might rape her baby daughter, just like he had raped Hussy when she was younger. I found out later that pretty much every word out of her mouth was a lie, so I'm not sure if her father ever even really raped her.

I found out two years later that Hussy really hadn't moved in with her parents, and never really left her ex Dick, but that she and Dick had moved in with Dick's sister Nicole for a few weeks, until I offered Hussy to stay at one of my rental houses for free, because I felt so bad for her after all the sob stories she had told me about her life.

At one point she claimed the tires on her truck were so bald, it was dangerous to drive around in it. Especially with her kids in the truck. I ended up giving her $400 for new tires.

When she moved into my rental house, a duplex in Lehigh Acres, she needed new furniture, and told me one of her friends was about to sell everything in their apartment for only $400, because they were moving up north. Supposedly she had to act fast, or the furniture was going to be sold to someone else. So I gave her another $400.

Hussy had a restraining order against Dick, and wanted to lift it, but one of the requirements was that she had to take domestic abuse counseling classes first. Those classes teach battered women how to recognize early warning signs of dangerous situations and things like that.

I asked her why in the world she would want to lift the

restraining order, if Dick is such an abusive asshole. She said so he could visit their baby daughter. Later I found out that it was really because they were actually living together.

One day, when I picked her up after one of those classes, she told me that in a weird way, getting hit made her feel loved. That blew my mind. But after thinking about it for a while, it started to make sense. Girls who grow up in abusive homes see violence as a normal part of life. And they start to believe that they deserve to be hit, if they step out of line. They tell themselves that if their man hits them, it's because she did something to upset him, and he'll say things like: "Look what you made me do!"

They tell themselves that their man only hits them, because his feelings are so strong for her, he just can't control his anger and frustration. And somehow their brains translate violence into love. I guess it's a coping mechanism, like Stockholm syndrome.

I had a hard time seeing the link between love and abuse. Then again, wasn't that exactly the same thing I always told myself about my ex-wife Donna's outbursts? She lost her temper all the time and threw hateful tantrums, if I didn't do exactly what she wanted. And I told myself it was a sign of how much she loved me, and how much she couldn't control her jealousy, because her feelings for me were so strong. But that was really just my way of coping with her emotional abuse.

Anyway, Hussy called me hysterically crying one day,

and said her mother had been arrested, because Hussy and her sister Amber had gotten into big fight. Amber was a drug addict and Hussy felt that Amber was not taking care of her two kids as well as she should. Hussy and Amber started hitting each other. Then their mother got in the middle of it. Someone called the cops, and their mother ended up getting arrested for smacking Amber.

Now Hussy was frantically trying to get bond money to bail her mom out of jail, because she had a heart condition, and without her medication, she might have a heart attack in jail. I ended up giving Hussy $500 to bail out her mother. Or so I thought. A few months later I found out her mother really didn't go to jail that night. Dick did, after hitting Hussy, and she called the cops on him. So I had wired Hussy money to bail out her abusive "ex" boyfriend, who really wasn't her "ex" at all.

After Linda had conned me into paying for several fake abortions in Pennsylvania a year or two earlier, of course I was weary. I had my suspicion that Hussy may be lying about her mother going to jail. Then again, what kind of a person would lie about something like that? And Hussy was so upset at my doubting her at a time like this, she threw the phone on the floor in despair.

Her father picked up the phone and texted me that Hussy was so upset about her mother going to jail, he was afraid she might try to kill herself again. Apparently Hussy had attempted suicide at least half a dozen times. This was not the time for annoying questions, I thought, so I wired her the money to get her mom out. Later I found out I really hadn't been texting with her dad. That was really Hussy pretending to be her dad texting me. How sick is that?

A few weeks later her dad suddenly went to jail. Or so Hussy claimed. Once again it was a life or death situation, and Hussy was about to kill herself unless I was going to send her money to bail her father out. Later I found out that whole story wasn't true either.

Then Amber died from a drug overdose. Hussy was distraught over the loss of her beloved sister. Sure, they had their fights. All sisters do. But deep down they loved each other. And now Hussy was beside herself with grief. Well, then later I found out there never was an Amber. Hussy had made her up. Amber was a figment of Hussy's imagination. Amber's two kids didn't exist either. But I didn't find all that out until much later.

Anyway, one day, after Hussy and I had spent some time together again, I went to Home Depot to buy some paint for the new crown mouldings in my condo. At the check out, I noticed that both of my debit cards were missing from my wallet.

I texted Hussy: "Damn! My ATM cards are gone. Did u see them lying around anywhere? Maybe I took them out of my wallet while paying some bills?"

Hussy replied: "I'm gonna turn around and come right back to help u look for ur cards."

I wrote back: "Nah, it's ok. I'm just gonna go home and look for them. If they're not there, I'll just cancel them."

For some reason her reply made me suspicious. Her eagerness to drive all the way back to help seemed suspect. My instincts told me she had stolen my cards and now she was scared and she was only going to "help" look for them, so she could pretend to find them somewhere, while really pulling them out of her pocket.

It reminded me of a joke Patty the drug counselor had told me: What's the difference between a drug addict and an alcoholic? An alcoholic will steal your wallet and then feel so guilty, he'll get drunk. A drug addict will steal your wallet, and then help you look for it.

On that day two other people had been at my place. A lady who measured one of the bedrooms for a new carpet, and the handyman who had been working on the condo for the past few weeks. So I didn't just want to accuse Hussy of stealing my cards, unless I was absolutely sure.

On my way home from Home Depot, the fraud department of my bank called to confirm some unusual activity on my personal debit card. I told them it had been stolen. They said that within the last hour, about $1000 had been charged to it at several different stores in the Coconut Point Mall, just down the street from my apartment. The suspicious charges began at 5:15 pm. Hussy had left my house at 5 pm. So obviously she had gone straight to the mall after she left my place and went on a wild shopping spree with my card, swiping it as a credit card, instead of a debit card, to get around the $500 daily spending limit.

I told the bank that I think I know who took my card, but that I wasn't 100% sure. They told me to call the police and tell them who I suspected. The police could get a copy of the security tapes at the stores, and have me look at them to identify the thief.

A few minutes later the fraud department called me again. This time they told me about suspicious activity on my business debit card. Someone had spent almost $1000 on that card in the past hour as well.

Then I texted Hussy: "I talked to my bank's fraud department. They said I should call the police."

"Yeah, definitely," she replied.

"I don't want to do that yet though. I want to talk to u first."

"Why? What do u mean?" she texted back.

"The bank people told me the cops can get the stores' security tapes and I can identify the thief. So I want to talk to u first."

"Are u saying I took ur cards?" she replied.

"I'm just saying I want to talk to u in person first, because whoever took my cards is going to jail."

That's when she broke down, and admitted that she stole them. She texted me that she didn't know what had come over her, and that stealing was totally unlike her. She said she was taking care of 7 children, and she just didn't know how to make ends meet, even with the money I had been giving her.

I felt really bad for her, so I didn't press charges. I forgave her, because I figured, if I was in her shoes, and I was a single parent taking care of 7 kids, I too may do things I'm not proud of.

A few days went by, and we made up. Suddenly, while we were having lunch at Bice, she mentioned that it was going to be her birthday the next day.

"What? Why didn't you tell me that sooner? We could have done something nice for your birthday," I said.

"It's ok. My parents are Jehovah's Witnesses, and growing up, I never had a birthday. So I'm used to nobody remembering my birthday or celebrating it," she replied.

"Aww, that's so sad," I said. "Well, that's all the more reason to make this birthday extra special. How about I take you to Miami Beach tomorrow, and we go to the beach for a while and then we'll have dinner at a nice restaurant?"

"I would love that! Thank you so much," she said with a big smile.

A day or two earlier, while we were grocery shopping for her kids at Walmart on Colonial Boulevard, she had longingly stared at a laptop and mentioned that she was so broke, she didn't even have a computer.

So I figured I'd make her birthday extra special by surprising her with that laptop she liked.

When she came over the next morning, we drove down Alligator Alley to get to the East Coast. During the car ride, I handed her the gift-wrapped laptop. She was ecstatic. Once we got to South Beach, we went swimming and then had dinner at a fancy restaurant on Ocean Drive. She told me this was the best birthday of her life. That made me feel really good. At the last minute, without any advance notice, I pulled off a pretty nice birthday for her. Later I found out that day wasn't even her birthday. It was just a scam to get a new laptop.

A few days later, I happened to check my bank account on the computer. I noticed a few checks I didn't recognize. Each one was for anywhere around $700 to $900. I clicked on each one, to see a scanned image of the front of the check. That wasn't my handwriting. All these checks were fake. Someone had stolen 8 checks from me, filled them out, and deposited them. Guess who? Hussy.

She was not exactly a criminal mastermind, because she didn't even bother to make the checks out to cash. She actually made them out to herself, and then faked my signature. I have no idea how she thought she was going to get away with that. I called her up and screamed at her: "I just saw you stole checks from me. ARE YOU OUT OF YOUR FUCKING MIND?!?"

Hussy started to cry and told me that it had been a moment of weakness. She said she had stolen the checks on the same day she had stolen my debit cards, she just didn't cash them right away. She said her sister Amber's death had made her crazy with grief. And now that she had to take care of Amber's two young kids on top of her own 5 children, she had lost it.

At this point I didn't know yet that the entire story about Amber was completely made up, but I had it with Hussy anyway. I had forgiven her after she stole my debit cards and charged $2000 on them. But now she had cashed 8 stolen checks, for a total of about $7000. This was not just a momentary lapse in judgment. There was method behind her madness. She cashed the stolen checks every few days. So she knew she was stealing from me again and again. There was no way I was going to let her get away with that. I was gonna put that fucking bitch in jail.

She said she hadn't even spent any of the money, and that it was all still in her bank account. I told her: "You better be here tomorrow morning before 10 am and bring me back all my money, and the laptop, or I'm calling the cops!"

I was going to call the cops either way, but I wanted to get my money and my laptop back first.

The next morning she brought me the laptop and handed me $600. I looked at the cash and asked: "What is that?"

Hussy was so nervous, while I counted the money, she

threw up. Then she said: "That's all that's left. I don't know what happened to the rest. I thought it was all still in my account, but when I checked today, it was all gone, except the $600."

"Get the FUCK outta here!" I said. She quietly cried, got in her car and left.

As soon as she was gone, I called the Lee County Sheriff's office. They sent a deputy. I filed a report and told him what had happened. He asked me to describe Hussy, so I did. Then he asked me for her date of birth. Since we had just celebrated her birthday a few days earlier, I knew exactly when her birthday was.

The deputy said: "I think I know who you're talking about, but that's not her date of birth."

"Yeah, it is," I replied.

"Come with me, we'll look at my computer," the officer said.

On the dashboard laptop in his police cruiser, the officer pulled up Hussy's mugshot. She had a bunch of prior charges for writing bad checks. Yupp. That was definitely her in the mugshot, and her birthday was definitely not last week. And that's when I realized that we had celebrated a fake birthday just so that she could con me into buying her a laptop. Motherfucker! What kind of a sick, twisted psycho does something like that?!

I told the officer that I wanted her to rot in jail for

playing me like that. He said she would, but first I would have to speak to a detective in the financial crimes unit. The deputy said he was just here to take the report, but I would have to wait for a detective to actually work on the case. And that was going to take at least a week.

"What am I supposed to do until then?" I asked. "If I don't talk to her anymore, she'll know something is up, and she'll skip town. Her parents recently moved to Ocala. So she'll probably hide up there."

"If she tries to run, we'll issue a warrant," the officer said. "She can't hide forever. We'll catch her eventually. But for now, just pretend everything is ok, so she has no reason to run."

So for the next few days, I pretended I had forgiven her, just like I had done when I found out about her stealing my debit cards. Hussy came over every day, as usual, and we had sex as usual, hung out, watched TV, or went to the mall, or out to eat.

About a week later, a detective called me. I told him what she had done and that I wanted her to go to jail. He said he couldn't just go arrest her. He said he would have to call her into his office and talk to her first.

A few minutes later, Hussy called me, hysterically crying: "You said you wouldn't call the cops!"

"No, that's what I said when you stole my debit cards," I replied. "But you stole my checks on top of that. Of course I'm gonna call the cops. You psycho stole $7000 from me!"

"If I have to go to jail, I'm going to lose my kids! DCF is gonna take them away from me! I can't live without my kids! If you press charges, I'm gonna kill myself!"

"Don't worry," I said. "Just admit everything. If you cooperate, they'll take it easy on you. You'll probably just get probation, or you'll have to pay me back or something. You're not gonna go to jail."

I was just lying to her to get her to confess everything to the detective. I wanted that bitch to go to jail so badly! I wasn't just mad about her stealing from me. My feelings were hurt, because she kept telling me she loved me, and then she just used me like that. And my pride was hurt, because she made a fool out of me. Now it was my turn to pay her back. And when someone fucks me over that bad, I get really vindictive.

Hussy went to the Sheriff station and admitted everything. She gave a full confession. Then the detective called me: "Did you tell this girl she's not going to jail if she admits everything?"

"Well, uhh, yeah. I didn't want her to run away," I said.

"You can't promise something like that. Check fraud is a serious crime. Each check she wrote is an automatic 1 year in jail. She wrote 8 checks, so she's going to jail for 8 years," the detective explained.

A few minutes later, after Hussy left the Sheriff station, she called me up, sobbing: "I'm not going to jail! I'm not losing my babies! I'm gonna kill myself! If you press charges I'll kill myself! I've tried to kill myself many times, but this time I'll really do it!" She was crying so hard, it was difficult to understand her.

I have a soft heart. I guess I'm what they call a bleeding heart liberal. When someone fucks me over, instead of feeling bad for myself, I end up feeling bad for them, because I think about what happened in their lives to make them the way they are. What got them to this point? If I went through what they went through, wouldn't I be at the same point now, doing the same things?

I wanted Hussy to go to jail for a bit. Maybe 6 months. Maybe even a year. But 8 years? Wow, that was harsh! Yeah, DCF would definitely take her kids away, and yeah, I really could see her kill herself over that. I didn't want to live with that guilt. So I called the detective back and told him to drop the charges.

Hussy and I didn't talk to each other for a few days, but she kept calling me over and over, asking me to forgive her, and that she loved me, and she wanted to make it up to me. A few days later I caved, and she started coming over again, and we had sex two or even three times every day again. At that point I didn't know yet that she was still with her "ex" Dick, and that they were living in my duplex together.

Easter was coming up. I took Hussy to Walmart to pick out some clothes for her kids, and candy. We planned to spend Easter together. But then, the day before Easter, she said her parents were coming down from Ocala, and they were going to bring along some other relatives, and that they were all a bunch of rednecks who argued at family gatherings, and that I wouldn't enjoy being around them. So suddenly our plans were cancelled. I was all alone on Easter.

That really bummed me out. Easter isn't that big a deal to me. Being alone on Christmas or my birthday would have been a lot worse. But just the fact that, for the first time in my life, I was spending a major holiday all alone, really got to me. Up until now, I had spent every holiday with my parents, or my ex-wife Donna, or my ex-girlfriend Alice. But now Hussy totally left me hanging on a big holiday. I was depressed. I felt really alone.

I spent Easter playing around on Facebook. I stumbled across Hussy's Facebook page. I didn't even know she had one. On her page, she was posting in real time about her Easter. Her family had not come down from Ocala. That was just another one of her lies. In fact, she posted on her Facebook page how much she missed her family this holiday. Instead she was spending Easter with her own little family at home: Dick and the kids. That was the moment when I found out she had been lying to me for months, about having left her "ex" and being a single mother. None of it was true.

I was really upset. I got on a plane and flew to Europe for a few days. Hussy had been trying to come over the day after Easter, but I wouldn't answer her calls or texts. She got scared and asked me why I was ignoring her. I texted her that I had found out the truth about her and Dick living together in my house and that I wanted nothing to do with her anymore. We didn't talk to each other for a few months.

I wanted to get them out of my house. At first I was going to evict them, but apparently that takes a long time in Florida. So instead I just sold the duplex, with them in it, on Ebay. A real estate investor in New York bought it. I told him that the tenants were nothing but trouble, with criminal records and a history of domestic violence. He thanked me for the heads up and evicted them.

PLENTY OF FISH

*"Online dating is just as murky and full of lemons
as finding a used car in the classifieds."*
Laurie Perry

Obviously the ad for a mutually beneficial relationship
backfired. So I put a half-assed profile on Plenty Of
Fish, or POF for short. It's a free dating website.

I ended up going out on a date with Maxine. She was
32, I think, and taller than I was. And she wore high
heels when we met at a little Italian restaurant on
Bonita Beach Road. She towered over me like a giant
Amazonian. And she had broad, manly shoulders. She
reminded me of a Football player. She probably could
have given me a piggyback ride around the parking lot.

Over dinner, she told me about some of her weirder
experiences on POF. She said one guy asked her if she
was into taboo stuff.

"What do you mean by taboo?" she asked him.

"You know, tabooooo," he replied mysteriously.

"You mean like child pornography or something?"

"Sex with dogs," he said with a sparkle in his eyes.

As it turned out, he wasn't really looking for a date for
himself, but for his dog. He asked Maxine if she'd like
to have sex with his pitbull.

Apparently there's this whole big underground dog sex fetish scene. Maxine told me that this guy said there are dating websites out there that specialize in this sort of thing. People post profiles for their dogs, and then other people pick which dog they want to have sex with.

She told me that dogs can cum over and over again, without needing a break inbetween, like men do. And she described different dog breeds' penises to me.

"Uhmm, you know WAY too much about having sex with dogs," I said.

"Oh, I just asked that guy a lot of questions," she replied and laughed.

After dinner we went back to my place and talked for hours. We were sitting on my living room couch, and Maxine was smoking weed. She lived in Naples and managed some sort of charity for low income families in Immokalee.

By 2 am she was so high, she said she couldn't drive anymore. She asked if she could spend the night. I said sure. We slept in bed together, but nothing happened.

The next morning she went home to change, and then drove to Immokalee. On her way to work she texted me: "Why didn't u try to have sex with me last night? R u not attracted to me?"

"I didn't know u wanted me to," I replied.

"Why do u think I spent the night in ur bed?" she asked.

"I thought u really were too high to drive home. I didn't want to take advantage of the situation," I texted. Man, I felt like a dodo.

Later that day she texted me again: "R u an ass man or a tit man?"

"What do u mean?" I texted back. Apparently I'm a little slow sometimes.

"Do u get off looking at ass or tits? What do you like better?"

"I like breasts. So I guess I'm a breastman," I replied.

A few minutes later she texted me some pictures of herself in her office. She wore a dark, professional-looking business suit. Her white blouse was unbuttoned and her bra was open. She was flashing her breasts at me.

I guess that shoulda really got me going, but I was so not interested. I didn't even text her back. She was just too damn weird.

A few weeks later, I met Flora on POF. She was 35 and kinda heavyset. She had monster boobs. Not the porn star kind. The ten ton tilly kind. She said she managed her own party business. We went out to dinner at her favorite restaurant in Naples.

Then she asked me to come over to her place for dinner

a few days later. She had a son. I think he was maybe 9 or 10 years old. She had told him all about me, before I arrived.

At the dinner table, he suddenly asked her: "Is Oliver going to be my new dad?"

Flora replied: "Well, Mommy and Oliver have just met a few days ago, but we'll see how things go. Would you like him to be your new dad?"

"Yeah, he's nice," her son replied.

She thought that was adorable. I thought it was crrreepy.

After dinner she put her son to bed and we talked on the couch for a while. She kept telling me that she thought I was brilliant and amazing: "You're such an amazing cartoonist. You are just so brilliant."

Did I mention she thought I was amazing and brilliant?

She kept flattering me so much, I was getting really uncomfortable. I guess I'm not very good at receiving compliments, and she was laying it on really thick.

She invited me over again a few days later, but I made some excuse. I really didn't feel like hanging out with her and her kid.

We didn't talk to each other any more after that, until we reconnected again a year or two later, when I was going through some drama with my girlfriend Veronica.

But I'll get to that later.

So, when I reconnected with Flora again, we hung out a few times. Usually at her place. She cooked dinner and we watched a movie.

Then one day she texted me: "How come u have never tried to have sex with me? Is it because I'm not European?"

"I didn't know u were interested in that. I thought we were just friends," I texted back.

The next time we met, she made sure I got the hint. She talked about sex a lot that night. She told me she had threesomes with some of her guy friends. And she told me she met a guy online who was into cuckolding. She said that's when a guy likes to watch his girlfriend have sex with another guy. I told her that was not my cup of tea.

Then she asked me if I was into breastfeeding. She told me she found a fetish website a few months ago, and all the guys on there were into breastfeeding. She said she joined the forum, and started talking to a guy from Alaska. A few days later, after she sent him pictures of her ginormous udders, he flew from Alaska to Florida to meet her for a wild suckling session.

She said it was the most intense, most erotic bonding experience of her life. She told me that he took great care to pay attention to each nipple equally, to not favor one over the other. And then he suckled on her clit for the grand finale.

Then she asked me if I would like to suckle on her breasts like an infant.

"Uhh, I'm not sure," I replied.

She got all emotional, and said: "You are so brilliant, so amazing. I would be so proud if you were my son." She teared up.

She had been drinking a lot that night, and this was just getting too damn weird. I wanted to get outta there!

She kept telling me how amazing and brilliant I was, and how honored she would be to breastfeed me.

"Hmm. I'm hungry," I said. "I need a snack."

"What do you want?" she asked. She probably thought I meant I wanted some of her milk.

"What do you have? You know what, I'll go take a look myself," I said, got up and walked into the kitchen. I was going to check her cabinets, and pick something that she didn't have, so I could pretend to go get it at the store. It was after midnight by now, but there was a 24 hour Walmart just down the street. I noticed she didn't have my favorite: Nutella.

"Hmm. I'm really in the mood for a Nutella sandwich right now. Too bad you don't have any. I'm just gonna run to Walmart real quick and grab some."

"Are you sure? It's late."

"Yeah, I'll be right back," I said, and quickly exited her apartment.

I had seen comedies and sitcoms, where two people meet on a blind date, and one of them pretends to go to the bathroom and then ditches the other one. I always thought that was so unrealistic. Nobody does that. Even if you have a bad date, at least you finish your meal and say good night. Nope, tonight I found out that sometimes people really do run away. I just did. I literally ran away from a girl who wanted to breastfeed me.

While I was driving back to Bonita Springs, she texted me: "R u coming back?"

I didn't respond.

A few minutes later she texted me: "Ur not coming back, r u?"

Then a few minutes later: "REALLY?"

Then: "Wow. Seriously? WTF"

The next morning, she texted me: "I guess I'll just never be pretty enough or skinny enough for u."

Aww. That made me feel so bad, because I really hurt her feelings. I had been a real jerk. So I texted her back: "No, it's not that. U were really drunk, and u know I don't like being around drunk people. So I thought it was better if I leave. I'm sorry."

I had brought over two DVDs the previous night, because I really thought we were going to watch a movie after dinner, not have her mammaries for dessert. A few days later she texted me: "I don't hate u for leaving like that. I still got ur movies. When do u want to come get them?"

I didn't reply. She could keep the movies.

I was not a fan of Plenty Of Fish, after meeting Maxine and Flora. I figured I might as well go back to plan A, and see if I'd meet someone nice with my ad for a mutually beneficial relationship.

MORE OF HUSSY'S LIES

"I can take any truth; just don't lie to me."
Barbra Streisand

"A single lie destroys a whole reputation of integrity."
Baltasar Gracian

"We tell lies when we are afraid... afraid of what we don't know, afraid of what others will think, afraid of what will be found out about us. But every time we tell a lie, the thing that we fear grows stronger."
Tad Williams

I started seeing three girls who answered my online ad. One of them was Manuela, a medical student from Equador. She was petite, skinny, with long black hair and a perfect body. She was only 20 and had this really timid, mousy little voice. She almost sounded like a cartoon character. But she was unbelievably beautiful. She could have been a professional model. And she was smart. We often made fun of those annoying illiterate American kids, who spell everything wrong, trying to emulate some idiotic gangsta rapper, and quoting asinine lyrics, because they think being dumb and shallow makes them look cool.

Manuela was going to go back to Ocala when the next semester started, but for now she was staying at her parents' house at The Forum on Colonial Boulevard. She didn't have a car, so I usually picked her up and we'd spend time together at the The Hyatt right there. But when her parents weren't home, we had sex in her bedroom. It was a typical teenage girl's room. It hadn't changed since before she went to college. There were teddy bears on the shelves, and a lot of pink everywhere. I felt like I was living in one of those pornos, where a guy has sex with his kid's gorgeous babysitter or something.

When Manuela moved back to Ocala, I saw on her Facebook page that she started dating a one-eyed firefighter. Apparently he was the love of her life. I never heard from her again.

I was also seeing another 20 year old girl at that time. Her name was Kayla. She was a quirky math student who grew up in Sayville on Long Island, New York, not far from where I had lived in Brooklyn. Kayla was 6 feet tall and a little chubby. She had long bright red hair. She was not nearly as pretty as the medical student from Equador, but also very smart. Kayla had a great personality and she always made me laugh with her silly little jokes. We both had the same strange sense of humor. She was a little punk, with a lip piercing and the word bitch tattooed right over her pussy. She liked to wear ironic t-shirts and paint each of her nails a different color.

Kayla wanted to become a financial advisor or something like that, but she had a drug problem and had been arrested and spent some time in jail. Now she was a convicted felon, and finding a job in the financial field was going to be difficult, if not impossible. But she wasn't going to let that stop her from finishing her college degree. She was on probation, so she wasn't doing any more heroin, but she still drank like a

Russian sailor, and smoked a lot of fake weed.

And I was seeing Crystal. She was a beautiful 30-year-old, with long blonde hair. She was skinny, tall and had amazing fake boobs. She had been a stripper for a while, and a model. Then she had worked at a real estate firm, but after the market crashed, she started working as a waitress at Applebee's. The first time I met her, she was as skinny as a skeleton. It made her huge fake boobs stand out even more. She was addicted to oxycodone pills and occasionally smoked crack. She was dating this guy Jerry, a wealth management advisor at some stock brokerage. He was almost 10 years younger than her.

Every time I had sex with Crystal, she brought this huge industrial-strength dildo, that plugged into a wall outlet. She loved rubbing it on her clit while we had sex, but to me it was kinda annoying and distracting, because it was in the way. And she was one of those girls who liked to scream and moan like a porn star. Her over-the-top theatrics sometimes made me feel inadequate, because I felt like I wasn't living up to the hype.

And then there was a fourth girl, Haley. I had met her the first time I had come to Florida. I'll tell you more about her later.

I had sex with at least one of these 4 girls every day, sometimes even with two of them on the same day. I was pimpin'. I was living the rockstar life.

In June, I suddenly started getting text messages from

Patty the drug counselor. It had been a year since she had been at my condo in Florida for two weeks, to spend her birthday with me. It was almost time for her next birthday now, so she decided to get in touch with me again. We hadn't talked to each other in a year, ever since our falling out after our road trip.

Patty texted me that she couldn't stop thinking about me, and that she knew she had been acting crazy last year. She said Rocky's death really messed with her head, and her anti-depressants were all off. She said now her medication was on point, and she was doing much better. She said she wanted to come spend her birthday with me again and see where things could go with us.

I really was not interested at all in ever seeing her again, so I just ignored her texts. Patty continued to text me several times a day, and had a one-sided conversation with me. Every evening she told me about her day, about work or going grocery shopping and cooking, about a cut on her foot and her visit to the emergency room, and so on and so forth. She acted like we had an ongoing conversation, although I never wrote back.

Then she texted: "Guess what? I booked a flight for tomorrow! I'll see u soon!"

That's when I finally wrote her back: "What? No, u can't just show up here! I'm seeing someone!"

I lied. I really wasn't in a relationship with anyone. My so-called relationship with Hussy was over at this point, and I just had sex with a different girl every day, but I wasn't going to tell Patty that. I really wasn't proud of being a manwhore. I just kinda fell into that situation, because I really liked and cared about all 4 of the girls I was seeing, but I wasn't in a serious relationship with any of them.

When I first met Patty at my big house in Pennsylvania, she had told me that pretty much every drug counselor used to be an addict, who got clean and then decided to help other addicts get their life back. Patty said she was the rare exception. She had never been an addict. Some of her patients felt that made her lack credibility. How could she possibly know what they were going through, if she had never been an addict herself and walked a mile in their shoes? Patty told me her reply to them was: "A doctor doesn't have to be a diabetic to understand diabetes and help a diabetic patient."

But after she had been acting so weird at my condo in Florida during those two sex-crazed weeks, and after she had been having a one sided text conversation with me a year later, I was starting to wonder if Patty really did not have some sort of substance abuse problem. She had told me that she takes Xanax to help her sleep, and that she likes to drink red wine.

When she texted me that she had bought a plane ticket and was coming to Florida uninvited, to spend her next birthday with me, and I told her not to come because I was seeing someone else, she totally lost it. She texted me over 40 messages between midnight and 4 am. Most of them didn't even make sense. She called me a snapping turtle. She said I lied to her. Apparently she thought I was still dating Alice, even though I hadn't seen Alice since she ran away from rehab in Rhinebeck, NY and I had moved to Florida by myself.

Patty texted me that she was going to call the cops on me for harboring a drug addict at my house. She said she'd have me deported, because this is America and she's an American but I'm only a guest here. She became totally unhinged and sent one hateful text after another.

Apparently she was still just as crazy as she had been a year earlier. I had the feeling she was drinking wine that night and mixed it with Xanax, and now she was drunk texting me this incoherent drivel. I texted her back that she was nuts, and that I never wanted to hear from her again. Then I blocked her number.

That didn't stop her. The next day, Patty really did fly down to Fort Myers, and really did come to my condo. She didn't knock on my door though. Or maybe she did while I wasn't home. I don't know. But a day or two later, she posted pictures of the outside of my condo on her Facebook page, as proof that she had really come to see me. How fucking weirrrd is that? I was starting to feel like I had an actual stalker.

I told Kayla the whole story with Patty. She thought it was hilarious that Patty the counselor was supposed to help other people get their shit together, but she was the biggest train wreck of them all.

A few months went by. Kayla met this guy Alex, and moved in with him. Meanwhile Hussy and I had started talking again.

Hussy told me that she was really sorry about all the lies she had told me in the past, and she felt really bad about the way she treated me. After I had called the cops on her for stealing my checks, she had not only handed me my laptop and $600, but she had also given me 3 or 4 letters. She claimed she had written them right after stealing my debit cards and checks. They were love letters and a full confession. She said she wanted to give me those letters before I found out on my own what she had done, but then she didn't, because she was too scared.

In those love letters, Hussy wrote how bad she felt about stealing from me, because I had treated her better than anyone else had ever treated her, and she really enjoyed being around me. She wrote that she had fallen in love with me. When I read the letters, I figured she had not really written them in the previous few weeks, before getting caught, but right after I screamed at her on the phone, once I had found out that she robbed me, and demanded that she bring me the laptop and my money back the next day.

Now, after we finally started talking to each other again a few months later, she said she had really meant the things she wrote in those letters. And she said she felt so stupid that she had still been living with Dick after meeting me. She claimed she had grown up a lot over the past few months, and realized that she did not want to be with a guy like Dick, who treats her like shit. She wanted to be in a relationship with me, because I had been so nice to her. She said, if I would give her another chance, she would show me that she could be a great girlfriend and make me happy.

I really didn't trust her, but I rrreally liked having sex with her. She had her tubes tied, so she wasn't worried about getting pregnant anymore. Actually she told me she would love it if I could get her pregnant again somehow. She let me cum inside of her every time. And she may not have been the prettiest girl in the world, but she had the tightest pussy I had ever felt. I'm not exactly small I guess, and I couldn't even get inside of her, when I got on top of her. We usually had to start having sex by her lying on top of me, and slowly, gently, easing her way down onto my dick, inch by painful inch, until it was finally completely inside of her after a few minutes.

I agreed to give her another chance, and she started coming over every day again. The New York investor who had bought the duplex she lived in had evicted her and Dick. Hussy said that after that, she and Dick split up, and she and her kids moved into a house near Sunshine Boulevard in Lehigh Acres. Her younger sister, Ferrara, who used to live with Hussy's parents in Ocala, came down to Lehigh Acres and moved in with Hussy.

Hussy had a teenage son who didn't live with her. He was being raised by Hussy's mother in Ocala. And she had two mixed boys with a black guy. She brought them over to meet me. They looked so different, I had a feeling they had two different black fathers. She got very offended by my question and told me her black baby daddy had accused her of the same thing, and he

47

had beaten her many times because he believed that she had been cheating on him and that the second black boy wasn't really his. I figured he was probably right.

Her 4th kid was a little baby girl, Bonny. Dick was Bonny's father. He was about 15 years older than Hussy, and he started having sex with her when she was only 14. As I found out later, he was a drug dealer who lived in a trailer with his mother, in North Fort Myers, near Suncoast Park. He sold his mother's pain pills to drug addicts in Suncoast.

The residents of Suncoast like to brag that it's the largest trailer park in the world, according to the Guinness Book of World Records. I'm not sure if that's really something to brag about, but oh well, I guess people cherish life's little victories wherever they may find them.

Dick had three children from a previous relationship. His kids were much older than Hussy's kids. Dick had a teenage boy, Little Dickey, and two older teenager daughters, Summer and Lucy. Lucy was the oldest, and only 7 years younger than her new stepmom, Hussy.

Hussy told me all sorts of horror stories about Dick. She said he had not only raped and beaten her in front of her children, but he also raped his much younger sister, Nicole, ever since she was 4 years old. Hussy told me he had even raped his younger brother Anthony repeatedly, until Anthony finally committed suicide. Nicole had also tried to kill herself many times, because of the near constant rape in her childhood. And Hussy had tried to kill herself several times, too. Apparently good ole Saint Dick spread his special Christmas cheer wherever he went.

I asked Hussy if Dick ever raped his teenage daughters Summer and Lucy. Hussy said she didn't think so, but she wasn't sure. Both of them were now drug addicts, just like Dick's sister Nicole. Big surprise. What I went through with my abusive father was pretty rough. But he never raped me. I can't even imagine how badly that would have fucked me up. And if someone had offered me some pills to make me forget my pain for a little while, of course I would have taken them, and of course I'd be an addict now, too.

A few months after the check debacle, Hussy and I made up and we started seeing each other every day again. After a few weeks I noticed that she always came over to my place, but never invited me over to her new place near Sunshine Boulevard in Lehigh. I thought that was odd. She said it was because her sister Ferrara, who was now Hussy's roommate, didn't like to have people come over to their house. I told her, if we're dating, then I'm not just "people" and Ferrara really has no right to tell Hussy that she can't have me come over. I started to get suspicious. My spider senses were tingling.

I decided to hack Hussy and find out where exactly she lived now. Then I drove by her house unannounced. I figured, if I had done that months ago, when she still lived in my rental duplex, I would have found out much sooner that she was lying to me all day long, and her "ex" Dick was still living with her, in one of my rental houses, rent free.

When I drove by Hussy's new place, she just so happened to be sitting outside, on the stoop, smoking a cigarette. I stopped in front of her driveway, and waved hello. I was gonna pretend I just so happened to be driving by and found her sitting there on the stoop by accident. Hey, it could happen, right?

When she recognized my car and saw me wave at her, her eyes got big. She was shocked: "Oh my God! You can't just show up here like that! You gotta leave right now! Right now! You can't be here!"

What the fuck?! Who acts like that, unless they have something to hide? I drove away without saying a word. Then I texted her: "What the hell is going on? Are u still living with Dick? Or some other guy? Are u just playing me again?"

"No, I'm not!!! I'm not seeing anyone else!!! But u can't just show up here like that. That totally freaked me out," she texted back.

I didn't believe a word. I texted: "U know what? Fuck u! I'm done with this bullshit. All u ever do is lie to me. Ur never gonna change. I'm going to New York. I'm sick of Florida for a while."

"No, please don't go! I need u. My rent is due. I need ur help," she replied.

I wrote: "Fuck u and ur rent!"

But then I felt bad for her. Well, not so much for her, really. I felt bad for her kids. I didn't want them to end up homeless, just because their mother is a lying, cheating piece of shit. The next day, before I headed to New York, I sent her $400 by Western Union.

A few hours later she texted me. Not to say thank you, but to pretend that she didn't have the money anymore. She claimed somehow the money fell out of her back pocket. Now she was still going to get kicked out, because she still couldn't pay her rent. Of course I didn't believe her. I heard these kinds of stories too many times by now. Hussy was just as bad, if not worse, than Linda.

I told Hussy if she didn't tell me the truth about what's really going on, I would find out for myself. She said there was nothing going on and nothing to tell. So I found out Ferrara's number and asked her what was up with her sister Hussy.

Ferrara was shocked when I told her that Hussy and I were supposedly dating. She told me that Hussy and Dick were living together at the house near Sunshine Boulevard. In fact Dick was in the living room, when I pulled up in front of the house. That's why Hussy had freaked out like that. She didn't want Dick and me to meet. Ferrara told me that her sister Hussy was a horrible liar and a terrible person. When even your own sister talks about you like that, you know you're a pretty shitty person.

Then I called Hussy's mother in Ocala. I introduced myself and asked her if she could tell me what the deal is with Hussy. Her mother told me that Hussy was a terrible person who made everyone around her miserable with her lies, and I should run the other way and never look back. Wow.

I asked her about Hussy's dead sister Amber. Her mother told me there was no Amber. That's when I found out all that had been a big lie. And Amber's kids obviously didn't exist either. I asked her mother whether she went to jail, when Hussy asked me for bail money to bond her out a few months earlier. Nope. Her mother had never been in jail a day in her life. And that's when I found out that when Hussy's father supposedly texted me that Hussy was so upset about her mother being in jail, she was going to kill herself, that was not really her father texting me, but Hussy herself.

THE BIG LIE

"In the big lie there is always a certain force of credibility... in the primitive simplicity of their minds the people more readily fall victims to the big lie than the small lie, since they themselves often tell small lies in little matters but would be ashamed to resort to large-scale falsehoods. It would never come into their heads to fabricate colossal untruths, and they would not believe that others could have the impudence to distort the truth so infamously."
Adolf Hitler

Linda still called me at least 2 or 3 times a week. At first she kept calling to help me get over Alice. But over time, my grief over losing Alice faded, and I was wrapped up in my adventures with Hussy. I guess there was a silver lining in everything I had been going through with Hussy. She helped me forget Alice.

When Alice ran away from rehab, I was so heartbroken, it felt like she had died. I grieved. I mourned. And for me, my Alice really did die, when I finally realized that the Alice in my head was not the same Alice that existed in the real world. The Alice in my head was a sweet, beautiful girl. My dream girl. But the Alice in the real world was a drug addicted hooker who fucked every guy in town and sucked any dope boy's dick for a hit. My dream girl with the sunny smile died, and all that was left was a rancid zombie who roamed the shadows, always looking for the next guy to fuck, the next dick to suck. I wanted nothing to do with the real world Alice.

After a few months, my phone conversations with Linda no longer revolved around Alice, but around the crazy girls I had met in Florida. Especially Hussy. Linda thought it was entertaining. To her, listening to my stories was like watching a soap opera on TV. Tune in tomorrow, to find out what happens next!

But Linda also had crazy stories for me. Some of them were about her own awkward experiences as a rookie hooker. But most of her stories revolved around her friend Stephanie. Stephanie was a heroin addicted hooker who had moved from New York to Atlantic City. She was homeless and prowled the Boardwalk. Linda told me that Stephanie used to be a beautiful girl. A tall, skinny blonde with a gorgeous face and a great body. But now she looked like a mangy toothless crackhead. Linda even sent me naked pictures of Stephanie, to show me how disgusting she looked now.

Stephanie had been raped, beaten and left for dead on the Atlantic City Boardwalk several times. You'd think she would have hit rock bottom after those experiences. But no. None of that made her quit. It just made her want to use even more drugs, to forget her miserable life. As long as she could get high, she didn't care if she was being raped in a dark alley. At this point in her life, a lethal overdose probably would have felt like her salvation.

Linda's stories about Stephanie really opened my eyes about how powerful drug addiction really is. It's easy for a sober person to say: "Just get over it and stop using drugs." But that's like telling a starving person not to eat. No matter how much will power you have, eventually you cave and you stuff your face with all the food you can get your hands on. And at that moment nothing else in the world matters.

Since those conversations with Linda, I read a lot about addiction. One medical article stood out to me. It explained that different parts of our brain are in charge of different things. The midbrain is the oldest, most primitive part of our brain. It's kinda like a cockroach. Not very bright. The midbrain is in charge of our cravings. If we only had a midbrain, we'd be fucking, eating and doing drugs all day long. We'd give in to every craving, every urge without any thought about the consequences of our actions.

Then there's the prefrontal cortex. That's the most advanced part of our brain. It's responsible for complex problem solving and abstract thinking. Basically it's the part of our brain that separates us from animals. The prefrontal cortex is where our brain considers the consequences of our actions. It's the part of our brain that lets us predict and contemplate future events, and how our actions will affect our future, or the lives of other people. The prefrontal cortex is what gives us empathy. A shark doesn't feel guilty when it eats someone. That's just what sharks do. But a typical human will feel bad for someone else, feel pity, guilt and remorse thanks to the prefrontal cortex.

It takes a long time for the prefrontal cortex to fully develop. Doctors say that part of the brain is not fully operational until you are about 25 years old. That's why teenagers think differently than adults. A teenage brain is simply not fully developed yet, and therefore not as good as an adult brain at considering the consequences of your actions, or truly comprehending how your actions affect someone else. That's why courts treat teenage offenders with more leniency than adult criminals.

It's also the reason why drug court is more lenient with drug offenders, because drugs like heroin or crack disrupt the development and function of the prefrontal cortex. The brain of a drug addict simply does not work the same way as a sober brain. A brain on drugs, with an impaired prefrontal cortex, is simply not capable of considering the consequences, or feeling empathy for your victims, in the same way as a sober brain.

To me, that right there explains why drugs turn addicts into selfish sociopaths who will hurt anyone to get the next high. Being mad at a drug addict for doing what drug addicts do, is like being mad at a shark for doing what sharks do, or being mad at a cockroach for doing what cockroaches do.

Addicts don't like when you tell them they are all the same. Of course not. Who would? But to me, addicts are like actresses, who all audition for the same role in a horror movie. It doesn't matter how they got to the audition. It doesn't matter how or where they grew up, once they get to the audition, all the actresses act in the same way and read the same lines. They all become the same character.

To me, the impairment of the prefrontal cortex explains why traditional rehab has such an incredibly high failure rate. The AA 12-step program is all about talking to the prefrontal cortex. They tell you to think about how your behavior has hurt other people. You're supposed to think about how drugs have ruined your life. Those are complex thoughts that happen in the prefrontal cortex. But when you put a bag of heroin or a crack pipe in front of an addict, the prefrontal cortex simply shuts down. It goes on vacation. All that is left is the midbrain, screaming for drugs: "Yeah! Let's do it! It'll feel sooo gooood! Fuck tomorrow! Fuck the consequences! Let's get hiiigh rrright nooow!"

You can train the prefrontal cortex all you want, with 12-step slogans and prayers, but none of that is gonna do you any good, if your prefrontal cortex isn't even home when your midbrain takes over and you're about to relapse.

I picture the battle between the prefrontal cortex and the midbrain like the cliché of the little angel and the little devil sitting on your shoulders. The angel (the prefrontal cortex) tells you not to do drugs: "Think about what it will do to your life! Think about your loved ones!" Meanwhile the little devil (the midbrain) on your other shoulder just chants: "Do it! Do it! Do it!"

And primitive urges are usually a lot stronger than rational thought. That's why people do things even when they know that they shouldn't. Drug addicts know they shouldn't take drugs. But they do it anyway.

People cheat on their spouses, even though they know that 5 minutes of sex with someone else is not worth ruining a lifelong relationship. But they cheat anyway, because the midbrain is winning. The poor little angel is fighting a losing battle.

Overweight people know they shouldn't eat 6 donuts in a row. But they do it anyway. Why? Because the little angel, who knows all about bad cholesterol and heart disease, was on vacation while the little devil screamed: "Do it! Do it! Do it!"

And that, in a nutshell, is why the AA 12-step-program has such a high failure rate in my opinion.

Anyway, let's get back to Linda:

The stories she told me about her own life often revolved around her kids. Her young son and her baby daughter. You know, the one she wanted to abort when we met in Pennsylvania a year earlier.

Linda told me she hated being a hooker. She hated having complete strangers touch her, get on top of her, be inside of her, and use her to get off. It disgusted her. The men disgusted her. And she was disgusted with herself. "But it is what it is. I need the money."

She told me that her baby daughter had a deformed foot. She needed to make money as a hooker to save up for the surgery. She said she didn't want just any random surgeon to work on her daughter. She wanted the best surgeon she could find. Honestly, I don't believe any of that was true. I think she smoked crack, and that's where all her money went.

One time she emailed me that she was stranded in New Jersey somewhere with a flat tire. She said she had no one else to ask, and she begged me to wire her $200 to get a new tire, so she could get home to her children. I told her that after everything I had been through with girls lying to me about make-believe emergencies to con me out of money, I wasn't going to wire a dime to anyone anymore. Especially not to her.

I hacked Linda's Yahoo Mail account and saw that she had emailed over 30 guys with that same story. And a bunch of them really did wire her $200 to get a new tire. I never told her that I had hacked her and knew she was conning a whole bunch of people.

Another time she claimed that she needed money to buy her mother a pair of fancy sunglasses for her birthday. A whole bunch of guys thought they were the only one she asked, and felt flattered that she would come to them, and they all sent her the money. She made thousands of dollars with these little scams.

Then one day I got text messages from her phone, asking me to bail her out of jail. Supposedly the texts were from Linda's babysitter, using Linda's phone. The texts said Linda had been arrested for unpaid tickets, and that Linda had gotten into a fight with one of the other inmates and was bleeding. She needed to be bailed out right now.

Texting was too slow and tedious, so I asked the babysitter to pick up the phone and talk to me. She said she couldn't, because the phone supposedly had gotten wet in the sink, and now the phone didn't work, except texting. I told her to use her own phone to call me, instead of Linda's. She said she didn't have her own phone with her. That's when I knew this really wasn't any babysitter texting me on Linda's behalf, but Linda herself. The whole jail story was just her latest scheme. I went into her Email account again and saw that she had been sending out emails that day, as well as the previous days. So she was obviously not really in jail. Later I found out that a bunch of guys fell for that scam again as well, and several of them sent her bail money.

This went on for a few months. I never sent Linda any money, but I also never told her that I knew she was lying about all this stuff to get money out of me and other guys. Sometimes it's better not to tell someone you know they're lying.

One day when Linda called me, she sounded really upset. She started crying and told me she had just found out her baby girl had cancer. Wow! Karma is a bitch, I thought to myself, while trying to sound compassionate and comforting on the phone. That's what she gets for always lying, to prey on other people's compassion. She had used her kids in so many of her lies and schemes, and now her baby daughter really was sick. And with cancer! Wow. Just wow.

Over the next few weeks, Linda told everyone she knew that her kid needed chemo therapy and expensive cancer specialists. A bunch of guys sent her money. Thousands of dollars. Then some of those guys even set up a charity for her baby daughter. And they organized a charity event for her. Linda asked me to be her date at her party. I declined. I told her I wouldn't be able to make it to New York in time for the party, because I was busy with some project here in Florida.

I was suspicious. Who could blame me, after watching her scam people over and over again with her stories? I kept asking her to tell me details about her daughter's health. About the type of cancer she had. Which hospital she was in. How she was feeling. Linda answered all my questions without skipping a beat.

Every time she called me, she kept me updated on her daughter's health. She told me about her appointments with cancer specialists, and what the oncologists and pediatricians told her about her daughter's condition. She told me about the Disney movies her daughter watched in the pediatric oncology department of the hospital. She told me about how kind the nurses were to her daughter, and what her daughter's favorite hospital food was.

The whole cancer thing was just way too big, way too elaborate not to be true. There was just way too much detail for all this to be a lie.

Then one day Linda disappeared. I was used to her calling me at least 3 or 4 times a week. Now I hadn't heard from her in over 2 weeks. So I searched around a bit, and found an online forum where people were talking about her. Apparently a lot of people were very pissed at her, because altogether they had donated tens of thousands of dollars to her and her sick baby. But when some of those guys wanted to go visit the baby in the hospital, and they started to ask more and more questions, it turned out that she wasn't in any hospital.

The whole cancer story was a big lie. Linda's baby daughter was in perfect health. People called the cops and tried to press charges against her, so she decided it was time to disappear. I never heard from her again after that.

I should have known. When Linda and I had spent time together in Pennsylvania a year or so earlier, she had seriously suggested that we should start a church together. She didn't believe in God or heaven any more than I did, but she thought it would be a great way to con gullible fools into donating lots of money to us.

HALEY

"Every harlot was a virgin once."
William Blake

"Prostitution happens to you because of troubles you had. In reality no woman would choose to do that."
Catherine Deneuve

"We fear violence less than our own feelings. Personal, private, solitary pain is more terrifying than what anyone else can inflict."
Jim Morrison

Haley was a pretty blonde with glasses. I had met her on one of my first trips to Florida, right after my divorce from Donna. She was thick, but it looked good on her. She had big, beautiful breasts. Not as large as Donna's, but not too shabby. She built websites and sold stuff on Ebay, so we had a couple of things in common. She also sold fancy shmancy wine bottles.

Haley and I had the same sense of humor. I really enjoyed hanging out with her. She had a great personality and was very easy to talk to. She was smart, witty, funny, and really sweet. We ended up having sex. Haley knew that I was only visiting Florida for a couple of days, and then I was going to go back to my house in Pennsylvania. She gave me a lift to the airport.

We kept in touch while I was up north, and every time I flew back down to Florida, Haley and I met up, hung out and had sex. We made plans to go to one of the resort hotels in Orlando together, but we never ended up going.

Over time I started to see a change in Haley. She wasn't as cheerful anymore. She always seemed exhausted and tired.

Then I met Alice in Pennsylvania, and I stopped seeing Haley on my trips to Florida. Haley still called me every few weeks though, to see if I was still with Alice, or if I might want to get together the next time I was in Fort Myers.

After Alice ran away from rehab, and I moved to Florida by myself, I just didn't have the ambition to meet anyone new. I was way too depressed. Then suddenly, out of nowhere, Haley called me again. I told her that Alice and I had broken up, that I was living in Bonita Springs now, and that I was utterly miserable. Haley told me that she had moved to Miami a few months ago, and asked me if I wanted to hang out. She said she'd cheer me up and help me forget Alice. Sure, why the hell not, I thought. I agreed to meet her in Hollywood, Florida, between Fort Lauderdale and Miami. We made plans for a romantic evening in Miami Beach.

While I was driving on I-75, through the swamps of the Big Cypress National Preserve, Haley texted me: "Oh, BTW, I live with a lot of people, so we can't hang out at my place."

After dealing with Alice and her druggie friends for a year and a half, my instincts told me that Haley was now a drug addict, too. If she lived in an apartment with roommates, she would have texted me: "I have a few roommates. So we won't have privacy." But she wrote "I live with a lot of people." To me, that meant she lived in a crackhouse with a bunch of random strangers. And only addicts live in crackhouses. So that one innocent little text made me think she was now a crackwhore. I was right.

When I arrived at Haley's home in Hollywood, some skinny dark-haired girl was standing on the sidewalk and got into my car as soon as I pulled up. It was a shady neighborhood. And now this girl just got into my car. I figured she was some crackwhore who assumed I was cruising the ghetto to pick up a "date." I was just about to tell the skinny strange girl to get out of my car, when she said hello and hugged me. It was Haley. I recognized her voice, but she looked nothing, n-o-t-h-i-n-g like the thick pretty blonde girl I remembered.

"Honestly, I'm too tired to go to Miami Beach. Let's just get a motel room," Haley said.

"Wow," I thought, "she doesn't waste any time."

She told me she knew a cheap place and gave me directions. On our way to some grimey motel in the worst part of town, I told her I didn't even recognize her, and asked her how she had been since the last time I saw her over a year and a half ago, before I met Alice.

"Not so good," she said with a sad smile. "When we are done at the motel room, do you mind if we pick up my friend Rosie? She's at my house right now. There's a lot of drugs there. I'm worried about her. She does drugs, but it's not safe at that house. Do you mind if she stays the night at the motel room with me, after we're done? At least that way I know she's not on the streets."

"Sure, I guess," I said. "So, your friend Rosie takes drugs, huh? What about you?"

Haley gave me a sad look and said: "Yeah, me too."

I had never told Haley about Alice's drug addiction. I was too embarrassed. It's not exactly something you brag about. But now that Haley told me about her own drug problem, I felt I could open up to her and tell her what I had been through with Alice.

Haley was a good listener. She was very sympathetic. "You poor thing," she said. "No wonder you're so miserable right now. That girl broke your heart every which way possible."

It felt good to be able to talk to someone who understood, really understood. I teared up. Haley did, too. We hugged and cried together. And I wasn't embarrassed about it at all. I had talked to Linda, Crystal and Kayla about Alice, but I never felt comfortable to let any of them know how deeply hurt I really was. Yeah, I told them I was really depressed, but I never cried when I talked to them about Alice. Instead I'd make sarcastic jokes about Alice fucking some dope boy and how stupid she was for ruining her life.

But talking to Haley was different. For some reason we connected on a deep level, and I felt like it was ok to be vulnerable in front of her. I didn't feel like I needed to hide my pain behind a tough front.

On our way to the shittiest motel in town, Haley opened up about what she had been through. The last time I saw her about a year ago, she had been so excited, because she had bought a little convertible. She was so proud of her new car.

But she had started snorting coke, because her baby daddy Rodney sold it, and she got it for free. Then they both got addicted to oxycodone pills. Those pills are basically legal heroin. Addicts in Florida call them Blues. They crush them up and inject them into their veins, just like the junkies in New York inject heroin.

At some point Rodney was arrested and went to jail, and Haley started hanging out with some black dope boy. He ended up killing someone, and used Haley's convertible during the murder. Her car was found at the crime scene, so now the police was on her trail. She told them she didn't know anything, and ran away from Fort Myers. That's how she ended up in Miami, and then Hollywood.

She didn't know anyone when she got there, but addicts have a sixth sense when it comes to finding drugs. It didn't take her long at all to find a dope boy in Miami. He pimped her out. She was raped and beaten regularly. Her life in Miami was absolutely horrible, so she moved to Hollywood. But things weren't much better there either.

She got arrested for prostitution and spent time in Miami-Dade County Jail. Shortly after her release, she went to jail again, for drug possession with intent to sell, because she was riding around in the car with a dope boy.

When we got to the dirty motel room, she told me that she was actually on the run from the police right now. She was supposed to be moved from jail to a rehab facility, but she jumped out of the car and ran. Great. So now I was aiding and abetting a wanted fugitive. Lovely. I was starting to get a headache.

Everything she went through came pouring out of her. It seemed like she was talking nonstop, without even taking a breath. I guess she was high on coke or crack. Then she asked me if we could go back to the house where she was staying, to pick up Rosie. But we had just gotten to the motel, and I really wasn't in the mood to drive all the way back to where we just came from. So she tried to bribe me: "You could fuck both of us! Rosie is really hot. You're gonna like her." That was the first time a girl asked me if I wanted to have a threesome.

Threesomes sound great in theory. But to me, the thought of disappointing not just one but two girls at the same time, seems like way too much pressure. I think I'd be way too nervous, and probably wouldn't even be able to get hard. I prefer being with just one girl.

Haley and I had sex. It was a pretty sad experience. She was completely different than I remembered her. She was so skinny and mangy. And where her big beautiful breasts used to be, she now had two saggy skin flaps that looked like deflated balloons. She used to be such a sweetheart. But now she was overacting like a porn star, grinding her pussy into me like she just couldn't get enough of my dick. She kept screaming and moaning so loud, I thought the people in the next room would complain about the noise. I didn't like it. And being around her in this condition was actually getting pretty stressful.

After we finished, we weren't even dressed yet, and she already wanted to go back to the house. Supposedly to get Rosie, but by now I was pretty sure she really just wanted to go back there to get more drugs. I told her I had a headache, and that I wanted to go back home to Bonita Springs. I offered to drop her back off at the house, and then she and Rosie would have to figure out a way to get back to the motel room on their own.

A few days later some guy, who sounded like a cop, left a voicemail on my phone. He said Haley got arrested, and she wanted me to bail her out. I called him back. He turned out to be a bondsman, not a cop. I told him that I didn't really know Haley all that well, and that I wasn't going to pay $1200 to bond her out. He told me that he couldn't blame me, because the charges she had were pretty serious, and people in her position tend to not show up for their court dates, and then I'd be on the hook for a lot of money. Haley spent the next 45 days in jail.

As soon as she got out, she called me and thanked me for not bailing her out. She said she had been totally off the chain and her drug use had become so severe, she probably would have died, if she didn't sober up in jail. Haley told me that by not bailing her out, I probably saved her life. She said she was all better now, and that she would never go back to using drugs. She was tired of that horrible life and she wanted to go back to school and make something of herself. I was really happy to hear that, and we made plans to get together again soon.

A couple of days later, she called me again and told me she had moved back to Fort Myers, and she found a room for rent. She said she just needed $20 to be able to move in.

"$20? To move into a room?" I asked. "Really? Are you sure, you're not just asking me for $20 to go buy some crack?"

At first she denied it, but then she admitted it: "Yeah, it's for crack. But I'm not gonna let it get out of control this time. I'm just gonna smoke crack casually, here and there. On the weekends. I'm never gonna let it get as bad as I was before I went to jail."

Yeah, right. I had heard that story before. I knew that if she starts smoking crack again, she'd be a wreck in a matter of days. I told her: "I'm sorry, sweetie. But I don't want to be the one to make you relapse, so I'm not going to give you money for crack."

She called me almost every day after that, and we started hanging out again. She stayed at a house off of Palm Beach Boulevard, with a man named Lorne. He was a 70 year old convicted drug smuggler who had spent his youth in prison. He only had one arm.

Haley had gained a lot of weight while she was in jail.

But she lost it again at an alarming rate, because she was smoking so much crack and not eating. Palm Beach Boulevard is one of the worst drug neighborhoods in Fort Myers. There seems to be at least one crack house, or trap house as kids like to call them these days, on every street.

Haley supported her drug habit by walking along Palm Beach Boulevard, getting in guys' cars and having sex with them. Sometimes for as little as $10. Or she spent all day and night in a trap house, having sex with whoever would stop by and throw her a couple of dollars or a hit of crack.

It broke my heart to see her like this. She was such a sweetheart, with such a great personality, and so much potential. She used to run a karaoke club a few years ago. She had a great voice and had auditioned for American Idol. She had even sung as the opening act for Rick Ross at a NASCAR race. And now here she was, nothing more than a sad shadow of her former self, sucking dick on Palm Beach, and spreading her legs for any random thug at a trap house on Ione Avenue.

Whenever she couldn't take it anymore, and she needed to get away from her miserable life for a few hours, she asked me to come pick her up. We'd go to the beach together, or to the little ice cream shop her dad used to take her to, when she was little. We watched movies at my place, and went out to eat. She told me my condo was the only place where she felt truly safe, and that being around me was the only time she felt like a normal human being and not just a piece of shit. She said I was her only real friend. The sad part was, she was my only real friend, too.

Every time we hung out together, she teared up when she told me how much she hated her life, and how badly she wanted to get away from it all. But she just couldn't quit drugs.

Over the years, Haley spent the night at my place many times, but in the beginning it was hard to get her to sleep in bed. She reminded me of a skiddish animal. She had been raped, groped in her sleep, and used by so many guys, that a bed had become a scary place for her. To her, a bed was not a place of rest, but a place of torment. She preferred the couch. She was used to sleeping with one eye open, always with her razor-sharp box cutter within easy reach.

She had to use that box cutter a few times to defend herself. One time a guy tried to rape her, and she stabbed him in his throat. Another time, 2 large Mexican girls tried to mug her on the streets, and she sliced one of the girls' cheeks.

GARY THE VIDEO GAME ADDICT

"All that we see or seem
is but a dream within a dream."
Edgar Allan Poe

After Hussy's mother and her sister Ferrara told me what a lying psycho Hussy really was, I needed to get away from her and Florida for a while.

I went to New York for a few weeks and visited my ex-wife Donna and her new boyfriend, Gary. He was in his 50s, a couple of years older than Donna, and he had Parkinson's disease. He was a retired cop. So you'd think he was a commanding presence, used to giving orders. But he was the most mellow, timid push-over I had ever met. He was like a big puppy. He didn't stand a chance against Donna's domineering personality, and she bossed him around all day long. There was absolutely no doubt that she was the one wearing the pants.

Donna didn't have a lot of friends, because she was a recluse who almost never left the house and didn't like being around other people, other than me. Our divorce had been really hard on her as well, because she didn't have a support network any more than I did. After the divorce she was all alone and she had no one to talk to, except a few online friends she had never met in person, and the occasional phone conversation with her childhood friend Roy. Roy was one of the few people who knew about Donna's agoraphobia. He was used to her not answering the door and pretending not to be home when he or anyone else came knocking on her door.

Roy's older brother Gary was a shut in, too. After he had been diagnosed with Parkinson's, he lost his job and his emotionally abusive wife left him. He went into a deep depression and lost his will to live. He escaped his lonely, miserable life by playing the online video game World of Warcraft. Everything he was missing in his real life, he found in the game. He became so addicted to it, he practically lived inside the game. The real world didn't matter to him anymore. The only thing he cared about was completing another raid in the game, or exploring a new dungeon and winning the admiration of his online friends in battle. He later told me that a lot of handicapped people become addicted to World of Warcraft, because in their online fantasy world, they are healthy, wealthy, and handsome. The game lets them forget about their broken bodies, and they become legendary heroes, saving the world, while riding dragons.

Gary really wasn't any different than a crack addict, when he was in the depths of his video game addiction. He wouldn't go to sleep for days at a time, and he'd play the game nonstop, day and night, only taking a quick break if he absolutely had to use the bathroom. He was totally addicted to the positive feelings he got from killing evil monsters or finding a new magical weapon or his game character raised a level and learned a new combat skill.

Anything that feels good triggers the reward center in our brains and a little bit of the feel-good chemical dopamine is released. Whether you get a raise at work, or you eat candy, or you have sex, or someone gives you flowers, or tells you they love you, or you watch a pretty sunset, or someone sends you a sweet text message, or you find a golden sword in a video game, it all releases a little bit of dopamine. You can get addicted to anything that makes you feel good, whether it's text messages, video games, food, sex, exercise, cigarettes, or drugs.

Drugs like crack or heroin flood the brain with so much dopamine, everything else in life pales by comparison. That's what makes these drugs so extremely addicting, and why addicts feel so miserable and empty when they don't have their drug. Once their brains get used to the endless flood of dopamine, life without drugs seems unbearably sad and dull. Nothing, no matter how pleasant, releases enough dopamine to even come close to crack or heroin. Once an addict gets sober, it takes their brain years to fully restore its chemical balance. It takes a while, before an addict can really appreciate life's simple pleasures again.

Gary's video game addiction was so bad, his younger brother Roy was getting really worried about him. Gary was so pale, his skin was almost translucent. He hadn't showered in weeks, and hadn't cut his hair or his beard in months. Roy figured that Gary and Donna would be perfect for each other, so he persuaded Donna to take a ride to meet Gary. He looked like a caveman when they met, but they hit it off anyway. They started talking on the phone, and then, after a few weeks, Gary moved in with Donna.

She told him that he wasn't allowed to play the game anymore, and he obeyed. But his beloved fantasy world never really left his mind. A year or so after he moved in with her, he begged her to let him play his game again. Just a little bit. Just on the weekends, after he finished all his chores around the house.

I'm sure you can guess what happened next. Well, not only did he get totally addicted to the game again, he got Donna addicted to it, too. When I visited them again a few months later, they both got on their laptops as soon as they woke up in the morning and played the game all day long, every day, until it was time to go to bed.

Anyway, after I talked to Ferrara and Hussy's mother, I spent a few weeks in New York with Donna and Gary.

A few days before I got there, they walked the dogs in nearby Seaview Park in Brooklyn late at night. All the parks in New York City close at dusk, because they're not safe at night. But Donna couldn't stand being around other people, so she only walked the dogs very late at night, when nobody else was in the park.

This one night there was someone else. A black guy on a bicycle. The dogs saw him from afar and started chasing after him. He was afraid for his life and tried to escape from what must have looked like vicious beasts to him. But the dogs were really just being friendly, when they barked at him.

He returned a little while later, holding a big stick. He wanted to beat the dogs with it. Donna freaked out and started screaming at the black guy. Gary slowly shuffled behind her. There was a big commotion, and Donna told Gary to call the cops. The black guy dropped the stick and ran off.

From that point on Donna didn't feel safe in the park at night anymore and decided that she needed a taser for self defense. But of course she didn't just order one. She ordered five.

She was a shopaholic. One of anything was never enough. She ordered so much stuff on the Internet every day, the whole house was full of crap. There were unopened boxes of kitchen appliances, dozens of unused purses, hundreds of plastic jars that were on sale, clown dolls that she bought wholesale in China and wanted to sell on Ebay but never did, and so on and so forth.

And when she ordered something on a Monday, she wouldn't be interested in it anymore by the time it arrived on Thursday, because she already bought different stuff on Tuesday and Wednesday. So the house was full of unused, unopened stuff, that she eventually threw away to make room for more stuff.

She had done that for years, ever since I started earning a lot of money on the Internet. There were times when she spent over $3000 a month on things we didn't need and that just cluttered up the house. She was still doing the same thing now, on a smaller scale, using Gary's credit card, instead of mine. I think shopping for things online filled an emotional void in her life.

Anyway, after the five tasers arrived, she put a few of them in her purse. One day she was rummaging through her purse, when she touched one of the tasers, and accidentally shocked herself. I was in Manhattan at the time, but she told me all about it when I got back at night: "Oh my God! I accidentally tasered myself today! It hurt like crazy! I felt like I hit a brick wall! Want me to taser you?"

"What? No, hell no," I replied and laughed.

"Gary, get over here, I'm gonna taser you," she yelled.

Gary said ok and obediently shuffled into the living room and sat down on a chair, to prepare himself for electrocution.

Donna had bought several different tasers. One shot 2 metal tips. And another was the kind that looks like an electric razor. But she decided to use the one that looked like a cattle prod to taser Gary.

"Ready?" she asked him.

"Hold on," I said. "Are you seriously gonna taser him? I gotta get my camera. I'm gonna tape this!" We all laughed.

I had given up on trying to stop Donna from abusing Gary. In the beginning I felt really bad, when I saw the way she treated him. One time she had ordered a cheap couch from Walmart online, and told him to put it together in the front room. His trembling hands accidentally dropped it while he was in the middle of assembling it, and one of the legs snapped off.

"You broke it! You are so useless," she screamed at him in front of me. "You're not even a real man!"

Emasculating a disabled man like that was bad enough. But to do it right in front of me, her ex-husband, was just cruel. I felt so bad for him.

Later that night we were all sitting in the living room, and when she talked to him like he was a piece of shit again, I told her she can't keep abusing him like that. She got all defensive and with a vicious, threatening tone in her voice she yelled at Gary: "Am I abusing you?!? Is that what you're telling people, you wimp?"

"No, no, you're not," he said quietly, with a shaky voice.

"Gary you need to stand up for yourself," I told him. I figured it was now or never. He had me as his backup right now, so this was his one chance to tell her to stop abusing him.

But he didn't. He couldn't stand up to her. He was afraid of her. She could make his life a living hell, and he knew I would leave eventually, and then he'd be alone with her again.

She had forgotten that I wasn't as easily pushed around as Gary was. So a few times, when I stayed in New York with them, she tried to start shit with me. For old times' sake, I guess.

But I just yelled right back at her. I didn't need to put up with her shit anymore. Unlike Gary, I could leave any time I want, so I had no reason to back down and let her boss me around.

I learned that she only enjoyed throwing tantrums and bossing people around with her hateful tirades, if she felt like she was in total control of the fight. If it started when she wanted it to, and it ended when she wanted it to.

Once I figured that out, I took that sense of power away from her, by keeping the fight going for 5 more minutes, after she decided she had enough. Suddenly the end of the fight was not hers to control anymore, because even when she was bored of it, I continued to berate her. Now she no longer felt like the bully, but like the one who was being bullied. Once I figured that out, we got along pretty well most of the time, because I don't start fights, and she was scared to pick fights with me. Gary was a much easier target.

Another time he was cooking. He did all the chores around the house, while she sat on the couch, playing Facebook games on her laptop, and issuing out orders. I guess he was taking too long or something, but suddenly the fact that he was cooking wasn't good enough. Nothing he did was ever good enough.

He was standing in front of the stove. The kitchen was small, and she shoved him with her shoulder while passing him. "Get out of my way," she said.

Then, when she passed him on her way back into the

living room, she body-checked him with her shoulder again, with a little more force.

She kept doing that a few times. Finally he mustered enough courage to stand up to her: "Stop shoving me!"

"Or else what?" she asked with an arrogant, condescending look on her face. "What are you gonna do about it?"

He decided to try to get physical. He slowly shuffled over to her, almost in slow motion, and tried to push her or wrestle her or something. But he was a featherweight with no body strength whatsoever. She took a step back and karate-kicked him in the stomach. I could not believe my eyes!

I was just quietly sitting in the living room, watching the drama unfold, and when she lifted her leg and kicked him, I wished I had my camera, to tape this insanity. I bet it would have gotten millions of hits on YouTube!

After kicking him, she mocked him and called him a wimp. Yupp, she bullied and kicked a cripple, and then laughed at him. Classy. And he continued to live with her after that, like nothing ever happened. It was just another normal day to him.

Anyway, let's get back to the day when she tasered him:

She turned on the cattle prod, stuck it against the skin on Gary's arm, and pulled the trigger. It crackled. There were blue sparks. She really tasered him! Holy fuck!

What a crazy bitch! And I got it all on camera this time.

And Gary just sat there. He didn't feel a thing. I guess his Parkinson's, or the medication he was taking for it, had dulled his senses so much, his nerve endings didn't even feel it when you tasered him.

After staying with them for a few weeks, I flew to Europe. I visited my parents in Germany, and together we went on vacation in Spain for a month.

Suddenly Patty called me. I hadn't talked to her in months, ever since she had tried to come to Florida uninvited, to spend another birthday with me.

She told me that I was still on her mind all the time. Remember, I hadn't seen her in about 2 years, ever since she had spent those two sex-crazed weeks with me in Florida.

Patty asked me how I had been and apologized for acting so crazy last year, when she texted hateful messages all night and then showed up in Florida the next day, even though I had told her not to. I told her I was in Spain right now.

She said she would like us to give it another shot. She told me she made me a key to her apartment in Scranton, and we could be snowbirds, living in Scranton during the summer, and in Bonita Springs during the winter. I didn't really know what to say, without hurting her feelings. Moving in with her was the last thing in the world I wanted to do. She was just too damn nuts. She was worse than any of the drug addicts I had met.

She said she had been thinking about her life a lot lately, and she wanted to make some changes, because she was miserable with the way things were. She wanted love in her life, but she couldn't seem to make any relationship work. So she decided to have a baby. A baby comes with built-in unconditional love, so Patty figured having a baby was going to fix her loveless life. She said she had thought about getting artificially inseminated, but then she decided she wants someone she really cares about to get her pregnant: me.

I had not seen this woman in two years, and we had not left off on good terms at all, and here she was, calling me in Spain, asking me to put a baby inside her. What. The. Fuck?

I told her I had to go and hung up on her. Then I blocked her number. Enough was enough.

BROTHERLY LOVE AND SISTER WIVES

"I think people should be free to engage in any sexual practices they choose; they should draw the line at goats though."
Elton John

After I got back from Spain, I still wasn't talking to Hussy anymore. I hung out with Haley, when she needed to get away from Palm Beach Boulevard for a while, or I hung out with Kayla, the quirky 20 year old math student.

Kayla was living in Cape Coral with her boyfriend Alex, an appliance repairman, but she still wanted to hang out with me. I asked her if she wasn't worried about her boyfriend finding out about us having sex. "He knows," she said.

"Huh? And he's ok with that?" I asked.

"Well, no, not really. But I told him that the only way I'll be in a relationship with him is if he'll accept that I'll keep having sex with you," she replied.

That was the craziest thing I had ever heard. How the hell is that a relationship? Did that guy have no pride? He's ok with his girl having sex with someone else? That's nuts. That would drive me insane. Then again, maybe he really didn't care about her. Maybe he was just using her for sex, and as long as he got what he wanted from her, he didn't really give a shit what she did on her own time.

"Alright, I guess," I said. "As long as I'm not gonna end up getting shot by some jealous boyfriend."

"Nah, don't worry," she said. "He's a pussy."

Kayla and I met up and had sex a bunch of times after that conversation. It was weird to know that I was fucking someone else's girlfriend, and he knew about it. Once again I felt like I was living in some kind of twisted porno.

She often told me about what a jerk Alex was. He treated her like crap. He even left her alone on holidays, because he was embarrassed to introduce her to his family. She called me up crying on the 4th of July, because Alex had left her all alone again, while he went to a barbecue at his parents' house without her.

I told her that Alex was a total douchebag, who obviously really didn't care about her, and that she deserved someone better.

"I know, but I kinda love him," she said. Somehow the people I had met in Florida so far seemed to have a completely different idea of what the word "love" means, than I did.

One day, when Kayla was hanging out at my place again, she asked me to bring her back to her house by the time Alex got off work. After we finished having sex, she called Alex and asked him where he was. He had been working in Naples, and now he was heading north on Route 41, towards Cape Coral.

"Hey, wouldn't it be funny if we saw him on 41?" she asked with a grin on her face.

Once we got in the car and we were heading north on 41 as well, she called Alex again and asked him where exactly he was. He was just a mile or so up the road from us.

"Speed up!" she demanded, laughing. "Let's try to catch him. That would be so funny!" She really did have a strange sense of humor sometimes.

"Uhmm, I'm not so sure about that," I said. "Knowing that I'm fucking his girlfriend is one thing. But actually seeing you and me in the car together might really upset him, because that's gonna make it real in his head, you know?"

"Nah, he'll be fine. He'll think it's funny," she said.

"Well, I guess you know him better than I do," I conceded.

So we were speeding on 41, and we really did catch up with Alex. He was driving an old white pickup truck. Kayla told me to pass him. So I did. She rolled down the window, leaned out of the car and waved at Alex, stuck her tongue out, and screamed: "WOOOOOOO!" She was acting like she was on Girls Gone Wild.

Alex was not amused. At first he gave her dirty looks, and then he completely ignored her, staring at the road in front of him.

"He looks angry," she said.

"Well, duh! You just rubbed in his face that we are fucking," I said.

'What the hell made me think that this was a good idea?" she asked incredulously.

"I don't know. But now he is driving right behind us. What's gonna happen when we get to your house? Is he gonna wanna fight me or something? I'm wearing flip flops. Those are not fighting shoes," I said, only half kidding.

She didn't think this was funny at all anymore: "Oh fuck, he is sooo mad at me right now. What the fuck was I thinking?!"

"I don't know. But seriously, what are we gonna do when we and Alex arrive at your house at the same time? If I'm gonna get into a street brawl, I'm gonna have to stop somewhere and get a sandwich first. I need my strength."

She finally laughed again. Then she said: "Let's take a different route than him, so we don't get there at exactly the same time."

By now the same kind of thoughts must have been going through Alex's mind, and suddenly he passed us and sped off, way over the speed limit.

We stopped at a gas station and Kayla got some fake

weed, to calm her nerves. When we arrived at Alex's house in Cape Coral, his truck was parked in the driveway. I gave her a hug and a kiss good bye and told her to call me, to let me know she was alright.

A few hours later I still hadn't heard from her, so I texted her: "Are u ok?"

"Yeah," she replied. "He was cursing me out when I walked in the house, but then he calmed down."

A day or two later, Kayla called me. I didn't answer, so she left a voicemail. She was hysterically crying: "Oliver, please come get me. Alex and I had a huge fight. PLEASE! I have nobody else!"

I tried to call her back as soon as I heard her message. She didn't answer and she didn't call me back. That was very unlike her. She always answered the phone when I called.

A few weeks earlier, Kayla had told me that she met a girl at drug offender probation in Fort Myers, who was also from Sayville, the same small town on Long Island, New York, where Kayla grew up. Small world, huh? The other girl's name was Morgan.

Morgan had also gotten arrested for drug-related charges, also ended up in jail for a few weeks, and now she was also on drug offender probation. Kayla and Morgan quickly became best friends, because they had so much in common. Kayla told me she wanted me to meet Morgan, and all of us to hang out together, because she was sure I would like Morgan, because she also had a weird sense of humor.

When Kayla didn't call me back after leaving that message, I decided to text Morgan and ask her if she knew what happened. Morgan replied that Kayla and Alex got into a big fight, and he called the cops on her, and now Kayla was in jail for violating her probation. Morgan and I agreed to let each other know as soon as either one of us heard anything from Kayla.

Morgan said Kayla told her a lot about me. I asked her what exactly. She said Kayla called me her sugar daddy, and that she said I'm a really nice guy. I was flattered, even though I hated that she called me that word. Morgan also said that Kayla told her I have a big dick. And she joked she'd like to see it for herself, and that she'd love to have a sugar daddy like me, too. I was gonna find out soon that she wasn't joking after all.

Later that day, Kayla called me from jail and explained what happened. She was sleeping, while Alex was talking about her to someone else on the phone. He called her a whore and a piece of shit. Then he started screaming at her to get the fuck out of his house, and she woke up while he was throwing her things out into the street. She told him: "Fine, I'll leave. I'll ask Oliver to pick me up."

That made Alex even more angry, and he blocked her path to the door and started hitting her. Kayla was about a foot taller than Alex. She defended herself and put up a pretty good fight. She ended up pinning Alex against the wall, with her elbow against his throat. Then she bit him. He called the cops, and told them she was beating him up. When the cops came, they arrested her, not him, even though she had just been defending herself. How fucked up is that?

After our conversation, I called Morgan to let her know what Kayla had just told me.

Kayla called me from jail every day. She told me I had been right about Alex and that she wished she had listened to me when I told her to leave that douchebag. Then she told me she loved me, and she started acting like I was her boyfriend.

I found out later that that's what girls do when they're in jail. They cling to someone on the outside and think they're madly in love with that person. Or they pretend to be, to get money out of them.

But at that point, when she started calling me from jail and told me she loved me, I had no idea that I shouldn't put too much stock in that. I was flattered that she felt that way about me. I didn't really love her, but I liked her, so I figured, what the hell, I guess I might as well be her boyfriend. We were already having sex anyway, and it's not like I really had anything else going on right now. I still wasn't talking to Hussy, Haley was just too badly on crack to be girlfriend material, and Crystal was still in a relationship with her much younger boyfriend Jerry, even though they were having problems, because she caught him cheating on her a few times, and he suspected that she was cheating on him, too.

So, suddenly I had a girlfriend in jail. Pretty bizarre. If

someone had told me a few years ago that I would hang out with drug addicts, or know someone in jail, never mind date someone in jail, I would have told them they're crazy.

The four most important things when you're in jail are:

1) getting visitors
2) getting mail (Only postcards are allowed.)
3) being able to call someone on the outside
4) getting canteen money from someone, so you can buy snacks (The food in jail is terrible.)

Kayla's dad sent her money, so I didn't have to. But I opened a prepaid account with Global Tel, so she could call me collect. And I visited her regularly. Inmates in Lee County Jail are allowed to have 2 one-hour-long visits per week. The inmate sits at a video screen in jail, while the visitor sits at a video screen in the visitation building.

And I sent her postcards. Since I had a background in newspaper publishing, I printed my postcards with a tiny font, so I could fit a lot more text on a card than if it was handwritten, and I made them look like newspaper pages, with funny little pictures. Kayla loved my postcards. They always cheered her up, and she showed them to all her friends in jail. They said that my cards were the best jail mail ever. It made me feel good when she told me that.

One day Kayla was all excited, because she had found out that there was a book called "Sex, Drugs and Taxi Cabs" written by some guy who had sex with a bunch of streetwalking hookers, who walked past his insurance office on Pondella Road. He called himself Captain Save-A-Ho. All the inmates were talking about his book, because he mentioned Lee County Jail in it. Kayla talked me into getting the book. It was poorly written, and painfully awkward to read. He bragged about humiliating these girls, because to him they were all just a bunch of worthless whores anyway. He sounded like a sleazy douchebag.

Kayla sent me a bunch of really sweet love letters. She wrote she couldn't wait to get out and have a life with me. She never wanted to touch drugs again, and she wanted to finish college. It all sounded oddly familiar.

Meanwhile her best friend Morgan kept texting and calling me all the time. She said we should hang out, and that I shouldn't feel guilty about having sex with her, because Kayla was going to be in jail for almost a year, and because Kayla had called me her sugar daddy, not her boyfriend, before she went to jail. Morgan said Kayla was just calling me her boyfriend now, because she needed to have someone to think about while she was in jail.

The way Kayla's best friend Morgan was moving in on me reminded me of the way Alice's best friend Kat had made a move on me, back in New York. The more I hung out with drug addicts, the more situations kept repeating themselves. Only the names changed.

Morgan was 25. She was much shorter than Kayla, had freckles and red hair. She wasn't beautiful in the classical sense, but she was cute in her own way. And she had a great sense of humor. She cracked me up with all her cocky little comments. She had a young daughter, and she told me her baby daddy said that without make-up Morgan looked like a hamster with down syndrome. I could see the resemblance.

Morgan lived with friends in San Carlos Park, between Fort Myers and Bonita Springs. She slept on the couch in the living room. It was a very uncomfortable situation for her. She fought with her roommates all the time, and one day, after yet another big fight, Morgan asked if she could stay with me.

Morgan was quiet whenever Kayla called me from jail, so that Kayla wouldn't find out about Morgan living with me. Then one day Morgan started telling me that she loved me, and asked me what was going to happen to her when Kayla gets out of jail. Would I kick Morgan out? I told her Kayla's release date was still months away, so we didn't have to worry about any of that yet. Morgan suggested that she and Kayla could both live with me and both be my girlfriends.

"Really? You would be ok with me having two girlfriends, and me having sex with another girl besides you?" I asked.

"Well, if it was any other girl, I would bite your dick off. But I love Kayla. She's awesome. I think the three of us could have a lot of fun together. So, yeah, I would be ok with you fucking me and her," she replied with a smirk.

Wow. Cool! Now I was really gonna live the rockstar

life! Before, when I was seeing Haley, Crystal, Kayla and Manuela, all at the same time, they didn't know about each other. But now I was gonna be living with two girls who both knew that I was fucking both of them, and having threesomes was going to be the new normal. As you know by now, I was never really into threesomes, because I'm just too damn shy to be naked in front of not just one but two girls. But I already had lots of sex with Kayla and Morgan individually, so they both knew what to expect. And I was comfortable with each one of them, so I could see myself having sex with both of them at the same time.

Remember when Patty had asked me to try anal? I really didn't want to with her. But when Morgan asked me to try it with her, I did. And I kinda liked it, although I could not even get it half way in, even with lots of lube, because my dick was too big for her, and she was in too much pain. But she seemed to like the pain and asked me to do it a few more times. She wanted to see if she could manage to take me all the way inside of her. Patty was a crazy freak, while Morgan was just the right kind of kinky. But at the same time she felt so self-concious, whenever she gave me a blowjob, she would only do it while she was hiding her head under the blanket. How adorable is that?

Now we just needed to find out if Kayla was on board with the Mormon lifestyle and having a sister wife.

At the next viso, I was going to test the waters. But that didn't go so well. As soon as I mentioned that I talked to Morgan recently, Kayla got this annoyed look on her face and asked: "Why are you talking to Morgan? Did that bitch try to get with you?"

And just like that, my career as Mormon MacDaddy ended before it even started. Bummer. I never did get to have a threesome with Kayla and Morgan.

At the next viso with Kayla, I tried to bring up the topic one more time. I pretended to be joking around when I asked her: "Wouldn't it be cool if you and Morgan both lived with me, and we all had sex together?"

Kayla looked at me like I had lost my mind. She crunched up her eyebrows and the expression on her face said: "What the fuck are you thinking, asshole?"

When I told Morgan that Kayla was not a fan of our awesome plan, Morgan realized that sooner or later I was going to have to make a choice, whether I wanted to be with Morgan or with Kayla. Suddenly Morgan started making snide remarks about Kayla whenever she got a chance. And now she purposely made noise whenever Kayla called me from jail. She wanted Kayla to know that Morgan was living with me, and she wanted Kayla and me to break up.

Morgan kept telling me she loved me, and she told me that she was worried that I was going to kick her to the curb as soon as Kayla got out of jail. I really liked Morgan at this point, and although I had explored the rockstar lifestyle for a bit, I really am a one woman kind of guy, so I stopped talking to Kayla.

Having lots of sex with a bunch of beautiful girls is a

lot of fun for a little while, but then it gets old. It leaves you empty inside. It doesn't even come close to the feeling you get when you are in a serious relationship with one special someone.

From that point on I just ignored Kayla whenever she called me from jail, and I didn't answer her letters anymore. I felt really guilty, but I figured things with Morgan were going really well, and she was right here with me. Who knew what would happen with Kayla once she gets out, and whether she was really going to come live with me, or go back to Sayville or what.

Morgan had lost custody of her little daughter while she was in jail. Her daughter was now living at the house where her baby daddy and his parents lived. His mother had custody of the child. Whenever Morgan wanted to see her daughter, she had to go to their house. She said she hated her baby daddy, and luckily he was never home when she went there to see her kid. Morgan and her baby daddy used to do drugs together, and he was a total loser with mental problems, she said.

My mother was going to come visit me for two weeks from Germany. I didn't want Morgan to stay with me while my mother was here, because I didn't want to officially introduce her to my mother as my girlfriend yet. And I wasn't going to be able to explain to my mother why this girl was living with me, and sleeping in bed with me, if she wasn't officially my girlfriend.

So to avoid all that awkwardness, I decided it would be better if Morgan stayed somewhere else for those two weeks. Morgan wasn't happy about that. She had nowhere else to go. She burned her bridges with her previous roommates. My mother's arrival was imminent, but Morgan kept procrastinating. I think she thought I was lying about my mother coming to visit, and she was worried that I was really just trying to kick her out and get back together with Kayla. At the last minute I rented a hotel room for Morgan for a few days, until she could find a place to stay until my mother left.

While my mother was here, Morgan and I texted each other on Facebook every day. And at night, after my mother went to bed, I snuck out a few times, to meet Morgan. She told me that her little daughter was staying with her at the hotel room, so we had sex in my SUV. The back of it was large enough so that we could lie down flat, as if it were a bed.

By chance I found out that Morgan's baby daddy was staying at the hotel with her. I flipped out. What the hell was going on? Morgan said he was only supposed to drop their daughter off, but then he refused to leave. I called the hotel and told them to cancel the room. Now Morgan and her baby daddy were standing outside the hotel, with nowhere to go.

Morgan did find a place to stay after all. Then she and I made up. She told me her loser baby daddy had relapsed yet again and that he offered her heroin at the hotel, if she would have sex with him. She swore she said no.

She ended up staying with some friends for a few days. We planned that as soon as my mother left, Morgan would be allowed to come back and continue to live with me. Her friends were a couple. Both of them were drug addicts, and both had HIV. I did not like the idea at all, that the girl I have unprotected sex with was staying with people who have HIV. I told her to stay as far away from them as possible while she was there: "Don't do drugs with them! Don't share needles with them! Don't use one of their toothbrushes! Don't use their razors!"

She told me that I didn't have to worry, that I knew very well that she was on probation and that she wasn't doing drugs anymore, that she had no interest in drugs, and that not even those two people she was staying with for a few days could make her relapse, even if they were doing drugs right in front of her.

But a day or two later, when I called the place where she was staying and I asked to speak to her, they told me that she had gone to see her daughter at her baby daddy's parents' house the previous day and never came back. She had spent the night with him. I knew exactly what that meant. He offered her heroin for sex, and she agreed, and she relapsed and cheated on me with her ex.

I was done with her. I packed up all her things, put them in a garbage bag, and dropped off the bag in front of the door of the house where she was staying. She called me and texted me and swore that they were lying, that she had not spent the night with her ex, that she didn't need to have sex with guys for them to give her drugs, that she couldn't continue to stay at her friends' house, that she loved me and that she wanted to come back to live with me. I told her to go fuck herself and that I never wanted to see her again.

Then Morgan got all arrogant and texted me that she didn't want to be with me anyway and that she was getting back with her baby daddy, and that it was her idea to leave my house in the first place. I got really pissed at her, so I wrote a Facebook message to her baby daddy and told him that Morgan had been staying with me for the past few months and we had been fucking every day.

The next day I got a message from Morgan's dad that said my message to her baby daddy had made him so unhinged, he went off the deep end. Her father said that this kid really was mentally unstable and may kill himself, or Morgan, or their daughter, or all three of them, because of the message I had sent him. And if anything happened, the blood would be on my hands.

I wrote Morgan's father back that if anything like that was going to happen, it's because Morgan is a lying cheater who has sex for drugs, not because I told someone that she's a lying cheater who has sex for drugs. The problem is that she is doing these things, not that I'm talking about her doing these things, so don't try to put the blame on me.

The next day Morgan's mother called me. She was really worried and asked me if it was true that her daughter had relapsed and was doing drugs again. I told her yes, it's true.

I never talked to Morgan again after all that. Later I found out that she was getting worse and worse on drugs, and she ended up back in jail.

Anyway, a few days after all that happened with Morgan, my mother returned to Germany, and I wrote Kayla a long letter in a tiny font on a postcard. I had stopped answering her calls and letters about two months earlier. In my letter, I told Kayla everything that had happened with Morgan. I figured she would find out sooner or later anyway, and I felt like I owed her an explanation and an apology.

To me, admitting when you do something wrong is a sign of integrity. A sign of character. I try to be a good person, but I'm not perfect, and I do fucked up shit sometimes, but at least I fess up to it afterwards, apologize for it and ask for forgiveness. I try to learn from my mistakes, and be a better person going forward.

Once Kayla got my card, she called me and we talked. She told me she understood how and why the stuff with Morgan had happened, and that even though she was really hurt, she still loved me and forgave me. She said since we really hadn't been boyfriend and girlfriend before she was arrested for beating up her boyfriend Alex, it wasn't fair to expect me to be faithful to her while she was in jail for almost a year. She told me she still wanted us to be together once she gets out. Her release date was only another week or two away at this point.

We made plans for me to pick her up on the day she got out of jail. But then just a day or two before her release, she suddenly told me that she had changed her mind. She said her dad, who lived out of state, had come to

Fort Myers to pick her up. She told me she hadn't seen her dad in forever, and he was only in town for a short while, so it would be rude not to let him pick her up.

She promised she would only spend a day or two with him, and then I'd finally get to see her again in person, and we would live happily ever after. The first thing she wanted to do with me, after having lots of welcome home sex, was to take a road trip to Titusville together, to visit her terminally ill grandma one last time before she passed away.

When Kayla finally got out, she spent some time with her dad. And she spent a night at her stepmom's house, with her brothers. Then her dad ended up driving her to see her dying grandma. After spending a day or two with her grandma in Titusville, she took a Greyhound bus back to Fort Myers, and I picked her up at the bus station. By the time I finally got to see her, she had been out of jail for almost a week already.

I took her home and we had sex for the first time in almost a year. She had spent Christmas in jail, so I gave her a late Christmas present: an Android tablet. She was really happy and played around with it in bed all night, installing apps and updating her Facebook page.

The next day she asked me to drive her to her stepmom's house again, because she hadn't seen her family in so long.

For some reason, I got suspicious. When I first met her over a year ago, she had told me that when she moved from Sayville, NY to Florida, she stayed with her stepmom and her brothers, Francis and Josh. She told me her dad and her stepmom had a son together: Francis. Then her dad and her stepmom split up, and her stepmom married someone else and had a son with him: Josh.

So technically Kayla and Josh were not related by blood, but she still grew up with Francis and Josh as her brothers. Josh was a drug addict too, and sold heroin. When Kayla first moved from Sayville to Florida, and lived with her stepmom, she was really badly on heroin. So bad, that she ended up having sex with her brother Josh to get drugs from him. She was actually dating her brother for a while.

When I first met her, and she told me that story, I couldn't figure out if she was embarrassed about it, or proud of being such a free-spirited, unconventional, crazy girl.

Anyway, now that she was out of jail, and wanted to go see her stepmom and brothers again, although she had just been there a few days ealier, my instincts told me something fishy was going on. So I hacked her Facebook page after I dropped her off at her stepmom's house.

I found private messages between her and her brother Josh. Ever since she got out of jail a week earlier, they had been talking about very explicit sex letters she had written him from jail a few months ago. Josh wrote how horny those letters had made him, and Kayla wrote she couldn't wait to bend over and feel Josh fuck her from behind.

And they also talked about how much they enjoyed fucking each other and getting high together when she had spent the night at her stepmom's house a few days ago, before I finally got to see her after I had picked her up from the Greyhound bus station. So the first person she fucked when she got out was not me, her so-called boyfriend, but her brother. Awww, good old family values.

When Kayla called me the next day to come pick her up again, I told her to go fuck herself. She was baffled and asked me why I was being so mean to her. I told her I wanted nothing to do with her anymore, because I knew she had fucked her brother. She called me crazy and paranoid, and denied everything. So I texted her screenshots of her and Josh's private Facebook messages to each other, where they explicitly talked about having fucked each other while getting high together. She didn't have much to say after that. She just gave me some bullshit about how she was sorry that she didn't tell me sooner that she had a problem being monogamous.

Honestly, I couldn't even really say anything about her cheating on me, since I had been cheating on her for months with Morgan. So it was not like I could sit on my high horse and preach about morals and loyalty. But, seriously, your brother? You're gonna fuck your own brother for drugs? That's just sick. I'm pretty sure even Jerry Springer would have a little problem with that.

I wasn't really hurt about her cheating on me with her

brother, because I didn't have deep feelings for her after she had been gone for almost a year and I had been living with Morgan. But I was insulted and disgusted. A few days later, Kayla ended up moving back to her real mother in Sayville. We never talked to each other again after that.

A few weeks earlier, Hussy had started texting me again. She told me how sorry she was about everything she had done to me, how ashamed she was of all her lies, and that she had grown up a lot since the last time I saw her, and if I could forgive her, maybe we could try it one more time. That all sounded oddly familiar again.

I told her I had someone else living with me, but Hussy and I kept in touch anyway.

Now that I was no longer seeing Morgan or Kayla, I started hanging out with Hussy again. I know, I know, I shouldn't have. I really didn't believe that she had changed, but I really liked her unbelievably tight pussy, and we did have some sort of emotional connection after having known each other for so long, and having had sex hundreds of times.

I figured as long as I always keep my guard up, and as long as I remember that I can't trust anything she says, I can still enjoy having sex with her. I didn't want her to be my girlfriend, but I liked that we were friends with benefits again.

I was also seeing Haley again, because I knew that no matter what Hussy said, she wasn't going to be faithful to me anyway, so I had no reason not to see other people, too.

After Hussy's landlord kicked her out of the house near Sunshine Boulevard in Lehigh Acres, she had moved back in with her so-called ex, Dick, the abusive child rapist who lived in a trailer with his mom and sold pills to addicts in the Suncoast Estates trailer park.

Hussy told me she hated Dick and really wanted to get away from him, but she didn't know how, because she had those two young boys and her baby girl, and her job at 711 simply didn't pay enough for her to get a place of her own. So she was trapped at Dick's trailer, unless maybe I could help her get her own place again.

Remember I mentioned earlier that Hussy had been in a bad car accident as a teenager, and she had lost all her teeth? One day she came over to my house without her dentures. She said something about Dick taking them so she wouldn't be able to leave the house, or something like that. I don't remember. Anyway, here she was, with no teeth. I had known for a long time that she wore dentures, but this was the first time I ever saw her without her teeth. She looked like a 90 year old woman. Her lips caved inwards and her voice sounded different. Her lower jaw sat much higher when she closed her mouth, and her face looked shorter. It was not a pretty sight. We had sex that day, like every other day, and I got my first toothless blowjob. (Don't knock it, til you've tried it.)

A few weeks later she told me she loved me, and that she had always known she loved me, but was scared that someone like me would never really be interested in someone like her. But if I would have her, she would like to come live with me, get married, have her tubes untied and have another baby with me.

Since my condo in Bonita Springs was too small for her three kids, she asked if we could move into one of my bigger rental houses. She knew I used to own a beautiful 3000 square foot house with 4 bedrooms in Lehigh Acres.

But when I told her that I had sold my last rental house in Florida a few weeks earlier, she asked if we could rent a 4 bedroom house in Naples and move in together. We actually went to look at a few different places, but I was hesitant to sign a one-year-lease anywhere.

I really did care about Hussy. How could I not? We had known each other for a long time now, and we had been through a lot together. And I knew that she didn't lie all the time because she was really a bad person. She was just really fucked up in the head, because of all the things she had been through in her life. Deep down she really was trying to be a good mother and a good woman. Lying was just the only way she knew how to survive in a cruel world.

But I really didn't trust her at all at this point, because she had lied to me so many times. I didn't want to put a lease in my name and be on the hook for a year, and then she was gonna pull some shady shit behind my back again and she'd end up living with Dick in a house where I pay the rent. No thank you.

Hussy knew me very well by now, and she knew that

when someone is in distress, I am always the first to try to help. It goes against everything I believe in, to leave someone hanging in an emergency.

I would like to believe that there is some sort of cosmic justice that maintains a natural balance between good and evil. Or in other words, I like to believe that Karma is real, and that it's true that what goes around comes around. It's just a comforting thought, that if someone does something bad, something bad happens to them in return, to restore balance to the universe, you know?

Well, I guess I'm not the only one who likes to believe that. I guess that concept is the underlaying idea behind heaven and hell. I don't believe in life after death, but I would like to believe that somehow Karma makes sure that good people are rewarded somehow, and bad people are punished for treating others like shit.

And I'd like to believe that if I do my best to help other people, then one day, if I ever need help, someone will help me, too.

Hussy knew that if she had an emergency, I would feel compelled to come to her rescue. She purposely got into a huge fight with Dick, so he would kick her out of his mom's trailer. She figured I would have no choice but to help her, and find a place to live for her and her kids.

And her plan would have worked, if I wasn't already busy dealing with someone else's emergency. I had met someone new. Her name was Veronica, and I had my hands full with her. So when Dick kicked Hussy out, she ended up on the side of the road with her suitcases.

Her parents had to drive all the way down to North Fort Myers to pick up her and her kids and bring them to Ocala. Hussy ended up living there for the next year.

VERONICA

Remember the online ad I placed a long time ago? The one that Hussy, Kayla, Crystal and Manuela had answered. Well, apparently it was still floating around on the web somewhere, and suddenly, out of nowhere, this girl Veronica wrote me an email. She said she had seen my ad online, and she was interested in a mutually beneficial relationship.

Veronica sent me a picture of herself. She was only 20 years old, 6 feet tall, skinny, with long blonde hair. She was beautiful. She looked like a model. I had a hard time believing that was really her in the picture.

She was staying at the La Quinta on Route 41. Right there I knew she was a hooker. 20 year old girls don't live in hotels, unless they are drug addicted hookers.

After all the crazy and painful things I had been through with all the other girls who had responded to my ad, I should have known better than to agree to meet her at the La Quinta. I should have run the other way. But she was freakin' beautiful, and I'll be honest: I wanted to have sex with her at least once.

I met Veronica for the first time on December 6th, 2011. When I got there at 11 pm, as agreed, she told me that she had to run an errand first, but she would be back shortly. I knew what that meant. She was on her way to get drugs.

When she got back, and I came up to her room, she was even more beautiful than her picture. She looked like an elf from Lord of The Rings, with her long blonde hair, pale skin, dark brown eyes, and her graceful features.

She wore a tight white v-neck t-shirt and skin-tight black yoga pants with the word PINK on her behind. We sat down on one of the two beds and talked. I told her I knew she was on drugs. She gave me a surprised look and asked if I was a cop. I said no. I told her about my experiences with Alice and the girls I had met in Florida. Now Veronica felt comfortable enough to tell me her story.

She suffered from severe anxiety and PTSD. She used to be a very good basketball player and was hoping to get a scholarship. But then she got into an accident and hurt her leg and back. Her promising basketball career was over before it started, and she ended up being addicted to pain killers. She told me she supported her drug habit by having sex with a handful of "friends."

I learned to hate when girls use the word "friend" when they talk about the dope boys and johns they have sex with. None of these "friends" really care about the girl. They feed her poison and use her for sex. With friends like that, who needs enemies?

Anyway, after talking for a while, Veronica and I took our clothes off and she began to gently suck my dick.

Suddenly there was loud knocking on the door. We both were startled, and I hastily put my clothes back on.

Veronica was still naked, when she opened the door just a crack and whispered to someone on the other side. Then she turned around and said: "Sorry, my friend needs to get something out of the room."

"Can't that wait?" I asked.

"No, the room is actually in her name. She's just letting me use it. So I have to let her in," she replied.

She opened the door, and some grimey, mangy old crackwhore with sun-damaged leathery skin, no teeth and strawy hair that looked like a bird's nest came into the room and frantically searched everywhere for something.

I felt really uncomfortable, because that woman obviously knew that Veronica and I were having sex in her room. Awkwarrrd. But Leatherface didn't care. Her mind was on whatever she was trying to find in the room. There was a hectic sense of urgency about her. Veronica gave me a look that said: "I'm so sorry. It's not my fault. My friend is crazy."

Then Veronica said to Leatherface: "Can I have some privacy with my friend?"

Leatherface was visibly annoyed and said: "I'm doing you a favor so chill the fuck out! I just need to find my fucking stem!"

Finally Leatherface walked out of the room, and angrily slammed the door behind her.

"She was looking for her crackpipe," Veronica explained.

I took my clothes off, and she started to suck my dick again. She had to start all over, because I lost my erection. I loved being inside of her mouth. She was so beautiful. I got hard again. Then Leatherface started banging on the door again. This was getting rrreally annoying.

Ever since my father tried to break down my bedroom door and kill my mother and me, I have been suffering from PTSD myself. I never really knew that that's what it was, until I happened to run across some articles about PTSD many years later. But all my life I've had a hard time being emotionally grounded in the moment. I have always been emotionally detached, removed from the situation. I've always felt like an observer rather than a participant. I often feel like I am an audience member watching my life, instead of being in the starring role.

Nothing that happens to me or around me ever makes me extremely angry, even if that is the appropriate reaction. And nothing makes me extremely happy, not even when I got my first $92,000 check for my Embarrassing Moments website. And nothing makes me extremely sad or scared. Everything is just sorta ho-humm, as if the part of my brain that's responsible for the appropriate emotional response is padded in styrofoam.

Things barely register on my emotional scale. It's as if my emotions are stuck in neutral. My divorce from Donna and the resulting depression were the only thing I really really felt in a long time. And the even deeper, almost suicidal depression after losing Alice too was the strongest, most painful thing I had ever felt in my life.

When my father killed himself, it didn't really faze me. I was kinda relieved that he was gone. And when my grandparents died, it didn't really bother me all that much either, because I wasn't that close with them. Divorcing Donna and then losing Alice were literally the two most painful things that had ever happened to me. Besides that, nothing really felt much like anything, good or bad.

Even when I have a naked girl right in front of me, the situation doesn't seem real enough, not intense enough, to get much of an emotional reaction out of me. Just being in the same room with a beautiful naked girl is not enough to get me aroused. Not even if she is lying in bed right next to me. I might as well be standing next to a little old lady at a bus stop.

A girl actually has to touch me before I get hard. And even then I have to force myself to really concentrate on the moment, really concentrate on what I'm feeling right now, and really focus on the fact that I'm having sex. And even the smallest distraction, like annoying rap music on the radio, will make me lose focus.

So when Leatherface kept banging on the hotel room door every few minutes while I was trying to have sex with Veronica, it was not helping at all.

"I'm sooo sorry, but she's not gonna stop until she takes a hit," Veronica said. "Just bear with me. I'm gonna have to let her back in and help her find her pipe. But you don't have to get dressed again. Just chill in bed."

Veronica let Leatherface back in the room, and they looked for the crackpipe together for a couple of minutes. Veronica was naked the whole time. She had no shame. Leatherface finally found the pipe in her bag on the floor next to the bed I was lying in, naked under the covers.

"What's up?" Leatherface asked me.

"Hey, what's up," I replied nonchalantly, pretending to be Mr. Cool, like this situation was totally normal and I wasn't weirded out at all. Just another Tuesday night. No biggie.

Leatherface left and Veronica started to suck my dick for the third time. She was very gentle and it felt really good. She got me really hard. Then I got on top of her. I couldn't wait to finally be inside of her pussy. And it felt amazing. Warm and soft. She lay there with her legs spread wide, quietly, barely moving her hips, kissing me, gently embracing me, softly running her hands down my back, and pulling me deeper inside of her. She didn't try to control the rythm and she didn't overact like a porn star. She was perfect.

For some reason I was more turned on by her than by any other girl I had been with before. Maybe it was her breasts. They looked completely different than Donna's. Veronica had smallish, perky, young girl breasts, with very small nipples. They were the most beautiful breasts I had ever seen, even if they were by no means the biggest. They were completely unspoiled by age or gravity. I kept looking at them, and kissing them, while thrusting my rock hard dick into her perfect little pussy faster and faster.

I was about to cum, when Leatherface started banging on the door again. "I need the room!" she yelled.

"God damn! What the fuuuck?!" I moaned.

"Go ahead, baby, finish. Cum inside of me," Veronica whispered.

"I can't now. All that banging on the door is really distracting," I said.

"Yeah you can. Let me feel you cum in my pussy. I want to feel your warm cum in me," Veronica whispered while kissing my neck.

But it was no use. It was all over for me. There was no way I was gonna cum now. Especially not while I was picturing Leatherface standing on the other side of the door, tapping her foot impatiently.

I got dressed. I was really frustrated. Veronica felt guilty. She gave me a worried look and apologized over and over. "I'm so sorry. I'll make it up to you next time, if you want to see me again," she said.

"Yeah, of course I want to see you again," I replied. "How about tomorrow?"

"Yeah, I would really like that," she said with a smile.

The next night Veronica was staying at the Budget Inn on 41, near Lee Memorial Hospital. It was pretty late at night when we met up. We both felt so comfortable around each other, as if we had known each other for a long time. While she was shooting up heroin right in front of me, she told me that she wished she could quit drugs. She told me her grandparents were about to come down from Boston in a few days, to try to get her into a rehab program. She told me about some sort of rapid detox. She hoped it would help her. While I was waiting for her to finish shooting up, I was lying on the bed naked, masturbating.

Then she smoked some crack and finally sat down next to me. She started kissing me while moving her hand between my legs. Then she slowly kissed her way down my stomach to my dick and started sucking it. I got on top of her and she wrapped her long legs around me, and pushed me deeper inside of her. Having sex with her was the happiest I had been in a long time.

After I came inside of her, she smiled and kissed me again. We talked for a while, and then we had sex a second time. Afterwards she washed up and said that she felt really comfortable around me. "I usually have a hard time making conversation with guys, but you are really easy to talk to," she said. "I like being around you."

I was going to leave, but she said: "Please don't go yet. Will you lie down next to me for a while?"

"Sure," I said. I really liked this girl. She was so sweet.

We lay down in bed and she snuggled up next to me. I had my arm around her, her head was resting on my shoulder, and one of her legs was lying across mine, with her foot between my feet. For some reason it felt like we were supposed to meet, and we were supposed to lie here together. She fell asleep in my arms. I never wanted this moment to end.

In her sleep, she put one of hands up to her mouth, and started to suck her thumb like a little girl. Like so many times before, one little word, one little gesture, told me volumes. And somehow her sucking her thumb told me that she had been sexually abused ever since she was a little girl. Sucking her thumb reminded her of the last time in her life when the world was still ok. It comforted her and made her feel safe, because it took her back to a time in her life, before she had been molested.

Young children are totally helpless. They depend on their parents to protect them from the harsh reality of the real world. Parents are supposed to create a protective bubble around their children. A safe, warm and friendly world of unconditional love. A non-threatening fantasy world of talking puppets, unicorns, Santa Claus and the Easter Bunny. When parents fail their child, and allow their child to be exposed to the rancid real world too soon, it does a lot of damage to the kid's psyche. A 4 year old girl is not supposed to know what it feels like to have a man touch her in a sexual way.

When that sort of thing happens to a young girl, the world is no longer a safe place for her. Especially if the man who molested her is her own father or some other close family member. If she can't even depend on her own parents, her protectors, to keep her from harm, how can she ever trust complete strangers not to hurt her?

Suddenly her protective bubble bursts, and she is exposed to the fact that the world is a scary, dangerous, dark place, at a time when her young mind is simply not able to cope with that reality yet.

Early childhood abuse or abandoment is so traumatic for a young child, it causes lifelong problems. It leads to trust issues, and that leads to relationship problems, because how can you love someone if you can't even trust them not to hurt you or abandon you? If your own mother or father didn't love you enough not to hurt you or abandon you, how can you trust complete strangers not to do the same or worse to you?

And that inability to love or bond with another human being often leads to depression, feelings of worthlessness, low self-esteem, and ultimately to drug abuse. I believe, in a nutshell, that most drug addicts are addicts, because they were abused or abandoned as children. They didn't get enough love as a child, consequently were incapable of forming meaningful relationships with other people, felt unloved and unlovable, lonely and miserable, and they started using drugs as a substitute for love.

They felt miserable, lonely and unhappy every day of their lives, even if they didn't realize it, because they didn't know aynthing else, so feeling miserable just felt normal. And then, when someone happened to offer them some drugs, they felt carefree and happy for the first time in their lives. For a few minutes, all their worries, all their fears and anxiety was forgotten.

If someone had offered me drugs when all that stuff with my abusive father happened, I would be a drug addict today. I was just lucky that there were no drugs around me when I was a young, impressionable child, going through difficult times.

And today, as a grown up, I know better than to start using drugs. I know I would like the way they'd make me feel. I know I would want to do them again and again to forget about my feelings and worries for a little while. And that's why I'm not even going to try them. I don't want to know how good they could make me feel, because I know I wouldn't be able to stop.

I read a study in which psychologists interviewed about 250 prostitutes in Los Angeles, New York, Chicago and a few other major cities. They found that almost all of these girls had been sexually abused in their childhood. And almost all of them suffered from Post Traumatic Stress Disorder. In fact, their level of PTSD was worse than that found among Vietnam veterans. Crazy, huh?

The study found that most of these girls had been trough very traumatic events in their lives and suffered severe emotional distress, so they ended up using drugs to self-medicate. They tried to make themselves feel better, and drugs made them feel better for a little while. I guess I was doing the same thing when I had sex with a bunch of girls after my divorce from Donna and after losing Alice. For a few minutes, while I had sex, I wasn't thinking about how unhappy I was. Just like Patty, when she kept raping me every day, while she was staying with me in Florida after Rocky's death.

Anyway, once the girls got addicted to drugs, they resorted to prostitution as the only means to make enough money to support their habit. The study showed that in almost every case, drug use lead to prostitution.

But occasionaly it was the other way around. Some girls thought prostitution would be a great way to make some quick cash. But once they started having sex for money, they realized that it's not easy at all, to have strangers touch you and use you. Walking into a room with a complete stranger, and being naked and totally vulnerable is a very traumatic experience. The study found that prostitution itself causes PTSD as well, because it's very scary to walk into a room and not know if the next guy is going to rape you, kill you, arrest you or just treat you like shit.

Drugs lead to prostitution, and prostitution leads to drugs. Those two go hand in hand. It's a vicious cycle, that's almost impossible to escape once you get caught up in it.

After meeting Alice and her friends, and then meeting a bunch of girls in Florida, and their friends, I have seen prostitution from the girls' point of view. And I have learned that no matter what girls write in their Backpage escort ads about how much they enjoy what they do, the truth is, they hate what they do. It makes them miserable. It makes them feel like garbage. And they can only do it if they get high before they walk into a room with the next guy.

And that's why today I'm against prostitution. Not because I'm trying to tell girls what they can or cannot do with their bodies, but because I know how much the girls who do it suffer.

Anyway, let's get back to Veronica:

When she snuggled up next to me and started sucking her thumb, I knew what that meant. She was regressing back to the last time in her life when she felt safe and carefree. I had seen it before. Alice used to like drawing in coloring books for little kids. So did Haley. Alice's friend Kat was obsessed with Hello Kitty childrens' toys. Every girl I knew who had been sexually abused as a young child, held on to childlike traits, from a time before she was abused, because it reminded her of a more innocent time in her life. Even my ex-wife Donna liked to watch children's TV shows, because she didn't like the grown up world she lived in.

While holding Veronica in my arms that night at the Budget Inn, I just wanted to hug her tight and protect her from the world. I just wanted to hold her forever. I fell in love with her that night. She seemed so sad, so lonely, so vulnerable and fragile. I felt like we were kindred spirits. I felt like we had met for a reason, and I was exactly what she needed in her life, and she was exactly what I needed in mine. But I didn't tell her any of that. I figured she'd think I'm crazy. I figured I was just one more guy among many other guys she had sex with.

The next night I saw her again. She said she was really dope sick, and she asked me if I could give her a ride to go get some drugs. I really didn't want to, but I was in love with her, so I said yes anyway. People do really stupid things when they're in love. She asked me to take her to a little blue house on Broadway.

She told me to park the car in the driveway and turn the headlights off. It was dark, but I could see a bunch of black thugs hanging out in front of the house. She walked over to two of them and they began to argue. Something wasn't right.

Meanwhile another one walked up to my car and knocked on the driver side window. I rolled it down. Don't ask me why. He leaned into the car and asked: "You party?" That's thug speak for "Do you take drugs?" I said no. I shoulda said yes. That probably woulda made me look less like a cop or a snitch or whatever this lowlife thought I was. "Lemme see your driver's license," he demanded.

"Hell no," I said.

"Gimme your license," he insisted.

"No fucking way," I said. Man, this shit was not cool. I wanted to get the hell out of here. I could tell that something bad was about to happen.

He looked to where Veronica was arguing with those two other thugs and yelled over to her: "Yo bitch, who dis nigga in da car?"

Suddenly she quickly walked back to my car, while those two thugs were following her. They were lifting the fronts of their shirts up and I could see that they had guns tucked into their belts.

Veronica was scared. Not a good sign. She wasn't even all the way in the car yet, when she yelled at me: "Go! Go! GO! GOOO! This is not a game! GOOOO!!!"

I backed the car out of the driveway as quickly as I could. I almost hit a passing car in the street. "Watch OUT!" Veronica screamed. "Oh my God, we gotta get outta here!"

My heart was pounding. This whole thing scared the shit out of me. Those two thugs with guns were almost at the car now.

I was about to floor the gas pedal and speed away, when Veronica yelled: "We gotta pick her up! We can't leave her here!" She was pointing at a girl with black hair who was standing in the driveway of the neighboring house.

"I can't stop right next door! They're gonna get us!" I yelled back. I wasn't sure who or why they were gonna get us, but I knew I didn't want to be gotten. They didn't look like happy campers.

"STOP THE CAR! WE CAN'T LEAVE HER HERE!" Veronica screamed.

So I stopped in front of the next driveway. The black-haired girl jumped in the backseat. Those two black thugs were only a few feet away from the car. They had the guns in their hands now. What the fuck was going on here?!

Some black guy climbed into my car right behind the girl with black hair.

Holy fucking fuck. We're dead, I thought.

"GO! GOOO!" Veronica screamed. We took off.

The black guy in my car apparently was not with the thugs who were chasing us. I guess he was friends with Veronica or the other girl.

"Those guys think I'm a CI," Veronica said.

"What's a CI?"

"A criminal informant. A snitch," she explained.

"Why do they think that?" I asked.

"Because there's an article in the newspaper about me being a snitch," she replied. "Last time I got arrested, I promised the cops that I'd cooperate. But then I didn't, so the cops gave the newspaper my name."

Oh, terrific! I had barely known this girl for what? Two days? And she already almost got me killed. I was totally stressed out. My heart was pounding like crazy. Veronica and the two people on my backseat were freaked out, too. They started smoking crack and passed the pipe around to each other. The whole car was filling up with smoke.

"Can you at least open a window?" I asked.

We were going to drop the black guy off somewhere. He didn't have his own crackpipe and asked if he could "borrow" Veronica's. She said no. He got more and more agitated. By the time we got to where he wanted to be dropped off, I was so stressed out, I hit a parked car while backing into the parking spot next to it. As soon as he got out of the car, we left. So I almost got killed and had a hit and run accident in one night. Thanks Veronica. Nice to meet you.

We met a few more times after that, but she was a typical drug addict, with all the typical drug addict traits. She was totally unreliable and unpredictable. If we made plans to get together, I never knew if she was actually going to show up. Sometimes she did, sometimes she didn't, without any explanation or apology.

I was still seeing Haley and Crystal as well, because Veronica was obviously seeing other people, too.

One morning I woke up at 8 am, because someone was knocking on my door. Nobody ever comes knocking on my door unannounced, because I live in a gated community with security and video surveillance. So people never just show up at my door. But someone was forcefully knocking on my door now.

I opened the door in my underwear. It was Veronica.

"What the hell are you doing here?" I asked. "You can't just show up here like that. What if I had company? What if I had another girl over? How the hell am I gonna explain who you are and why you just show up here like that?"

She started to cry: "Please don't be mad at me. I didn't know where else to go. I'm in sooo much pain. I need help. Can I please stay with you for a while?"

Veronica couldn't even stand up straight. She was hunched over in pain, holding on to the wall next to the door with one hand. I let her in. "What happened? What's wrong?" I asked. I was really worried about her. She looked terrible. He had scabs all over her face. Crack addicts like to pick their face when they smoke crack.

She put one of her arms around my neck and hobbled towards my bedroom, while using me as a crutch. "It's my leg," she said, still crying. "It's hurts sooo bad. I can't take it anymore!"

I helped her lie down in my bed. She told me she thought she had pulled a muscle, or torn a ligament, or maybe broken a bone or something. She wasn't sure how it happened, or why she was in so much pain. I ran the water in the bathtub. I figured maybe a hot bath would help her feel better.

She needed my help to use the toilet, to get undressed, and to get into the tub. Once she was in the hot water, she felt a little bit better for a little while. She told me she needed to tell me something. She had a warrant. So now this was the second time in my life I was aiding and abetting a wanted fugitive. Great. I was really moving on up in the world. She begged me not to call the cops on her, and said that she would leave if I didn't want her in my house. I felt so bad for her. She was a crying, helpless little pile of misery.

After she got out of the tub, she was in too much pain to put her clothes back on, so she got back into bed naked. She asked me to look at the back of her right leg between her butt and her knee. She asked me if it looked swollen or red. No, it looked like her other leg. I couldn't see anything unusual.

I gave her some Ibuprofen and some over-the-counter sleeping pills. I thought maybe some sleep would help her feel better. I lay down next to her, and she fell asleep in my arms again. The next morning she was still in terrible pain. I brought her breakfast in bed. She fell asleep again afterwards. Later in the day she asked me to get her drugs. I told her I wouldn't do that.

She said she couldn't take the pain without drugs and asked me to bring her to a drug dealer's house. She spent the night there. The next day she asked me to come pick her up again. This went on for a couple of days. She kept leaving to get drugs and then came back to me, because my place was now her safe haven.

This was the time when Hussy got into a big fight with Dick, and she thought that once she had nowhere else to go, I would come to her rescue and move into a house in Naples with her and her kids. But I was way too busy with Veronica, so Hussy ended up moving to Ocala.

Veronica always asked me to pick here up at a different place, because she bounced around from one cheap motel to the next. One day she asked me to come get her at the Gulfview Motel. When I got there, she was staying in a room with several other hookers. She told me that she had changed her mind and that she wanted to stay there, but she wanted to have sex with me before I leave.

She couldn't even walk or move her leg without being in terrible pain. I told her I really didn't want to have sex with her in that condition. She said it would be ok, as long as I was careful and didn't thrust into her too hard. I told her I would feel horribly selfish if I would cause her pain to make myself feel good at her expense.

She wouldn't take no for an answer, and asked me to pull her yoga pants off, because she was in too much pain to do it herself. So I helped her take them off. She spread her legs for me and told me with a strained smile that I should feel very special, because she was in too much pain to have sex with anyone else, but she wanted to have sex with me. Just with me, and nobody else.

While she said that, I saw that someone else's cum was slowly dripping out of her pussy. She obviously had sex with someone else right before I got there. I didn't have sex with her in a few days, since before she showed up at my door unannounced that morning at 8 am. I just felt it was wrong to take advantage of her in her condition.

But now that I saw a glob of someone else's thick white cum slowly dripping out of her pussy, and I knew that she had obviously been having sex with other people despite the pain, I figured I might as well have sex with her, too. And it's not like I was forcing myself on her. She was literally begging me to fuck her. I took my pants off and rubbed my dick with one hand until I got hard, while using my other hand to wipe the cum off her pussy lips with the sheets. But I didn't say anything about it.

Then I got on top of her and gently eased my dick inside of her. She squirmed in pain. "I can't do this," I said. I felt so guilty for even trying to have sex with her like this.

"It's ok. Don't stop. Keep fucking me," she said with her eyes closed and pain in her voice. In some sick way, it was starting to really turn me on that she was begging me to fuck her while she was in this much pain. Every single time I thrust my dick inside of her, she was in unbearable pain. She had tears in her eyes. Her hands were clutching the sheets. Meanwhile I got hornier and hornier. I knew she wouldn't be able to handle this agony for long, and sooner or later she would tell me to get off her, so I had to make every thrust count.

I pushed myself inside her as slowly and gently as I could. I moved my dick inside of her in slow motion, from the very tip of the head to the very bottom of the shaft and back again. Every time I was balls deep inside of her, I paused for a few seconds, just concentrating on what it felt like to be inside of her, while her warm soft pussy lips were wrapped around me. I think I only had to push my dick inside of her for maybe 9 or 10 times before I came. After I finished, and I could think clearly again, I almost felt like I had just raped her.

Day after day, the pain in her leg was getting worse and worse. The next time she was at my house, she asked me to buy her a crutch. Then she called her stepdad, a doctor, and asked him what the pain could be. He told her he needed to see her, but she didn't trust him or her mother not to call the cops on her. I offered to take her to the emergency room, but she didn't want to, because she was afraid she'd get arrested.

I ended up giving her some antibiotics, just in case the pain in her leg was some sort of infection. Then she asked me to drop her off at the Value Place on Colonial, because some of her hooker friends were staying there, and she said they would give her some drugs. I didn't hear from her anymore for a few days after that.

When she finally called me again, she told me the police had been at the Value Place, to arrest the people in the room next to the one she was staying in, and when they asked her for her ID, they arrested her, too. When they saw how much pain she was in, they took her to Lee Memorial Hospital instead of jail.

I visited her in the hospital a few times. The doctors pumped her so full of painkillers, she wasn't even lucid the first time I visited her. She didn't even know I was there. Her mother Rachel was by her bedside, and we talked for a few minutes. Rachel said Veronica had been asking for me in her daze.

When I visited Veronica the next day, she was awake and I brought her pulled pork sandwiches from Burgerque on 41, and raspberry ice cream from Love Boat. She was really happy and started to cry because she was so touched that I went out of my way to visit her and bring her her favorite foods.

She told me that the doctors said she had a life-threatening MRSA infection and that if I hadn't given her the antibiotics, she'd be dead now.

She said she was done with drugs for good, and that she really liked being at my house. She asked if she could come live with me once she gets out of the hospital. I told her yes, of course. I still didn't have the balls to tell her I was in love with her, because I felt I'd look like a fool.

Veronica told me that she would delete all her phone numbers and not talk to any of her johns or dope boys or her druggie friends anymore. She said the only people she wanted to have in her phone were me, her mom, her dad, her stepdad and her grandparents. That made me feel really good.

My Dodge Durango had been stolen in New York a few weeks earlier, and I was going to go to a car auction in New York to buy a new SUV. She promised she'd be good while I was gone, and I promised to be back in time to pick her up from the hospital, so she could come live with me.

While I was in New York, her mother called me and told me that the infection was so bad, the doctors were afraid Veronica would die, unless they amputate her leg. She went through several surgeries. They were able to save her leg.

I saw on her Facebook page that she hadn't kept her word. She was still talking to a bunch of her old drug friends and had them come visit her in the hospital. I was glad I didn't tell her how I felt about her, or I really would have felt like a fool now.

After a few weeks in the hospital, she was supposed to be released on a Thurday. She asked me to return to Fort Myers and come get her. I told her I would. But before I left New York on Tuesday, I saw on her Facebook page that she was posting rap lyrics about smoking crack and that she already left the hospital, against doctor's orders.

She didn't get very far. The cops arrested her in the hospital parking lot, because she still had that warrant. They took her to jail.

I wrote her some postcards in jail. I told her I was mad at her for leaving the hospital prematurely, instead of waiting for me to come pick her up and take her home with me as we had planned.

She wrote me back and told me how sorry she was and that she hoped I would still let her come live with me once she gets out of jail. She told me how grateful she was that I took care of her when her leg was so infected.

We both knew she was going to be in jail for a while. Now I really had no reason to come back to Florida any time soon. So I told her I would stay in New York for a few more weeks.

She wrote me a bunch of letters and started calling me every day. She told me that she loved me and that when she was going to come live with me after getting out of jail, she didn't want it to be as roommates, or friends with benefits, but as boyfriend and girlfriend. She told me she wanted to be in a real relationship with me, and she didn't want me seeing any other girls besides her anymore. She said she wouldn't be able to handle living with me and then seeing me walk into the bedroom with some other girl. And she said she knew that she had no right to tell me not to see other girls while she's in jail, but it would make her really upset if I did that. She said she wanted us to be faithful to each other.

I asked her if she was sure she wanted to be my girlfriend. She had told me earlier that she had dated a few girls before she and I met. And when Kayla was in jail, she had told me that a lot of girls in jail become "gay for the stay" and start dating other inmates. I figured Veronica would do that too, if she was going to be in jail for a long time. So I felt it was better if we just stayed friends for now, and then, once she got out of jail and she came to live with me, we could be boyfriend and girlfriend. That way she could do her thing in jail, and I could do my thing outside. I was going to keep seeing Haley and Crystal, until Veronica got out.

But Veronica told me she loved me and she definitely wanted us to be faithful to each other and not see anyone else. She promised she wouldn't talk to any other guys anymore, and she would not date any girls in jail. She said: "I do like having sex with a girl every now and then, but I don't want to be in a relationship with one. Too much drama. I only want to be with you."

And that's how I ended up with my second jail girlfriend.

LCJ: FORT MYERS' BIGGEST WHOREHOUSE

"The mentality and behavior of drug addicts and alcoholics is wholly irrational until you understand that they are completely powerless over their addiction and unless they have structured help, they have no hope."

"It is difficult to suffer the selfishness of a drug addict who will lie to you and steal from you and forgive them and offer them help. Can there be any other disease that renders its victims so unappealing?"
Russell Brand

Have you ever noticed that actresses being interviewed on late night talk shows always pretend that they have nothing but good things to say about other actors, directors and producers? They all pretend to be one big happy family. They all pretend to love each other oh so much. The reason for that is obvious: networking. If you have a lot of friends in Hollywood, or pretend to be friendly with a lot of people, chances are, you might land a role in one of your friends' next movies. If you want to get a lot of movie roles, it's not what you know, it's who you know.

Most drug addicted girls do the same thing. They not only tell a bunch of guys that they supposedly love them, hoping that one or more of the guys will bite and be a devoted slave to the girl from that point on. Drug addicted girls also tell each other all the time how much they supposedly love each other. And just like in Hollywood, the reason is networking. The more junkies you know and call your dearly beloved friends, the higher your chances that one of them might throw you some free drugs, or introduce you to a new connection. A lot of drug addicted girls pretend to love other drug addicted girls, to get drugs. Or, while they are in jail, they do it to get sex, or some free candy from the other girl.

In Hollywood they sell dreams. Ironically, inmates in Lee County Jail (LCJ) also call it "selling dreams" when they pretend to love someone in order to manipulate them to get money, food, drugs or sex.

But while these girls pretend to love each other oh so much, they talk shit about each other behind each other's backs, because in reality they are neither lovers nor friends, but competitors. Each drug addicted hooker wants to get her hands on the guy with the big wallet. And if another hooker gets in her way, she'll defend her territory.

And no matter how much they pretend to love each other, there is no honor and no loyalty among drug addicts. Drugs turn them into selfish sociopaths. They only care about the next high, and it doesn't matter who they have to betray to get it. That's how they survive on the streets, and that's all they know when they go to jail. Drug addiction is the number one reason why females commit crimes, and LCJ is full of sociopathic drug addicted girls. It's a snake pit of fake love, lies and betrayal. And if they have no problem screwing over their real families and their real loved ones, of course they will screw over other addicts as well.

Almost every drug addicted girl will try to move in on some other girl's man, if she feels she has a chance to get him on her team, and it will benefit her in her quest for more drugs. So what Alice's friend Kat did when she had sex with me, and what Kayla's friend Morgan did, was not uncommon. That sort of thing happens all the time.

When Veronica started writing me letters and calling me from jail every day, I remembered what Kayla had told me when she was in jail. All the girls in Lee County Jail try to get money out of guys on the outside, by selling them dreams, and pretending to love them. Some girls call a bunch of different guys every day, telling each of them that he's her one and only true love. They scam so many guys into sending them money, that they end up having more canteen money than they can spend on snacks. So by the time they get released from jail, they have hundreds of dollars in their accounts, or on the books, as they call it. As soon as they get out, they cash the jail check and go buy drugs with the money.

Remember the sleazy douchebag who wrote a book about the hookers in LCJ, called Sex, Drugs and Taxi Cabs? One of his little stories stood out to me. One of the streetwalkers he had been fucking went to jail. He started to visit her regularly, talked to her on the phone all the time, and put money on her books. She sold him dreams and convinced him that she loved him and that she was his girlfriend.

Then some other girl was released from jail, and that other girl met up with the guy, to tell him that his so-called girlfriend was really in a relationship with that other girl. Those two girls had been dating in jail the whole time, and to prove it, she showed him love letters his so-called girlfriend had written to the other girl. He was crushed, because his so-called girlfriend had him fooled the whole time. She had even put some of her inmate friends on the phone so they would tell him that his so-called girlfriend was really faithful to him and loved him oh so much.

He had a bit of advice for his readers: If you date a girl in LCJ, don't believe anything, anything, ANYTHING she or her inmate friends tell you. They will lie for each other to con guys on the outside. They lie all day long, about everything, because that's what they're used to doing on the streets.

I told Veronica all that. And I told her about my experiences with Alice and those other girls I had met. Veronica was offended. Or pretended to be. She said: "Don't compare me to those other whores. Can't you tell I'm totally different? I would never do to you what those other girls did to you. I will never ever hurt you the way Alice hurt you."

Of course I knew that a con artist will never admit that they're conning you. But I really believed that Veronica was being sincere. I believed that she really hated being a drug addict, that she really hated what her life had become, that she really hated the things she had done for drugs, hated herself for doing them, and that she genuinely had feelings for me and wanted to have a better future with me.

Everyone who has ever dealt with a drug addict knows that they lie all day long. Lying is their most important tool, when they try to con people into giving them money or drugs, or trying to hide the true extent of their addiction. They are so used to lying, sometimes they don't even realize they're lying. It's just habit. And old habits die hard.

So I already knew I would catch Veronica in lies occasionally, and that that didn't necessarily mean that she didn't love me. Becoming a sober person and living a sober life required her to not only stop doing drugs, but stop living like an addict. Stop hustling. Stop cheating. Stop conning. Stop lying. That's a pretty big, difficult change, if that's all you know.

When Alice and I went to Florida together for the first time, her friend Becky called her and asked where we were. Alice told her we were in Canada. Afterwards I asked her why she lied to one of her best friends. She replied: "I don't know. I'm just so used to lying every time I open my mouth, sometimes I can't turn it off. Lies just slip out for no reason at all."

I was willing to give Veronica the benefit of a doubt, if I caught her in a lie. I knew she had a difficult life and that the transition to a new life with me would not be easy for her. But I really believed she genuinely loved me. She had told me a lot of things about herself that I didn't think she ever told anyone else. Like the fact that she had been sexually abused by her mother's boyfriends ever since she was a little girl. It was very difficult for her to talk about that. I believed it was a good sign that she was able to tell me things like that. It showed me that she was not a completely broken human being yet. Despite everything she had been through, there was still hope that she might be able to develop a deep, meaningful bond with me. And that's really all love is.

During the first few weeks in jail, her letters were long and thoughtful. She wrote about the things she wanted to do with me once she got out. She wrote about our future together, and that she wanted to get married and have a baby with me, and live happily ever after. I felt the same way. For the first time in my life, I actually wanted to have a baby with someone. She drew hundreds of little hearts along the top and bottom of her letters.

Then her letters changed. They looked and sounded different. Sloppy. Like she wasn't really putting all that much effort into them. Or like she was writing them hastily, maybe while trying to hide the fact that she was writing me from some other inmate. Maybe a girl she was dating in there? I found out later that my instincts were right again.

A week or two later, Veronica told me that she had a fight with some other inmate, and that the other girl threatened to write me a letter, to tell me what Veronica was up to in jail. Veronica was clearly worried that I would be upset about the letter, and she swore that whatever the other girl was going to write me, was all lies.

I told Veronica that if there was anything I should know about what she was doing in jail behind my back, it would come out sooner or later, and that it was better if I hear it from her, rather than from someone else.

In her next letter, Veronica wrote that she had made a friend in jail. Her name was Theresa. She said she didn't mean for it to happen. Right there she gave herself away again. People only say that kind of thing if they cheat, not if they simply make an innocent friend.

She wrote that she needed a female companion in her life to be truly happy, but that I didn't have to worry about it, because she still loved me and wanted to be with me, but she was going to do things with Theresa, that she couldn't do with me.

Apparently she really thought that was an acceptable thing to write, and didn't even realize how badly it hurt me. When I'm in a relationship with someone, that girl is the center of my world. She's not just my lover, but also my best friend and confidant. She is closer to me than any other person in the world. There is nothing I could do with someone else that I can't do with her.

And here Veronica was telling me that she was gonna do all the things with Theresa, that she couldn't do with me. That obviously implied that she felt closer to Theresa than to me. I was always going to be the third wheel.

Rather than trying to explain that with a million words, and risk being misunderstood, I decided to show Veronica exactly how I felt when she wrote me that stuff about Theresa.

I wrote her a letter back, and wrote pretty much exactly the same stuff she had written me. I wrote that I had met a new friend, and that her name was Faith. Faith didn't really exist. I made her up. She was simply a mirror image of Theresa. But of course I didn't tell Veronica that. I made her believe Faith was a real person.

I told Veronica that I didn't mean for it to happen, but that I needed a friend like Faith in my life, because with her I can do all the things that I can't do with Veronica. Veronica and Theresa had been living together in the same dorm for weeks, so I told her Faith and I had been spending a lot of time together every day for the past few weeks.

Veronica had asked me how I would feel about her "occasionally" having sex with Theresa and if I would be ok with that. The concept of being faithful to someone seemed foreign to her. So when I wrote her back, I asked her if it was ok if I had sex with Faith every now and then. I wrote that it would work out perfectly, because then I could do all the things with Faith that Veronica may not want to do with me. Like, if Veronica didn't like going to museums, I could do that with Faith. And if Veronica didn't like anal, I could do that with Faith, too.

When Veronica got my letter, she freaked out. She was livid. She threatened to beat the shit out of Faith. "I'm gonna drag a ho!" she screamed on the phone. She was sooo upset and jealous about Faith moving in on her man. Then I told her that Faith didn't really exist, and she was really just an imaginary mirror image of Theresa that I had created to show Veronica how her letter made me feel.

Finally it sunk in, and she said I really fucked with her head. She said she understood now why all that stuff with Theresa was not ok. She told me she would never cheat on me with Theresa or anyone else. She said she was 100% faithful to me and I had nothing to worry about. Later I found out she was lying to me the whole time, and that Veronica and Theresa were officially a couple and had been dating in jail for months.

But at the time I didn't know that yet. I did get more and more suspicious though, because I caught Veronica in more and more lies and keeping secrets. Kayla had told me a few months earlier that girls in jail date each other and have sex with each other all the time.

I didn't tell Veronica I knew that was going on. I just asked her, if girls in jail have sex with each other. She said: "No of course not. Don't be ridiculous. This isn't a youth hostel. It's jail. You can't have sex here."

She was clearly lying. And why would she lie about that, unless she was having sex with someone in jail and didn't want me to know about it?

Kayla always told me the latest gossip that was going on in jail, about who was making out with each other, who got caught writing love letters, who was taking showers together, and so on and so forth.

But Veronica kept her jail life completely secret. I realized later that she was afraid she might accidentally let slip out a bit of information that would reveal that she was dating Theresa. So she figured the less she told me about what was happening inside the jail, the better. But the more I realized that she was purposely keeping things from me, the more suspicious I got.

While she was cheating on me all this time with Theresa, I really had been 100% faithful to Veronica. I had never cheated on Donna in over 15 years of marriage, and I wasn't going to cheat on Veronica either. I completely stopped talking to any other girls. I wouldn't even answer the phone when Haley or Crystal or any other girl tried to call me.

A lot of people say Romeo and Juliet is the most romantic love story every told. I disagree. I think seeing an old couple who has been married for 40 years is way more romantic. They truly are each other's best friends and soulmates. They truly have grown together as one, like one soul in two bodies. That's beautiful.

That's the kind of relationship I want to have. I want to grow old with someone. I want to go through life together, face storms together, enjoy the happy little moments together, and be there for each other always. But in order to have a loyal partner, you have to be a loyal partner. You can't expect someone to be loyal to you, if you're not loyal to them.

Unfortunately people who have abandonment issues don't grasp that simple concept. People like Veronica, who have been abused and abandoned by their parents at an early age, believe that if their own parents don't love them enough not to leave them, then nobody will ever love them enough, and everyone will leave them eventually. And being abandoned or betrayed like that hurts terribly.

Nobody has ever killed themselves over a broken arm. But every day, thousands of people kill themselves because of a broken heart. Why? Because emotional pain hurts much worse than physical pain.

When someone you love leaves you or betrays you, it hurts like nothing else in the world. I know, because I went through it with Alice. Queen Elizabeth II of England once said: "Grief is the price we pay for love." So true.

People who have been abused or abandoned during early childhood, people like Veronica and all the other drug addicted inmates in LCJ, are so scared of being abandoned and hurt again that they are afraid of real relationships. Many of them prefer to be in shallow, meaningless, fake relationships, because they think those relationships can't hurt them. Someone you don't really care about can't really hurt you all that bad when they leave you or cheat on you. But those meaningless fake relationships leave you empty inside. You will never find real love like that, because you will never develop a deep, meaningful bond with someone.

They all want to find someone who will truly love them and never leave them, but they don't even realize that by acting slutty, and bouncing from one shallow fake relationship to the next, always cheating, never faithful, they're sabotaging themselves. Nobody will ever take you seriously as a potential life partner, if all you ever do is cheat on people and jump from one shallow relationship to the next.

And yet that's all the love-starved drug addicted girls in LCJ do. They're afraid to put all their eggs in one basket and really commit to one person. One day they profess eternal love for this person, and the next day they proclaim they are madly in love with the next person. And they constantly cheat on everybody with everybody else. They really have no idea what love actually is, because they don't know how to really bond with another human being. They confuse sex with love.

And that's exactly what Veronica was doing, just like all her so-called friends. They all had dated each other in various combinations. And most of them had dated the same guys, usually dope boys, at one point or another. They all supposedly loved each other, and then cheated on each other 5 minutes later.

Veronica wasn't just cheating on me with Theresa. She was cheating on Theresa with a dyke (or a "stud" as dykes in jail like to call themselves) who was known as Snickers. I guess she liked those candy bars a lot. She had short blonde hair and she liked to say she looked like Justin Bieber. Everyone in jail knew Snickers. She had gotten arrested so often, she had spent more time of her young life inside of jail than out. She looked like a boy. She had dated pretty much every girl in jail at one point or another, because she was just as love-starved as everyone else in LCJ. And now she and Veronica were dating, too. Behind Theresa's and my back.

Snickers thought Veronica had broken up with Theresa. But then she realized that Veronica was still cheating on her with Theresa. Theresa and Snickers both got really pissed at Veronica, and decided to date each other to make Veronica jealous. It worked. She was really upset about it and wrote me letters about how depressed she was. But she didn't tell me what exactly she was depressed about. I didn't find all this out until much later. At the time I thought she was simply depressed about being in jail, so I tried to cheer her up by sending her funny postcards every day.

She told me that Snickers was a stalker who wouldn't leave her alone. At the same time she told Snickers that I was a stalker who wouldn't leave her alone. Veronica told me that she wanted to get a tattoo with my name right over her pussy. At the same time she told Snickers she wanted to get her name tattooed over her pussy. She told me she couldn't wait to get out of jail and cuddle up with me under her pink Disney princess blanket. She told Snickers exactly the same thing.

That's how Veronica operated. She threw herself at a bunch of different people and kept telling them all that she loves them. And then, when someone finally said it back, she acted like they were chasing after her instead. She talked shit about them behind their backs, and acted like she wanted nothing to do with them while she was around other people. It was her way of trying to make herself feel wanted, powerful and in control.

While all this stuff between Veronica, Snickers and Theresa was going on, Veronica was also sending love letters to a bunch of other girls. She was fishing. She was throwing herself at a dozen different people at the same time, selling everyone dreams, using the same lines with everyone, hoping someone would actually love her back for real. She was desperate for love, and she was always worried that whoever she was with would leave her once they got to know the real her, so in every one of her fake relationships, she was always with one foot out the door right from the start, always looking for the next fake relationship already. She thought she was completely unlovable, because not even her own parents loved her. So why would anyone else ever really love her?

In all her fake relationships, she actually bribed people to be with her. She bribed guys with sex. And she bribed girls by giving them drugs, or candy while she was in jail. She thought nobody would ever want to be with her, unless she had something to offer them.

While living on the street, she had sex with a bunch of different guys for money, so that she could use the money to buy drugs for herself and her girlfriend, which was always another crackhead. Of course the only thing the other crackhead really cared about was crack. So as long as Veronica fed them drugs, they pretended to be her girlfriend, even if they weren't gay at all.

But as soon as Veronica had nothing to offer them, they moved on to the next person who would give them money or drugs, unless she left them first. There was no loyalty, no love among any of them, although they all constantly threw around the word love. And the more

Veronica dated other crackheads, the more she reinforced the idea in her head that everyone will leave her sooner or later, and nobody will ever truly love her. It was really sad to watch.

At one point, right after she had told me that she wanted to be my girlfriend, she asked me to log into her Facebook account and link both of our accounts in a relationship. She couldn't remember her password, but her phone was set up to automatically log into her Facebook. She asked me to get her belongings, including her phone, out of the jail's property storage.

Once I picked up her phone, I went through all her text messages. I was being nosy. Shoot me. What I found shocked me. While she had been in the hospital, she threw herself at every single person in her contacts, male or female. She told everyone she loved them and wanted to be in a relationship with them. She was hoping that someone, anyone, would say it back. That's how desperately lonely she was. And she was networking, hoping other junkies, who "love" her, would bring her drugs into the hospital. It worked.

A bunch of her so-called friends brought her crack and Dilaudid pills, or "Ds." Those are even stronger opiates than the oxycodone Blues. She was also on a Dilaudid IV drip in the hospital, because of the excruciating pain in her leg. Between all the drugs she was doing, she was more fucked up in the hospital, than she had ever been while living on the streets, bouncing from one cheap motel to the next.

Then I found text messages that proved she had been

having sex with guys while she was in the hospital. One of her johns texted her how much he enjoyed eating out her pussy in her hospital bed. Her mother Rachel later told me Veronica not only had sex with johns, but with some of the doctors, too. How sick is that?

But Rachel was by no means innocent. The text messages that shocked me the most were the ones that involved her. Rachel was a benzo addict. She was hooked on Xanax and alcohol. When she mixed those, she completely blacked out. And she had turned her daughter into an addict by feeding her Xanax whenever she had a bad hair day at school, or felt anxious, like teenagers with low self-esteem often do. When Xanax didn't do the trick anymore, Veronica moved on to harder drugs, until she ended up on heroin and crack. And Veronica learned from her mother how to survive by manipulating men with sex. Like mother, like daughter.

Veronica and Rachel had such a disturbed relationship, they really didn't act like mother and daughter at all. They were drug buddies.

Both of them were tall, skinny and beautiful, and they had the same strange rivalry that I had noticed between Alice and her mother. Like I said, the more time I spent around drug addicts, the more I saw the same situations repeat themselves over and over. Only the names changed.

Rachel pretended to be holier than thou when I had met her at the hospital, but now in the text messages on Veronica's phone, I could see that Rachel not only knew about Veronica having sex with guys for money and drugs, but encouraged it, because she benefited from it. Whenever Veronica had drugs, Rachel got some. Veronica was Rachel's most reliable source for her own drugs. Rachel left the dirty work up to her daughter. In the past, Veronica had sex with johns for money or with dope boys for drugs right in Rachel's house, and Rachel not only knew about it, but got a cut.

The most recent text messages in the phone were from Veronica's stay in the hospital, right before she went to jail. She and her mother Rachel were texting back and forth about buying drugs from dope boys who visited Veronica in the hospital. Her condition was so critical, the doctors thought about amputating her leg to save her life. She was literally on her death bed. Meanwhile her mother made Veronica meet dope boys and buy drugs for her. On her death bed! Rachel gave her money for drugs, to get Xanax, but gave her a few extra dollars, which Veronica used to buy herself more crack and Ds.

During one of these text conversations, one dope boy had been delayed, so Rachel was afraid he'd be a no show, and told Veronica to call another one. Then both of the dope boys showed up, and Rachel told Veronica to meet one of them in her hospital room, while Rachel would meet the other one in the parking lot.

With a mother like Rachel, who could blame Veronica for being a totally screwed up train wreck?

When I found out Veronica was cheating on me with Theresa and then with Snickers, and that she had been throwing herself at a dozen other girls as well, I just felt sorry for her. I should have been livid, because my so-called girlfriend was a total whore, cheating on me nonstop. Instead I felt bad for her, because she was so damaged, and this behavior was all she knew. She was beautiful, smart, and had so much potential, but she was a totally broken human being.

I thought I could fix her. I believed that if only I hung in there long enough and showered her with love, affection and kindness, if only I could show here that not everyone was going to leave her or use her, then one day she would snap out of being such a lying, cheating, selfish, sociopathic whore. If I could show her unconditional love, and if I could get her to bond with me in a deep, meaningful way, I could save her from the drugs and from her own self-destructive behavior, I thought. I was a poster child for codependency.

Anyway, I didn't know at the time what she was doing behind my back while she was dating Theresa and then Snickers. Now, after 7 months in jail, her time was almost up. She had been sentenced to serve jail time followed by a six month rehab program. So upon her release she was going to have to stay at the Salvation Army. I was really worried about it, because I figured whatever she may or may not have done behind my back in confinement was going to be much worse once she had more freedom. And that's exactly what happened.

HALEY'S EMERGENCIES

"One of the greatest diseases is
to be nobody to anybody."

"Being unwanted, unloved, uncared for, forgotten by
everybody, I think that is a much greater hunger, a
much greater poverty than the person who has
nothing to eat."

"Even the rich are hungry for love, for being
cared for, for being wanted, for having someone
to call their own."
Mother Teresa

I was faithful to Veronica, so I hadn't talked to Haley, Crystal or any other girl in months. By now Haley had realized that this was no coincidence, and that I was ignoring her phone calls on purpose. During one of our last conversations I had told her that I had met Veronica. Since I was used to being completely open with Haley, I also told her that I had a feeling that there was something going on between Veronica and her new "friend" Theresa, and that I felt kinda stupid for being faithful to Veronica, while I was pretty sure that she was cheating on me.

Haley was heartbroken when I kept ignoring her calls after that. She and I had been through so much together. We had been so close. She felt I was the only person in the world who really cared about her. And now I was giving her the cold shoulder, like she was nothing, because I was in some bullshit relationship with a jail whore who cheated on me the whole time.

Haley left me a bunch of really sad voicemails on my phone, whenever I ignored her calls. One time she sobbed: "Why are you treating me this way? Why are you just ignoring me? I love you. Veronica doesn't give a shit about you. She's just using you. You and I have known each other for so long now. Why don't you love me the way you love her? What does she have that I don't have? I wish someone would love me as much as you love her."

That voicemail broke my heart. I hated the thought that Haley was in pain because of me. I really did care about her a lot. I did love her. But I had never really thought of her in a girlfriend kind of way, because she was so bad on drugs. I didn't think she was interested, or even capable of being in a relationship, because she was so high on crack or heroin or alcohol all the time. I don't think I had seen her sober for even one minute in the past year or two. And she was getting worse and worse.

In the beginning, Haley and I had still been able to do normal things together when she stayed at my house to get away from her miserable life on Palm Beach for a little while. But lately she had just been hiding in the bathroom for hours, smoking every bit of crack that she had brought with her. It was supposed to last her all night, until the next morning, but instead she smoked it all at once. Every damn time.

When she finally ran out of crack, she'd come out of the bathroom and ask me to take her back to Palm Beach or

Ione. That was bad enough. But then she'd beg me to give her a couple of dollars, so she could buy more drugs. The first couple of times she did that, I felt bad for her and gave her some money.

But then I realized that she did this to me every time now. I was getting fed up and I told her that it wasn't fair to make me drive all the way from Bonita Springs to Palm Beach Boulevard to get her, drive her all the way back to my home, thinking we'd spend some quality time together and watch a movie or something, and then she'd just hide in the bathroom the entire time, and as soon as she got out, she'd ask me to drive her all the way back to Palm Beach. What the fuck?!

I told her if that's how it was gonna be now, then at least I wanted to have sex with her first. That made her cry. She said: "Please don't talk to me like that. Please don't make me feel like a whore. Everyone treats me like I'm a piece of meat. I can't handle it, if you talk to me like that, too."

She said she didn't want it to be like that between us. She said she wants to have sex with me when she stays at my house, but she wants it to happen naturally, not on command. She said she wanted to feel like a normal girl, and like I care about her, and like we're making love, not like I was just fucking her like some cheap whore.

I knew her well enough by now to know that she was telling the truth. She really did want to feel loved. But how was that ever gonna happen, if all she did was hide in the bathroom, smoking crack for hours, and then wanting to go right back to Palm Beach, as soon as she got out? And that's why I didn't see how we could be in a relationship while she was on drugs like that.

When I met Veronica, I obviously knew she was on drugs, too. But she still seemed to be able to function on a somewhat normal level. And when she asked me to be in a relationship with her, she had been sober for a few weeks in jail.

Anyway, now that I had made a commitment to be faithful to Veronica, I stopped talking to every other girl, including Haley.

But like Hussy, Haley knew that I would never say no if she had an emergency and needed my help. So when Haley realized that I was ignoring her calls on purpose, she started to fabricate all sorts of emergencies to get me to talk to her and spend time with her.

One time she told me that she had an offer for a regular job, that would allow her to stop tricking on Palm Beach. She told me she needed to go to the DMV and get a copy of her driver's license, before they gave the job to someone else, and only I could drive her to get her papers.

Every time I saw Haley, I tried to convince her to go to rehab. I told her all she had to do was say the word, and I would drop everything and drive her to rehab right away. So one day she told me she finally decided to go to rehab, and she needed me to take her there before she changed her mind. I drove all the way to Palm Beach to get her and drive her to detox in Port Charlotte. But after I picked her up, she said she wanted to make a quick stop and say good bye to an old friend first. She disappeared in his house for a few minutes and then told me to take her back to where I had picked her up. She really wasn't going to Port Charlotte. She had just conned me into taking her on a quick drug run. She did that a lot. She always came up with new stories why she needed me to come get her. It was an emergency! And then it always ended up being just another drug run.

Then one night she called me with yet another so-called emergency. Her baby daddy Rodney had just gotten out of jail again recently, and they were staying together at a dirty little trap house off of Palm Beach Boulevard. Now he was supposedly trying to kill her, because he thought she had stolen his last bag of heroin.

It was late, and I was already in bed. I had taken some melatonin, a natural supplement that's supposed to help you fall asleep. I really wasn't in the mood to get up and drive all the way to Palm Beach for one of her fake emergencies again. She had cried wolf one too many times.

But I could tell by the panic in her voice that she wasn't kidding this time. She really was scared for her life: "Please come get me! PLEASE!!! He's going to kill me!"

I got up, got dressed and drove to Palm Beach to get her. I had no choice. Even though she had fooled me a bunch of times with fake emergencies, what if this one was real? And it really did sound like the real deal this time. What if I didn't go get her and then the next day

I'd read in the paper that her dead body was found in a ditch somewhere? I wouldn't be able to live with myself.

When I pulled up in front of the run down house where they were staying, I called Haley. She didn't answer the phone, but she came running out from behind the house. Rodney was right behind her, chasing her with a baseball bat, taking swings, but narrowly missing her. Holy shit! I'm as anti-gun as they come. But in moments like these, I really wished I had a gun.

Haley was quicker than Rodney. Taking swings slowed him down. She easily jumped the broken chainlink fence in front of the house and got in my car. "GO!" she yelled, while he was clumsily trying to jump over the fence as well. The baseball bat in one hand made it difficult. We took off down the road.

Haley was hysterically crying, trying to explain what had happened, but I couldn't understand a word, because she was sobbing so hard. And it didn't really matter anyway. It was just another normal day in the life of Haley the crackwhore. Although it was a different story every time, all the stories were the same somehow. This wasn't the first time she sobbed so hard that I couldn't understand her, and it wouldn't be the last. Rodney tried to call her a few times, before her phone died. She slowly calmed down. "Thanks for coming to get me, Oliver. You just saved my life."

I gave her a hug with my right arm while holding the steering wheel with my left, and said: "You need to get clean, sweetie. If you keep doing drugs and hanging out

158

with these lowlives, you really will end up dead one day."

By the time we got back to my place, it was 2 am, and I was dead tired. The melatonin really worked. "I'm going to bed," I said.

"I'm way too hyper right now. I can't sleep. Is it ok if I sit in the living room for a while and play around on the computer?" Haley asked.

"Sure. Just don't wake me up at 4 am and ask me to drive you back to Palm Beach," I said.

Haley laughed and promised she wouldn't.

At 4 am, she came into the bedroom and woke me up anyway. I fucking knew it. "I'm sorry, but Rodney keeps calling me, and he knows where you live. He said if I don't come back he'll come here and start problems," she said.

"Bullshit," I mumbled half asleep. "Your phone is dead, and we both know Rodney doesn't know where I live, and he has no way of getting to Bonita Springs anyway."

"No, really, he keeps texting me," Haley insisted.

"No he's not. Show me his texts," I demanded.

Of course she couldn't. Her phone really was dead, Rodney really didn't call or text her, and she just wanted me to take her back to Palm Beach so she could get more crack.

I was so pissed at her, but I knew that I wasn't gonna get any more sleep until I drive her back. I dropped her off at the same house where Rodney tried to kill her with a baseball bat, and by the time I got home, the sun came up. I went back to sleep.

I woke up around noon and tried to get some work done on my computer. That's when I noticed my two external hard drives were missing. Haley had stolen them while I was sleeping. Motherfucker! I went out of my way for her in the middle of the night and literally saved her life, and she thanked me by robbing me in my sleep. Nice.

I was so pissed at her, I needed revenge. I was thinking about pretending not to have noticed that she robbed me and then, when she calls me the next time, I'd pick her up and beat the shit out of her. Oh, who was I kidding? I had never hit a girl, and I wasn't going to start now, no matter how pissed I was at her.

While I was plotting my revenge, she called me: "Hey sweetie, wanna come get me again?"

"Are you fucking kidding me?" I blurted out. "You stole my fucking hard drives!"

"What are you talking about? No, I didn't," she claimed. "We have known each other for so long now. You know I would never steal from you! I would never jeopardize our relationship like that. You mean too much to me."

"Spare me the bullshit and give me back my hard drives, or I'll call the cops," I demanded.

"Fuck you! Now you're gonna threaten me with the cops? FUCK YOU! I don't have your stupid hard drives," she yelled. She acted like she was highly offended.

"I'm warning you. I never make empty threats," I said. "I'm telling you, I really will call the cops if you don't give me my drives back."

She kept denying it, so I hung up on her and called the cops.

A deputy arrived a few minutes later. Haley was blowing up my phone, calling over and over, trying to convince me that she really didn't have my drives, and that I shouldn't call the cops. She even tried to threaten me. She said she knew a lot of bad people who could make my life very difficult. She should have known better, because that only pissed me off more.

I answered the phone right in front of the police officer and told Haley one last time to give my drives back, and told her that if she continued to deny it, I would just hang up and file a report with the officer who was standing right in front of me. She denied it again, so I hung up on her.

The next time the phone rang, I picked up again, and a voice said: "Please come get me! Ron hit me again. This time I broke up with him for good."

Wait. What?

"Huh? Who is this? And who is Ron?" I asked.

"It's me, Jennifer," the voice said. "Can you come and get me?"

Remember Jennifer the gold digger who looked better than Jenna Jameson? I used to see her for a while, while I was living in that big house in Pennsylvania. She and I had talked about moving in together a few times, and she had asked me to come rescue her a couple of times, when she and her alcoholic boyfriend Ron had yet another violent fight.

But after I met Alice and stopped seeing Jennifer, we didn't talk for a few weeks, and then I saw on Jennifer's Facebook page that she and Ron moved to Dallas. I didn't hear from her in well over a year, and suddenly, out of nowhere, she called me to come and get her in Texas. While I was in the middle of filing a police report, because Haley had stolen my hard drives. You can't make this shit up. Well, you could, but why would you want to?

I told Jennifer that I was sorry I couldn't help her right now, and that I was dealing with my own crisis at the moment. Then I sat down with the officer and filled out the paperwork for the report. He asked me how much the drives were worth.

"Well, they're used," I said, "so they're probably not worth more than $50 each. But to me they are irreplacable because all my photos are on those drives. I can't replace those. And all my work is saved on them."

"Sorry, but if the value of the stolen property is less than $300, we don't do anything," the deputy explained.

"What? So you're not gonna do anything?" I asked in disbelief.

"Nope. I'm going to take your report, but as soon as I walk out of your door, I'm going to close your case," he said.

Unfuckingbelievable. I was about to lie and pretend that Haley had stolen some cash, too, so that the total value would be over $300. But then the phone rang again. It was Haley.

"Look, I swear I didn't take your drives. But to save our relationship, I'll do whatever I can to help you find them, ok?" she said.

Remember that little joke, about the alcoholic and the drug addict? The addict will steal from you and then help you look for it.

"Whatever," I said. "As long as I get my drives back, I really don't care who took them."

"I swear I didn't take them. I think maybe Rodney stole them. I know a lot of people, so I'll ask around for you, ok? Please don't file a report, I promise you'll get your drives back tonight," she said.

"Ok, if I get my drives back tonight, I'll drop the

charges," I promised.

"She agreed to give me my stuff back," I told the officer. "I'm going to meet up with her on Palm Beach."

"Oh no you're not," the officer said sternly. "You're going to get yourself killed."

"Well, if you guys aren't gonna do anything, I really don't have a choice. I need my drives back," I said.

"That's really foolish," the officer said.

I gave him her full name and the address where I was going to meet her. I told him that if I turned up dead, it was her fault.

On my way to the shitty little trap house off of Palm Beach, Haley called me. She was hysterically crying again: "OH MY GOD! HE HAS A GUN! HE'S GOING TO KILL US!!"

"What? Who? Who has a gun?" I asked. I thought maybe she was talking about Rodney. Or some other dope boy at that house. Maybe he got pissed when he heard that because of Haley I had alerted the police and now he was afraid he was going to get arrested, too.

"Do you want me to call the cops?" I asked.

"No, they're already outside," she cried. I could barely understand her, because she was sobbing so hard again. But from the little that I did understand, I think she said something about some kind of a stand off between some guy with a gun and the cops. She was hiding in the closet, waiting for me to come get her.

"There better not be some guy with a gun waiting for me when I get there," I said. "Or I won't even stop. I'll drive right by and call the cops and they'll put you in jail."

When I finally got to the house, I realized just how stupid I really was. What the hell was I thinking, driving into the hood, to a house where some angry guy with a gun was waiting for me because I had called the cops? Did I have some kind of death wish? Apparently yes.

I stopped about 40 feet away from the house, while leaving the engine running. I figured that distance would give me enough reaction time to speed away if I saw anyone other than Haley come out of the house and approach my car. Man I wished I had a gun right now.

I saw two or three shady characters prowl around the house, but none of them was paying any attention to me. Then someone else emerged from the house and approached my car. It was Rodney. My heart was pounding. He had something in his hand. A gun?

I could tell by his body language that he was not aggressive. He was scared. When he reached the car, I rolled down my window. He was clearly more afraid of me than I was of him.

"Haley said you called the cops," he said.

"Yeah, I did. She stole from me."

"Please don't have us arrested," he begged.

"I gave her my word that I won't, as long as she gives my drives back," I said confidently. I felt like Dirty Harry there for a minute. I got the hood running scared!

He handed me one of my hard drives and told me she was going to come out and bring me the other drive. When she finally came out, she was still crying. She opened the passenger side door, but wouldn't get in yet. "Do you promise not to have me arrested?" she asked me.

"Yes, I promise. And you know I always keep my word."

She got in the car and told me she had sold my hard drive to Lorne, the 70-year-old who only had one arm. On our way to his house, she explained that there had been some sort of drug dispute between one of the dope boys staying at the trap house where she was staying, and some other dope boy. The other guy showed up with a gun and threatened to shoot everyone. Then the dope boy who stayed at the trap house called his buddies for back up, and those were the guys I had seen prowling around the house. They were standing guard in case the other guy came back.

Once we arrived at Lorne's house, Haley asked me for $30 so she could buy my drive back from him.

"Are you fucking kidding me? Get my fucking drive

back! Tell him I will have him arrested for dealing in stolen property if he won't give my stuff back," I yelled.

She got out of the car, walked up to the door, talked to Lorne for three or four minutes, and then returned with my drive.

"I am so sorry," she cried. "I can't believe I stole from you."

"I can't believe it either," I said with a sad tone in my voice.

"It's those fucking drugs. When I take Xanax and drink, I black out. I do all sorts of crazy shit, and then I don't remember anything afterwards," she said.

I didn't really know what to say, so I just gave her a hug. Veronica was about to be released from jail and go into the Salvation Army rehab program. I wasn't going to hang out with Haley anymore anyway, because I had promised Veronica I'd be faithful to her, and I had kept my word so far. So I figured this would be the last time I'd see Haley. I was wrong.

A few weeks later, Haley called me and told me that she had a really bad infection in her cheek. She had been picking her face while smoking crack, and one of the scabs got really infected. As it turned out later, it was MRSA. She needed me to take her to the emergency room. Of course I did.

SALVATION ARMY REHAB

"Addiction should never be treated as a crime. It has to be treated as a health problem. We do not send alcoholics to jail in this country. Over 500,000 people are in our jails who are nonviolent drug users."
Ralph Nader

When Veronica was finally released from jail in September 2012, she had gained about 50 pounds. She was still pretty, but she had chubby chipmunk cheeks now. She didn't look like a tall, blonde Lothlórien Elf from Lord of The Rings anymore. They brought her to the Salvation Army on Edison Avenue. It's not only a homeless shelter but also a rehab center.

Inmates/patients are not allowed to have cell phones in rehab, but Veronica asked me to bring her one anyway. I had a bad feeling, but she told me she wanted it so she could text me from her room at night. She said it would help her pass the time until she could finally come home to me.

Veronica also wanted to color her hair, from blonde back to her original dark brown, because in jail her roots had grown out so much, her hair was a mess. They're not allowed to have hair dye in rehab, but after being there just two days, Veronica told me she had met a guy who would get her some from Walmart. Right there I knew something was going on. Why else would this guy risk going back to prison for violating the rehab rules, to bring her illegal contraband?

His name was Dee. He had been in prison for selling drugs. He was a short black kid who tried to look like Lil Wayne. He had long dreads and lots of tattoos. He only had about one more month to go, before completing the 6 month program.

During the first 2 months, patients are not allowed to leave the rehab center. In the next 4 months, they are allowed to leave and look for work. Once they have reached certain milestones, they get day passes on Sundays and are allowed to spend a few hours at home with family.

The fact that Dee was willing to risk going back to prison by smuggling contraband into the rehab center, so close to completing the program, made me suspicious. Right after I gave Veronica the cell phone, I hacked it, to see what she would do with it. My instincts were right again.

As soon as she turned the phone on, she started texting Dee, not me. She told him she would send him naked pictures of herself and asked him for a picture of his dick. And she asked him to bring her chicken wings from KFC.

Then she started texting me and told me how much she supposedly loved me. I didn't really know how to respond to that. Should I tell her already that I could see everything she was doing on her cell phone? Or should I wait and gather some more intel first? If I waited, she would send that piece of shit thug naked pictures of herself and then she'd probably fuck him in some dark corner. I couldn't handle that. Then she called him. I could hear everything she was saying. She called him babe, and the way they were talking to each other left no doubt that there was something going on between them.

When she texted me again a few minutes later, and asked me why I was acting weird, I told her I had hacked the phone and saw that she was about to send naked pictures to some lowlife thug. I told her I was done with her and that I wanted nothing to do with her anymore.

She was shocked that I knew what she was doing. Then she put one of her 3 roommates on the phone, and had that girl lie to me, pretending that this other girl had borrowed Veronica's phone and that she was the one who had been texting and calling Dee, not Veronica.

I told the other girl that I knew she was lying. The fact that Veronica was not only cheating on me, but that her so-called friends knew all about it and they were all conspiring against me by helping her deceive me, pissed me off even more.

When Veronica got back on the phone I told her she was a lowlife piece of shit and a worthless whore. I told her never to call me again. She was really upset and asked me to please come to viso the next day, so we could talk. I didn't really see what there was to talk about, but the next day, on Sunday, I went to visit her at 2 pm anyway.

In jail I had only been able to see her on a video screen during visos, but at the Salvation Army, patients and their visitors were allowed to meet in the same room, in a small chapel. Chairs were arranged in about 15 different little groups of 2 or 3 chairs each, that faced each other.

I quietly sat across from Veronica with my arms crossed and an angry look on my face. She was so upset, she was trembling. At first she tried to make light of it: "I didn't do anything! I didn't cheat on you! I was just texting him!"

"No, you weren't just texting him. You were flirting with him, and you were about to send him naked pictures, if I hadn't stopped you and told you I knew what you were doing," I calmly replied in a hostile tone.

"I really don't care about Dee. I don't even like guys. You're the only guy I want to be with," she said with tears in her eyes.

"Then why the fuck would you send him naked pictures?"

"I was just gonna send him those pictures so he would bring me chicken wings," she said. As if that was a legitimate excuse. As if the fact that she was whoring herself out for chicken wings made it all ok somehow. How fucking damaged in the head was this girl?!?

"We both know what comes next. First you send him naked pictures for chicken wings, then you suck his dick for cigarettes or fuck him for drugs," I said angrily. I was so disgusted with her.

"I'm so so sorry," she said, still trembling with anxiety.

"You're not sorry for cheating on me. You're just sorry you got caught," I replied. I had seen on her phone that she had not only cheated on me with Dee, but also logged into her old Gmail account, and downloaded all her drug contacts into the new Android phone I had given her. She was texting all those guys too, telling them she couldn't wait to hook up with them. She was drug networking, while she was in rehab. Obviously that's exactly the reason why addicts aren't supposed to have phones when they're in rehab. I felt like an idiot for letting her talk me into giving her a phone.

"I love you! Please give me another chance. I want to prove to you that I can be a good girlfriend. I'm never going to cheat on you or hurt you again, I swear!" she said. Her face was pale and sweaty. She was so anxious, she looked like she was going to throw up. She wasn't faking that. She really was genuinely upset.

She had fucked so many different guys and girls while she was living on the streets, walking along 41 as a crackwhore and bouncing from one cheap motel to the next, did one more guy really make any difference at this point? Not really.

Yeah, I was really really hurt and upset. But I wasn't naive. I knew she was a crackwhore, and I knew that that life was all she knew for the past few years, ever since she was a teenager. I knew it wouldn't be easy for her to change. I had anticipated that she would cheat on me. I was by no means ok with it, but was I really

172

willing to throw her away just because she was damaged?

"Ok, I'll give you one more chance," I said. "But if I find out you're still talking to Dee, or texting him, or even just looking at him in the hallway, I'm done. And don't even think about texting any of those other dope boys again."

She told me again that she loved me and how sorry she was, and that this was never going to happen again. She promised she was going to have nothing whatsoever to do with Dee or any other guy from now on.

She calmed down a little bit, but she was still very anxious. Then she told me that when she's really nervous, she gets diarrhea. So that's why she had been sweating and looked so pale. She was trying not to shit her pants. We hugged and kissed, and then she ran to the bathroom.

As soon as I left, I hacked her phone again. I was going to check for myself if she was really being good now. I wasn't just going to take her word for it.

Not even half an hour after the end of our viso, Veronica asked Nancy, one of her roommates, to call one of Dee's roommates and relay a message to him. The guy Nancy was talking to wasn't sure who the message was for at first, so Nancy said: "It's for Dee. You know, Veronica's dude. Tell him Veronica wants to meet him in the cafeteria."

Veronica's dude? So everyone in rehab knew they were

dating. What the FUCK?!?

I didn't know what was more baffling, her audacity, or her stupidity. Veronica thought by having her roommate talk to Dee's roommate, somehow I wouldn't catch on to the fact that she was still talking to Dee, still flirting with him, still hanging out with him, still dating him, and probably still fucking him. I guess she thought I could only read her texts, but not hear actual conversations.

I texted her that I knew she was still dating Dee and that they were about to meet in the cafeteria, and I told her once again what a lying lowlife piece of shit she was, and that it was over. I really wanted nothing to do with her anymore.

I had complete control over her phone, so I was able to turn on the microphone even while her phone was not in use. While I was texting her, I could hear everything that was going on in her room. Her roommate Nancy had the phone in her hands and was texting some other inmate. They were dating and having sex. They were texting about where they were going to meet up next to fuck without getting caught by the rehab staff.

As my texts arrived, Nancy was reading them out loud to Veronica, and they were both laughing at me. They thought they were cool as shit. I hated them both so much at that moment, hearing how arrogant and obnoxious and condescending they were.

When Veronica was around other inmates, she liked to pretend that she was a hustler and a bigshot drug dealer, and that she made enough money selling drugs so she didn't have to trick. She liked to talk down to other girls. She called them nasty hoes, and she pretended that she was above tricking.

The truth however was that she was much worse off than most other girls who tricked. She was homeless when I met her, and she literally had nothing except the clothes on her back. Veronica had walked 41, selling her body to anyone who passed by. She was on the lowest rung of the ladder. Being a streetwalker on 41 or Palm Beach is the lowest form of prostitution in Fort Myers. There is nothing lower than that. It's the final destination on the downward spiral of drug addiction.

Veronica didn't want the other hookers to know that she was even lower than most of them, and that she had sucked dick for as little as $20 and that she had let thugs fuck her for a single hit of crack. So she liked to put on a grandiose act of what a successful hustler she supposedly was.

When Nancy read my text messages out loud to Veronica, she commented: "That Oliver dude is getting to be a headache. You should ditch his ass."

Veronica replied: "Yeah, that dude is stalking me. He's obsessed with me. He's like totally in love with me or something. I never even had sex with him, but he does everything I say and buys me everything I want. I used to have a whole bunch of dumb motherfuckers like him."

Then they both laughed again. I was really really hurt.

And then all I could think was: payback is a bitch.

I called the front desk at the rehab and told them Veronica was hiding a phone. I told them exactly where to find it: in a hole she had cut into the bottom of her mattress. It was her first infraction, so I knew she wouldn't be sent back to jail, but she'd get 2 weeks of room restriction. Basically she was going to be grounded and couldn't leave her bedroom for 2 weeks. Not that big a deal, but at least she wasn't going to be able to use the phone I gave her to cheat on me anymore.

Then I hacked Dees phone and told him if he didn't stay the fuck away from Veronica from now on, I would make his life miserable. Then I hacked his Facebook page, and got in touch with his wife and told her that he was cheating on her with Veronica.

To me that was the end of the story. I really wanted nothing to do with Veronica anymore. She was, without exaggeration, the worst human being I had ever met in my life.

I decided to go back to New York for a while, to lick my wounds and forget about Veronica. For the next 2 weeks I didn't hear from her anymore.

But while I was in New York, her mother Rachel kept calling and texting me. She was getting awfully friendly with me, when I told her that Veronica and I were no longer talking to each other. Rachel started sending me poetry and her favorite songs. And she asked me to read her blog.

Then she told me that her husband, Veronica's stepdad, the doctor, was a horrible person. Supposedly he treated Rachel like shit, and she said she wished she could meet a nice guy like me. Suddenly I had a sense of Déjà vu. This was a replay of what I had gone through with Alice and her friend Kat, and Kayla and her friend Morgan. Rachel was hitting on me. She was moving in on Veronica's man. Later Veronica told me this wasn't the first time her mother had hit on one of Veronica's boyfriends.

I didn't tell Rachel that I saw the text messages between her and Veronica, while Veronica was on her death bed in the hospital. I didn't tell her that I knew she and Veronica were more drug buddies than mother and daughter, or that I knew Veronica had learned how to be a slut from her mother.

Rachel told me that her husband had cancelled her health insurance, and now she was no longer able to get her medication. She was talking about her benzos. He really wasn't a horrible person. He was trying to get Rachel clean. But when you try to get between an addict and her drugs, you are the enemy in her eyes. Just like I was suddenly Alice's enemy when she ran away from rehab and I tried to get her to go back.

Rachel texted me that she needed a couple of hundred dollars to get her prescription filled. I'm certain if I had told her that I'd give her the money for her drugs, if she'd let me fuck her, she would have. But I didn't reply. Having sex with Veronica's mother was a taboo I wasn't going to break, no matter how much I hated Veronica at that moment for cheating on me and talking shit about me behind my back with her little crackwhore friend Nancy.

In the past, Veronica had told me a lot about how mean her mother was. She said Rachel would be pleasant one minute, and then a total bitch the next. She'd become totally unhinged and viciously aggressive over nothing. The more Veronica told me, the more Rachel started to remind me of my ex-wife Donna. They seemed to be personality twins. These stories about Rachel were the first time I ever even heard the word benzo. I had no idea what benzos were, until Veronica told me that Rachel was addicted to them. She explained to me that they were a class of tranquilizers that were even more addicting than opiates, and even harder to kick. She listed a few: Valium, Xanax, Ativan, Lorazepam...

Lorazepam? That name sounded familiar. Donna had been taking Lorazepam for as long as I could remember. After meeting Veronica, I finally realized that I had been married to a drug addict for over 15 years and didn't even know it. Suddenly Donna's bizarre behavior made perfect sense. I read up on Lorazepam, and the side effects listed sounded very familiar. Donna had almost all of them. The information I read about these pills also said that you're not supposed to take them for more than a few weeks. Donna had been taking them every day long before I ever even met her, so she had been on those pills for at least 20 years at this point. Wow. Mind blown.

Over the next few days, while Veronica and I weren't talking, Rachel told me two more times that she needed money. She and her husband were on and off. Right now they were separated again, and he had shut off the cable in her apartment, so now she couldn't even watch TV anymore. She said she needed a couple of hundred dollars to pay her cable bill and a few other bills, and asked if maybe she could come over and watch TV at my place. I could hear baum chicka baum baum porno music in my head, while reading her texts. I know I could have had sex with her if I wanted to. But I was in New York.

While I was up there, I placed a new online ad. I didn't have the ambition to start dating. I was way too depressed. But I wanted to forget about Veronica, and I figured the best way to get over her was to cheat on her with someone new and make sure that Veronica finds out about it. I don't know. It seemed to make sense at the time.

This girl Erin answered the ad. I already knew what to expect, so I hacked her and my instincts were right: she was a drug addict, who had spent the last few months in Collier County Jail. Erin and I texted back and forth. I didn't tell her I knew everything about her already. I wanted to see what she was going to tell me on her own. I told her that I had just broken up with my girlfriend and was looking for some meaningless sex. She was ok with that.

After a few days, she told me that she used to have a drug problem and went to jail, and lost custody of her daughter. Now her baby daddy's mother had custody of her and didn't want to give her back. I had heard it all before. It was the same story like with Morgan and her daughter. Erin and I made plans to meet, once I got back to Florida, even though I wasn't really sure yet when I was going to leave New York.

I didn't hear from Veronica for two weeks, while she was on room restriction. Then she started calling me again. She asked me to come back to Fort Myers, and pick her up, because something had happened and she wanted to run away from rehab.

We had talked about this earlier. I read up on the Salvation Army rehab program. The statistics weren't very encouraging. For addicts in her age group, the success rate was barely 50%. The other 50% didn't complete the program. The average time spent in rehab, before they ran away, was 2 months and 2 weeks.

It made sense. While they were confined to the rehab center during the first 2 months, it was relatively easy to resist temptation. But once they had to go out into the real world and look for work, it only took about 2 weeks before they relapsed. I told Veronica all that early on, and we made a backup plan: She said if she relapsed, she'd run away from rehab instead of being sent back to jail. She'd come live with me, like we had planned all along, and we'd have a baby. Then, a few months later, after her belly was big enough where anyone could clearly see that she was pregnant, we would hire a lawyer and we'd ask the judge to give her house arrest, or "community control" as the courts in Florida call it, instead of jail time. That way she could be home with me and raise the baby.

She and I hadn't talked in 2 weeks, ever since I caught

her cheating on me with Dee. I really shouldn't have even answered the phone when she called. But I loved her, and I missed her. So when she called, I was happy to hear her voice, despite everything.

"Why are you in New York? I need you! Please come back as quickly as possible. Leave there today," she demanded.

I asked her if she was absolutely sure she wanted to leave rehab. She said yes, because two of her roommates had gotten caught having sex with male inmates at the rehab center. She said her roommates were sent to jail based on hearsay, and she claimed it was only a matter of time before she would be sent back to jail because of hearsay and false accusations, just like the other girls.

Since I knew for a fact that it wasn't just hearsay, because I had read Nancy's text messages to the guy she was fucking in rehab, I figured Veronica was worried about going to jail, because she did have sex with someone, too.

But hadn't I already been over that in my own head when I first found out about Dee? She had sex with so many people before I met her, was one more really going to make a difference? If she wanted me to pick her up, take her home and have a baby together, maybe this relationship was still salvageable.

"Ok," I said. "But don't make me drive 1200 miles down there, and then you'll change your mind before I get there."

"No, I'm not going to change my mind," she replied. "I'm definitely leaving rehab. Either you come pick me up and I come live with you, or I'll be on the street and you know what's gonna happen then. I'll start tricking on 41 again or I'll live in a trap house with a dope boy."

I got in my car that same day and drove back to Florida.

Of course she changed her mind before I got there.

She said she would call me during every break between her rehab classes, until I got to Fort Myers. But instead I didn't hear from her any more for the next two days. By the time she finally called me again, I was home in Bonita Springs.

"I changed my mind. I think I should stay and complete the program, you know?" she said.

I couldn't really say anything. She wanted to try to finish rehab and complete the sentence, instead of getting new warrants and going back to jail. It was the right decision. But I was still pissed that I drove almost 1200 miles for her and she didn't even say thank you, or that she was sorry for making me drive all this way for nothing.

Erin kept texting me, and I told her that I was back in Florida now, but that I had changed my mind about having sex with her, because Veronica and I were trying to work things out, and I didn't want to cheat on her anymore now. Erin said she understood and it was cool. She still wanted to keep in touch though, just in case.

A week later Veronica told me again that she wanted to run away from rehab. I figured it would be a replay of last time and she'd change her mind at the last minute again. But no, this time she really did run away from rehab. She didn't even last a month and a half.

MORE OF HALEY'S EMERGENCIES

"It is little wonder that rape is one of the least-reported crimes. Perhaps it is the only crime in which the victim becomes the accused and, in reality, it is she who must prove her good reputation, her mental soundness, and her impeccable propriety."
Freda Adler

While Veronica was at the Salvation Army, Haley kept calling me every day. I didn't answer, because I was still trying to be a good boyfriend and be faithful to Veronica, so Haley left me voicemails.

One night, the messages sounded particularly urgent again. It was another one of Haley's emergencies. She said she had a really bad infection in her cheek, because she had been scratching the scabs on her face. She said she needed me to take her to the emergency room, or she might die. She said she was sitting in Lorne's front yard. He wouldn't let her in the house, and she had nowhere else to go.

I figured she'd just want to come to my house for a while, lock herself in the bathroom for a few hours, smoke crack, and then ask me to take her back to Palm Beach the next morning. But she really did sound bad when she left the message, so I decided to go get her, just in case it was a real emergency. It was.

When I got there, I didn't even recognize her at first. She looked like the Elephant Man. The left side of her face was swollen to at least twice its normal size. She looked grotesque. I took her straight to the hospital. In the emergency room they asked her if she took any illegal drugs. She was going to lie and say no, because she was ashamed. She thought they would look down on her, as if she was human garbage. I told her she needed to tell them the truth, in case this was an allergic reaction to something she shot up, or some of the medication they were about to give her may have bad side effects if they are mixed with the stuff that she already had in her system.

She was surprised that they didn't treat her any different after she admitted that she was a drug addict. They gave her morphine to make sure she was ok and didn't get dope sick. The doctors and nurses at Lee Memorial Hospital were really nice to her.

After a few hours in the emergency room, they admitted her into the hospital and brought her up to a room in the contageous disease ward. She had a severe MRSA infection in her cheek, and it was close to her eye. There was a chance she might go blind in that eye. I stayed with her the whole time and she told them I was her emergency contact. She had nobody else. It was really late by the time she finally got a room, and they gave her some sleeping pills. She fell asleep and I went home.

I went back the next day. She was in the contageous disease ward, and I had to wear a gown and gloves before entering her room, just like when I used to visit Veronica a few months ago, when she was at the same hospital with a MRSA infection in her leg. She had been in the same ward, in the same room. Déjà vu.

I brought Haley candy, coloring books, Burger King and a little laptop. I told her she could keep it. She was so happy, she cried. She told me how much it meant to her that I was there for her, and that with her new laptop she'd be able to get back into selling things on Ebay. She said this infection was a wake up call, and she would finally turn her life around now. I had heard that one before.

I visited her every day and spent a few hours with her each time. We watched TV together, or we'd just talk and joke around. The swelling in her face was slowly going down. We had always been very close, but her little adventure as a freaky looking mutant brought us even closer.

A few days later she left the hospital against doctor's orders, because she wanted to go smoke crack. It all sounded awfully familiar.

The next day she called me up hysterically crying. I couldn't really understand what she was saying, because she was sobbing so hard again. I felt so bad for her. She was so upset, so hurt.

"He raped me!" is pretty much all I understood. "Call the police!"

"What?" I asked.

"He stole everything! My shoes, my bag, my clothes, and the new laptop you gave me! And then he raped me! I'm naked! I don't even have any clothes! If I call the police they won't listen to me. They know I'm an addict and I turn tricks. They're not gonna believe me. But you're an upstanding citizen. They'll believe you!"

Maybe. But the problem was, I didn't really believe her either. I figured this was just another one of her stories, to make me drive all the way up there and come get her.

"Well, I wasn't there," I said. "So I really don't know what happened. I don't even know where you are. If you want I'll come get you, but you're going to have to call the cops yourself."

She told me she was at some dirty little trap house on Ione. When I arrived, the cops were already there. The cruiser was parked in front of the house with its lights flashing. Haley was standing in the street, crying, while talking to two officers. She really didn't have any clothes or anything else anymore. She was wearing some guy's t-shirt. No pants or shoes or anything else. Just that t-shirt. Good thing I brought her some of her clothes, just in case. She always left some at my house.

The officers really didn't take her seriously. They thought she was just a tweaking crackwhore who was drunk or high out of her mind. They couldn't really understand anything she was saying either. So I told them about the laptop, her bag, her clothes, and that she said she had been raped. They looked sceptical.

"Without evidence or witnesses, there's nothing we can do," they said. They didn't seem very interested in Haley or what she had to say. I had seen this attitude before, when I had tried to file a missing person report for Alice, and the cop told me to forget about her, like she was worthless garbage.

Haley obviously was used to being treated this way by cops. "They don't give a shit," said cried. I gave her a hug, led her to my car and handed her some clothes. She got in and changed. She said: "They think just because I turn tricks, I can't be raped. Any guy can do whatever he wants to me, and I'm supposed to be ok with it. Like I'm not even a person."

She told me that she was doing drugs in the back room of that house. Then she passed out on the bed. When she woke up, she was naked and all her things were gone. Her vagina hurt, and she could tell that someone had raped her while she was passed out. I had never seen her this upset. She was ranting and raving about setting the house on fire and killing the guy who did this to her.

When we got back to my house, she calmed down a little. She had asked me to buy her some alcohol at a gas station, and it relaxed her. She told me this wasn't the first time she had been raped. She said at least this time she was passed out while it happened and she didn't have to go through it awake. Somehow that made it better in her head.

The next morning she asked me to drop her off at another trap house on Ione.

A few weeks later, Cirque du Soleil was performing at the Germaine Arena, and we made plans to go see the show together. I made her promise not to stand me up, because the tickets were expensive. She promised she wouldn't. But of course she stood me up anyway. Drug addicts are so damn unreliable, you can't make any plans with them at all.

But we did spend my birthday and Thanksgiving together. We went out to eat at Golden Corral, her favorite restaurant.

A couple of days after that, she called me up with yet another emergency. She was hysterically crying again, and I couldn't understand anything she was saying, as usual. At some point I gathered that she was in Cape Coral somewhere and had a court date, and if she wasn't going to be there, they would issue a bench warrant for her and she'd go to jail. She asked me to give her a ride to court.

I drove all the way to Cape Coral, and when I got there, she wouldn't answer the phone. Great. If she made me drive all the way out here for nothing, I was really gonna be pissed. But after a few minutes, she finally came out of the house. She was either totally drunk or high as a kite. I don't know, but she wasn't wearing a shirt, just a bra. And she didn't have her glasses on. Without them, she was blind as a bat.

"If I take you to court like this, you're gonna get arrested," I told her.

She started crying again, really bad.

"What the hell happened to you?" I asked. "Did you get raped in that house or something?"

189

I couldn't understand anything she was saying at first, but then I think she said that a bunch of guys were in that house and they had sex with her and they wouldn't let her leave.

"Wow. So do you want me to call the cops?"

"No," she cried. "They don't help girls like me anyway. Just take me to court, or I'll get arrested."

"Ok, but can you at least put a shirt on?"

She went back in to get a shirt. I waited for about 10 minutes, but she didn't come back out. Suddenly some black guy walked out and approached my car. Great. Now what?

He seemed scared, and said: "Look, I don't know what Haley told you, but this is not a trap house. This is a family residence. Nobody did anything to her. There's children here, and she's running around the house naked. You need to get her outta here."

"Well, I'm trying! She said she wants me to take her to court. Can you get her out here?" I replied.

He went back inside. Then nothing. I waited for about another 10 minutes. Then some fat girl came out. She also looked nervous and told me the same thing he said: "I don't know what Haley told you, but this is not a trap house. This is a family residence. There's children and she's running around naked. She needs to leave."

"I'm TRYING! Can you please get her out here and make sure she has a shirt on?"

Then Haley finally came back out. Still with no shirt or glasses. Still totally blitzed.

The fat girl brought her a shirt. Haley was so fucked up, she couldn't figure out how to put the shirt on. Her head and arms kept getting stuck in the wrong holes. I tried to help her, but even then she couldn't get it on until the third attempt.

She told me the black guy was a dope boy who had just been released from prison, so he got himself 3 hookers and he kept feeding them crack and fucking them.

Then she called her lawyer to ask him what was going to happen at court. She was still sobbing, and he couldn't understand her, so I took the phone and told him she was in no condition to go to court right now. What did he want me to do? He said I should take her back to the house and leave her there. Then the judge would order a bench warrant and she'd go to jail and get help. He said that's the best thing for her right now, or she'd end up dead. I agreed. Haley overheard the conversation, and threatened to kill herself if she had to go back to jail. She insisted that I take her to court. Alrighty then.

As we were going over the bridge from Cape Coral to Fort Myers, she suddenly started taking her pants off.

"What are you doing?" I asked.

"I gotta pee," she said.

"Do not pee in my car. DO NOT PEE IN MY CAR!!!" I yelled, while she was getting ready to relieve herself on the passenger seat.

"I can't hold it in. I really gotta go," she said.

Luckily there was a McDonald's right after the bridge. "Look! I'll stop there and you can go pee in there," I said.

When I pulled into the parking lot, she got out of the car and said: "Don't leave me here."

That thought had never even occurred to me, until she said that. Normally I would never dream of just leaving someone behind somewhere, but that was the perfect solution right now. Someone would call the cops, and she'd get arrested for public intoxication. They'd take her to jail and then she'd go to rehab. Perfect plan! So I drove off without her.

A few hours later Haley called me from jail. The plan worked, I thought. She was confused: "How did I end up in jail? I don't remember anything."

I looked up her charges on the Lee County Sheriff's website a few minutes later. She didn't get arrested for public intoxication. She got arrested for grand theft auto! What the hell?! When I left her at McDonald's, she decided to steal a car. She spent the next year in jail.

THE ESCAPE

"She goes from one addiction to another.
All are ways for her to not feel her feelings."
Ellen Burstyn

"Romantic love is an addiction."
Helen Fisher

When Veronica told me that she was really going to run away from the Salvation Army rehab this time, I thought she was going to change her mind again, like the first time. But she really did run, together with 3 other girls.

It was dark. I was parked in the back of the building, as agreed. Veronica was carrying a big garbage bag with all the clothes and stuff I had bought her, when she ran out of the back door of the rehab dorm and jumped into my car. A second girl, Alexis, followed her. Veronica asked if Alexis could come home with us, until she could figure out where to hide from the police.

The two other girls, Kim and Sandra, got into someone else's car. I later found out the other driver was Erin. Small world! All the drug addicts in Fort Myers know each other. And Kim, Sandra and Erin had grown up together in Cape Coral.

Veronica and Alexis were totally hyper, talking a mile a minute. When we got to my condo, Alexis called her baby daddy, a 40 year old black drug dealer. When he heard that she had run away from rehab, and now had a new warrant, he told her he wanted nothing to do with her. She called her back-up boyfriend, a latin drug dealer who lived in Lehigh Acres. He agreed to pick her up at the Miromar Outlet Mall and let her hide at his house.

After we dropped Alexis off at the mall, we went home. Veronica said she really wanted to smoke some crack. I tried to talk her out of it for hours. I told her she was just nervous and excited right now, but in a day or two she would calm down, and then the urge to do drugs would pass.

But she wouldn't take no for an answer: "I just ran away from rehab. Now I have new charges. There's no way I'm not gonna do drugs now. Either you let me smoke crack here, or I'm gonna run away, fuck some dope boy for drugs, and smoke crack in some trap house. Is that what you want?"

I replied: "If you smoke crack even just once right now, you won't be able to stop. You'll be back in full-blown addiction in a matter of days, and you'll end up on the streets or tricking on Backpage again. Is that really what you want?"

I was trying to appeal to her common sense. But her prefrontal cortex wasn't home right now. There was only her midbrain, screaming for drugs. Right now there was not a single part of her brain capable of considering the consequences of what would happen after she smoked crack. I felt like I was talking to a mentally challenged person. Someone with advanced Alzheimer's maybe, who couldn't understand even the most basic logic.

She pleaded: "I'm just gonna smoke crack tonight, and then I won't even touch any more drugs at all. I swear! Let me show you! Let me prove it to you! Just let me smoke some crack tonight so I can get it out of my system, and then tomorrow I'll be clean. I'm not saying I'll never smoke crack again, but I won't touch that shit for at least a week. I swear! Let me show you! If I ask you within the next 7 days to let me do drugs, you can even call the cops on me and have me put back in jail. I'm serious. Let me show you! Just let me smoke some crack tonight. Please? It'll make me really horny. You'll love it. When I smoke crack, I just want to fuck all night."

This went on for hours, like a broken record. I couldn't take it anymore. She was relentless. Finally I caved: "Alright, fine. But only tonight. And then don't even ask me for drugs for at least a week, ok?"

"Ok," she promised. Then she grabbed a prepaid pone that I had lying around and she started calling and texting a bunch of dope boys. When addicts try to line up their next hit, they furiously text and call, as if their life depended on it. They have a singular focus, and they completely forget the world around them. Then she asked me for some money and told me to drive her to some little dead-end street in the hood off of Martin Luther King Boulevard. She said she would buy some crack and ecstasy pills. "They make me really horny. You should try some," she suggested with a smirk.

After Veronica picked up her drugs, she asked me if we

could pick up her friend Kim. She said the others had dumped Kim by the side of the road in the hood somewhere, and now she had nowhere to go.

I really didn't want to. I was sick and tired of driving around all night. I hadn't been able to have any alone time with Veronica in almost a year, ever since she went to the hospital with the MRSA infection in her leg. I just wanted to cuddle up in bed and make love to her. But we went and picked up Kim anyway.

When we got back to my place, we sat in the living room and watched some music videos on YouTube. I showed them what they had been missing while they were in jail and rehab. First and foremost: Gangnam Style by Psy.

Kim and Veronica were making calls on the prepaid phone. Kim called her parents. They were really pissed at her for leaving the program and wanted nothing to do with her. Veronica called one of her roommates in rehab and asked if their escape had been discovered yet. It had. They were both full of nervous energy. It was getting later and later. By 4 am I decided to go to bed. I figured Veronica would follow. But she didn't. I was pissed.

At 6 am she walked past my bed to go to the bathroom in the master bedroom. I woke up and gave her a dirty look. She asked if I was mad at her. "Yeah, of course I am," I said. "I can't believe you would rather sit in the living room with Kim than come to bed. We haven't seen each other in forever!"

Of course she'd rather sit in the living room and do drugs with Kim than come to bed. She's a drug addict!

"I'm sorry. I'll come to bed in a few minutes," she said. She went back in the living room, and by 8 am she finally came back into the bedroom, and we had sex for the first time in almost a year.

Then she said she would like to go to the beach today. Sounds like a good idea, I thought. Wholesome. A non-drug-related activity. Yayy! I got almost no sleep that night, but I figured we could doze off at the beach.

"Ok, let's do that," I said with a smile. Then we had sex again and fell back asleep.

When we woke up in the afternoon, Veronica said: "Let's get some weed for the beach."

"What? I thought you said after last night you wouldn't ask for any more drugs for at least a week," I replied.

"Weed isn't like a real drug. It's not like crack or heroin," she said. "Wouldn't you rather have me smoke some weed than crack?"

"Yeah, I guess." I figured if smoking weed keeps her happy, and away from crack, fine. It's definitely the smaller of two evils.

I should have known better than to trust her. She told me to drive her and Kim back to the same drug dealer's house near Martin Luther King Boulevard where she had bought crack last night. That should have tipped me off to the fact that she really wasn't buying weed, but more crack. Let's blame my stupidity on the fact that I didn't have enough sleep that night.

Before we got there, Veronica had conned her father into wiring her some money, by telling him on the phone that she was still in rehab and that she needed money to buy some books or something. He wired her $100. After she picked up her drugs, she said she was too tired to go to the beach, and just wanted to go back home and get some sleep. Of course. Figures.

On the ride home, she asked me to stop at a fast food joint on 41, so she could use the bathroom. She and Kim went into a single person bathroom together. I knew what that meant. They were going to do drugs together. That's when it dawned on me that they hadn't bought weed and ecstasy, but crack and Ds.

Kim came out of the bathroom first. I was pissed: "You two just shot up some Ds in the bathroom, didn't you?" She tried to deny it at first, but her mind wasn't working right because she was high, so she started tripping over her own lies.

Then Veronica came out of the bathroom. We all got back in the car. I gave Veronica a dirty look and told her I knew she had lied to me and they did pills in the bathroom.

"No we didn't. I swear," she said.

Meanwhile Kim was nodding out on the backseat. I had seen those droopy eyes and open mouth often enough by now. I knew she was high on opiates.

"No, Kim just took a Xanax," Veronica claimed.

"Bullshit. I've seen people on Xanax, and I've seen people on Ds, and she's high on a D," I said angrily.

"No, it's just a very strong Xanax. It's a new kind. Extra strong," Veronica said. She didn't make much sense anymore, because she was starting to nod out, too.

When we got back to my place, we went back to sleep for a while. When we woke up, we sat on the porch while Veronica was smoking a cigarette. I told her I was really upset, because she didn't keep her word about not doing any drugs for at least a week.

"I just said that because I really wanted to smoke crack. I'm a drug addict. I lie. What do you expect? I'll say anything so you'll let me smoke crack," she said, like it was ok. She obviously didn't even feel guilty about it.

We argued for a while, and she was getting more and more agitated. She told me she was more fucked up in the head than any other person I'd ever met, and that if I didn't stop telling her not to smoke any more crack, she would kill herself.

Then we agreed not to argue anymore for the rest of the night. I assumed we were all gonna watch a movie in the living room. Instead Veronica disappeared in the guest bedroom with Kim. I was really pissed that this was Veronica's second night home, and just like the first night, she didn't spend it in bed with me, but doing drugs with Kim.

The next morning I woke up really early around 6 am, because I had to use the bathroom. Then I decided to get something to drink in the kitchen, before going back to bed. I saw Veronica standing by the sink, crushing up a D with a spoon. I just gave her a dirty look, but didn't say anything at first. She looked back at me, didn't say anything either, and quickly tried to flush the crushed up powder down the drain.

"What the fuck are you doing?" I finally asked.

"I'm making Jello," she said.

"What the fuck are you talking about? We don't have any Jello," I said.

"Yeah, it's Jello. Lime Jello," she claimed.

"We don't have Lime Jello. That's a crushed up pill. You haven't just been smoking crack. And those pills you bought weren't ecstasy. You bought Ds! What the fuck is wrong with you?" I said. I was so disgusted with her and her neverending lies. I went back to bed.

At 10 am I woke up again. When I walked out of my bedroom, I saw that the guest bedroom door was open. I could see inside. Veronica and Kim were in bed together, making out.

"WHAT THE FUCK?!" I yelled. "Get over here right now! We need to talk!"

Veronica came into my bedroom and we closed the door.

"That girl gotta get the fuck out of here right NOW!" I yelled.

"Babe, it's not what it looks like. I was just rubbing her back. She had a backache," Veronica claimed. Lamest excuse ever.

"Please, spare me the bullshit," I said. "She better get the FUCK out of here before I lose it!"

"It's really not what you think, but ok, I'll tell her to leave," Veronica said. She went in the guest bedroom and talked to Kim. A few minutes later she came back into my bedroom. She said Kim would be gone by 4 pm. That's the soonest she could get a ride. I said ok. I was relieved that Kim was gonna be gone soon. Hopefully things with Veronica would get better, once we were alone, and she'd actually focus on me for a change. Then Veronica cuddled up next to me, told me she was sorry and that she loved me. We had sex again and fell back asleep in each other's arms afterwards.

I woke up around 4:30 pm. Veronica was still sleeping. I went in the living room, and there was Kim, sitting on the couch, watching TV.

"What the fuck are you still doing here? You were supposed to be gone by 4 pm," I said.

She was acting all snooty and said: "Don't talk to me like that."

"Get the fuck out," I demanded.

"I need to talk to Veronica first," she replied, even snootier, while texting on the prepaid phone I had let Veronica use earlier.

"No you don't. You need to get the fuck out RIGHT NOW!" I yelled. "And give me back my phone."

"That's not your phone. That's Veronica's phone," Kim said.

I approached her to grab the phone out of her hands, but she jumped off the couch and ran around the table, while yelling: "Don't touch me!" She looked like she was afraid I was going to hit her.

All the yelling had woken Veronica up, and she came into the living room. "What's going on?" she asked.

"He was trying to take the phone," Kim said.

"What the fuck is she still doing here?" I demanded to know.

"I gotta talk to you," Veronica replied. We went back in my bedroom and closed the door. "Remember I told you a while ago, I need a female friend? I can't relate to a guy the way I relate to a girl. I'm sorry I was so in your face about it when you found me in bed with Kim this morning. We'll be more discreet from now on. We won't rub it in your face anymore, so you won't know when we're having sex."

Did she just tell me she was going to be fucking Kim behind my back from now on, like she was doing me a favor? Yes she did! I was speechless. What the hell was going on in her fucked up head? Did she really think I was going to be ok with her having sex with someone else, and I would still want to be in a relationship with her, and be the third wheel?

"Kim and I could both live with you, and then you can still fuck me any time you want," she said. "Wouldn't you rather do that, than break up with me and then you have to find someone new and start a relationship with a new girl all over again?"

She was suggesting the same type of sick drug "relationship" she and many other crackwhores are used to. She was going to date another crackwhore to have someone she could relate to, and she was going to date me as her means of survival and source of money for drugs.

This is how she had lived for the past few years. She wasn't used to having a guy treat her like a person with actual feelings. No wonder she thought she couldn't relate to a guy. But didn't she realize I was different than those other guys she was used to? She was used to being some guy's sex slave. And to make herself feel better about that arrangement, she got herself some crackwhore as her sex toy. She had no idea how to be in a normal, monogamous relationship with a guy who actually respected her and treated her as an equal.

"Are you fucking serious right now?" I asked.

"Isn't it better you share me with Kim, than not to have me in your life at all?" she asked.

"Uhmm, no. I'm not a dope boy. And you're not just some whore to me. I'm not looking for some girl I can fuck whenever I want. I don't just want to use you for sex. I actually love you. I really care about you. I can't handle the thought of sharing you with someone else. I want you all to myself," I explained.

"If you're kicking Kim out, I'm leaving too," she said.

"What? So you're gonna pick her over me?" I asked.

'It's not that, but she's my friend, and I can't just kick her out into the street and let her fend for herself," Veronica replied.

"Kim is older than you! What the fuck are you gonna do for her? Trick on Backpage? Suck dick to buy her drugs?" I asked with a vicious tone in my voice.

"No, I'm never ever going back to that," she claimed.

"Yeah, you are. If you leave now, you're going to be bouncing around from one cheap motel to the next again, and you'll go back to fucking dope boys and tricking on Backpage within a matter of days."

"No, I'm not," she said, while opening the closet door.

"Yeah, you are."

"I don't want to leave," she claimed, while opening the closet drawers to pack up her clothes. In her mind she was already gone, already smoking crack in some motel room with Kim. She was just going through the motions right now, pretending that I was making her leave, when really she wanted to leave to get high without me getting in her way all the time.

The reason why drug addicts feel closer to other drug addicts is because sober people try to get them to quit. And that gets annoying. Sober people get in the way when all you want to do is get high. So if Veronica had to make a choice between living with me and being clean, or living with Kim or any other crackwhore or dope boy, and getting high, of course she was going to chose Kim.

"Look, you don't have to leave. I'm not kicking you out. You can stay. But Kim has to go. What the fuck were you thinking making out with her?"

"I can't believe you're making me leave," Veronica said with fake indignation. She wasn't even listening to a word I was saying. Her mind was completely preoccupied with how and where she was going to go smoke crack with Kim.

I was so upset at this point, I started to cry: "Don't go. I'm not kicking you out. I want you to stay."

"I want to stay, but you're making me leave," she said. She didn't even care that she wasn't making any sense. I gave up. I had no choice. I wasn't going to try to force her to stay.

Veronica told Kim to call Alexis and ask if they could stay with Alexis and her crack dealer boyfriend in Lehigh Acres.

They were going to meet us at the Miromar Outlet Mall. I dropped Veronica and Kim off at the mall. Kim and Alexis hugged. This was the first time those two saw each other since they all ran away from rehab together.

Veronica stayed in the car with me for a few seconds, and said: "I love you." She was waiting for me to say it back, but I didn't. "I really do love you," she tried again. But I didn't say anything. I was so heartbroken, if I was gonna say anything, I would just start to cry again, and I didn't want to give her that satisfaction.

She got out of my car and into the car of the crack dealer with the others. As they drove away, I could see that Veronica was on the phone with someone already. No doubt she was calling some john, to meet up with him and fuck him. I couldn't hold it in anymore and started to cry, while driving back to my apartment.

When I got home, I checked Backpage. And sure as shit, there she was. Veronica was already back on Backpage! I couldn't take the thought of my girl fucking every guy in town. I was beside myself. I had waited for her for months while she was in jail. And now this. This was my worst nightmare.

The next morning I called my ex-wife Donna and told her I wanted to come visit her and Gary in New York for a while. I needed to get away from Florida before I was going to lose my mind. I couldn't sit in the house alone right now. But of course I didn't tell Donna any of that. I never told her anything about my personal life since our divorce. She still thought I was celibate.

While I was packing my stuff, I found a big envelope in the closet, chock-full of letters. They were love letters to Veronica, from other inmates and some from guys on the outside. They were replies to love letters she had written them. It took me a few hours to read them all. They were from about a dozen different people. She had been telling all these people that she loved them and wanted to be in a relationship with them. Like some sort of deranged psycho.

Some of the love letters I found in my closet were from Theresa and Snickers. That's when I found out that Veronica had been cheating on me the whole time while she was in jail.

Later I found out she had also been cheating on me the whole time at the Salvation Army. Not just with Dee, but also with some guy named Danny, who kept buying her cigarettes and kept giving her money, and obviously with Kim. And she was still writing letters to Snickers in jail. There were probably others, too.

I hated Veronica so much right now. I decided not to go to New York just yet, but to have lots of sex first, and then rub it in Veronica's face. I was hoping that it would upset her at least a little bit.

I called Haley and told her everything that had

happened with Veronica and that I was done with her. I told Haley I wanted to see her and have a whole lot of revenge sex with her. She laughed and told me to come pick her up. She hated Veronica and relished the thought of her finding out about Haley and I having sex.

Then I called Crystal and told her the same thing. She hated Veronica, too, so she suggested that I should take some pictures while we were having sex and text them to Veronica. She came over and I took some pictures of my dick inside her pussy right before I came. I texted them to Veronica with some spiteful comments about how much prettier Crystal was, and how much better she was in bed. I really wanted to get under Veronica's skin.

Veronica called me right after she got the pictures. Her speech was slurred, because she was so high. She tried to act all arrogant: "The only thing those pictures prove is that you're still thinking about me and you're still all fucked up about me."

Well, duh! Of course I was still hurting. Of course she was all I could think about. All the stuff with her and Kim in my guest bed, and then driving off with a crack dealer, had just happened 2 or 3 days ago. For almost a year, I thought we were going to have a future together. She had told me a bunch of times she wanted to marry me, and we had talked about where to have the wedding, and where we'd spend our honeymoon, considering she was on probation and we couldn't leave Lee county. She said she'd like to rent a beachfront home on Captiva Island for a week or two. And we had talked all the time about having a baby together. And from one day to the next, my whole future with her evaporated into thin air.

I also called Erin, and told her that Veronica and I didn't work things out after all, and I was ready to meet Erin now. When I told her the whole story of Veronica and her friends running away from rehab, she started laughing and told me that she had been the other driver, who had picked up Kim and Sandra that night. She kicked Kim out of her car in the hood a bit later, because she hated Kim. What a freaky coincidence.

Erin told me Sandra was a good friend of hers. Sandra was a heavyset stud. She and Kim used to date, before Kim started cheating on Sandra with a bunch of people, including Veronica. That's why Sandra hated Veronica now. Erin told me if I wanted to, she could have Sandra call me and tell me everything that Veronica did behind my back, while she was at the Salvation Army.

While Veronica was in rehab, I had met up with her at AA meetings a few times. It was against the rules for inmates to have friends or family attend the meetings, so we had to sneak, but it worked, until Veronica asked her mother Rachel to attend a meeting with her as well. Rachel got offended at the mere suggestion that she might have a substance abuse problem, and called the rehab people to tell them that her daughter asked her to come to a meeting with her. After that, Veronica was no longer allowed to attend meetings outside of the Salvation Army.

But prior to that, I had met Veronica at several AA

meetings, at the Cape Coral Hospital and at the church on Hancock Parkway, and she had introduced me to some of her rehab friends, including Sandra.

During one meeting, Veronica suddenly got up and whispered that she had to use the bathroom. Sandra, who was sitting on Veronica's other side, leaned over to me while Veronica was gone, and said: "You know, it's none of my business, but I just wanted to let you know that Veronica is doing really good. You should be proud of her. She's not talking to any other guys or girls. She's totally faithful to you."

For some reason, the way she said that made me suspicious and I had a feeling that Veronica had put her up to saying that.

Sure enough, when Erin asked Sandra to call me, and I asked her about that meeting a few weeks earlier, she admitted that Veronica had made her say that. Then she told me that Veronica was cheating on me the whole time in rehab.

After Sandra ran away from rehab with Veronica and the others, she was now hiding at her friend Coconut's house. Coconut was also a drug addicted stud, and like Snickers, Coconut had also spent more time in jail than out. And she had also dated almost every other girl in jail at some point or another. Veronica had been hitting on her, too, while she was in jail. Coconut didn't like Veronica, so when she heard Sandra talking to me on the phone, telling me what a lying cheater Veronica had been in rehab, Coconut wanted to speak to me as well, and she told me what a lying cheater Veronica had been in jail prior to rehab.

When Sandra had lied to me during that AA meeting a few weeks earlier, it wasn't the only time Veronica asked other people to lie to me for her.

The morning when I caught Veronica crushing up a D at my kitchen sink, and she claimed she was making Lime Jello, she primed Kim to lie to my later that day and pretend that she and Veronica had really made Jello. And I caught her having people lie to me a few more times later on.

Anyway, Erin was a pretty 25-year-old with long dark hair. When we finally met, after Veronica ran away with Kim and started posting ads on Backpage, Erin and I ended up having sex twice that evening. The next day I drove to New York.

Patty had emailed me out of nowhere again, just a few days before Veronica was about to run away from rehab. She wrote: "I'm going to be at my sister's place in Tampa for a week. Let me know if you feel like getting together. I miss you. We haven't seen each other in ages. You're welcome to come stay with me at my sister's. I still want to get pregnant and have a baby, so if you want, we could have sex as often as you want every day, and whatever happens happens."

Tempting. But nooo thank youuu. I didn't want to have a baby with a crazy lady. I just ignored her. I wanted to have a baby with Veronica, and nobody else.

Now, about a week or two later, while I was on my way

to New York, I saw on my cell that Patty had emailed me again: "Please call me. It's important. I need to talk to you."

I was on I-95, driving north through the woods in South Carolina. I was bored, so I called her: "Hey, it's been forever. How ya been? What's up?"

She sounded really upset: "Remember when I emailed you last week and told you I'd like you to get me pregnant? Well, to be honest, you weren't the only one I asked. There's this guy, Aaron. I met him about 4 or 5 years ago. We dated for a few days, and then I never saw him since, but we talked on the phone every now and then. A few weeks ago I also asked him, if he wanted to get me pregnant. He said yes. He lives in Tampa. I've been staying with him for the past week, not with my sister."

"Wow." I didn't really know what to say. By now I was used to love-starved drug addicts desperately throwing themselves at a bunch of people at the same time, but the fact that Patty asked me and another guy at the same time to get her pregnant just seemed really sad and sleazy at the same time. I felt a little hurt and insulted, because I wasn't as special to my stalker as I thought I was.

Her "relationship" with this guy sounded just like her "relationship" with me. Both Aaron and I had only spent a little time with her years ago, and now we were her A-team for putting a baby in her? That's just sad.

Patty started to cry while she continued talking: "So I've

been staying with Aaron for the past week. And we had sex at least once a day every day. I was really falling for him. And I thought he liked me, too. But then I went through his phone and saw that he's been texting this other girl. And he's been talking shit about me to her. He texted her that I'm really annoying, and that I give the worst blowjobs ever!"

Aww. I felt so bad for her. She was so deeply hurt.

"When you told me a few years ago that my blowjobs are the worst ever," she cried. "But now Aaron told that other girl the same thing about me. So I guess it's really true. What am I doing wrong?"

I just felt sooo bad for her at that moment. I tried to calm her down: "It's not that you're doing anything wrong, sweetie. It just... well... everybody is different. Some people like really fast, hard, sloppy blowjobs. But I prefer it slow and gentle. Romantic. Sensual. And I guess Aaron does, too. I'm sure a lot of guys would love your sloppy blowjobs."

Somehow that didn't sound right.

Patty told me that she was so hurt, she wanted to hurt him back. She told me about her revenge plans. They sounded pretty crazy, but I could empathize. I knew exactly how she felt right now. I told Patty what happened with Veronica. Somehow it made Patty feel a little bit better, knowing that I felt just as wounded and betrayed as she did, because Veronica had hurt me so badly, when she ran off with Kim.

HURRICANE SANDY

"Just as a heroin addict chases a substance-induced high, sex addicts are bingeing on chemicals. In this case, their own hormones."
Alexandra Katehakis

"Romantic love is mental illness. But it's a pleasurable one. It's a drug. It distorts reality, and that's the point of it. It would be impossible to fall in love with someone that you really saw."
Fran Lebowitz

It was October 2012 when I was back in New York. Halloween was right around the corner. I kept looking at Veronica's escort ad on Backpage. It was driving me crazy. I kept picturing her in my head, spreading her legs for other guys, letting them touch her beautiful breasts, letting them ram their cocks in her soft little pussy, sucking them off, swallowing their cum, and getting high with Kim. I was miserable. It was torture to have these images play over and over in my head. I couldn't take it anymore. I had to make it stop!

When an inmate absconds from the Salvation Army rehab program, it takes a few days before their probation officer files the paperwork that leads to a new warrant.

It took over a week until there was a warrant out for Veronica's arrest after she left rehab. As soon as the warrant came out, I hacked her phone, got her location, told Crimestoppers that she was staying at the Days Inn in North Fort Myers and gave them her phone number. A cop called her to set up an escort date. She and Kim were arrested the same day. I finally felt better. Balance had been restored to the universe. After all the pain she had caused me, now she was going to rot in jail again. Good. Fuck her. Karma is a bitch.

As soon as Veronica was back in jail, she started to call me again. She told me how sorry she was for running off like that and cheating on me, and that she loved me and she hoped I still loved her. I told her to lose my number and go fuck herself, and that I wanted nothing to do with her anymore. I hung up on her.

Then I wrote her a really vicious postcard, telling her that she was a lying, cheating crackwhore sociopath with no conscience, the scum of the earth, and that no matter how pretty she thought she was on the outside, she was ugly on the inside. I told her she was the worst human being I had ever met in my life and if she dropped dead tomorrow, the world would be a better place.

Then Hurricane Sandy hit New York, right before Halloween. The streets were flooded. Almost every block had one or more huge old trees that were uprooted by the storm and knocked over, blocking the road. The power went out. The cell phones didn't work anymore, except in a few rare spots. The gas stations had no more gas. It was horrible. The chaos reminded me of the days right after 9/11.

It took my postcard over a week to get to Fort Myers. In the meantime, Veronica kept calling me. When I finally had a signal for a few minutes, I answered the phone. She told me she had heard about the hurricane on the news and she hoped I was ok. She said she knew I wanted nothing to do with her anymore, but she had to tell me something: she was pregnant, and I was the father.

Considering she just fucked every guy in town a few days earlier, I had a hard time believing she was so sure I was the father, if she was even pregnant at all. She replied that she had used a condom with all those guys she met on Backpage, and I was the only guy she let cum inside of her without a condom. And she told me that if it had been any of those other guys, it would be too soon for the jail pregnancy test to be positive already. She said the baby could only be mine.

Veronica had lied to me so much, I didn't believe anything at all she said at this point. And since Linda had already lied to me about being pregnant with my baby a year or two earlier, this all seemed oddly familiar again.

But what if Veronica really was pregnant? What kind of a horrible guy would I be if I left her hanging, broke, homeless, all alone, and in jail... and pregnant? I decided to give her the benefit of a doubt. I still loved her, despite all the fucked up things she had done to me, and I still wanted to have a future with her, because I believed that deep down, under all that grimey drug addict bullshit, she was a sweet, kindhearted person, who had been through a lot, and needed someone to love her. So we made up.

She called me every day, and I figured out a spot where my cell phone worked, even though the power was still out in Brooklyn. I went to that spot every day and waited for Veronica's call.

Donna started to wonder why I was always leaving the house around the same time of day. She finally began to suspect that I wasn't celibate after all, and that I was seeing someone. She kept telling me that I was keeping a secret from her, and she demanded to know. But I still didn't tell her anything. I knew it would only cause problems.

A few days later Veronica got the vicious postcard I had sent her after her first call. She cried on the phone and told me the card really hurt her feelings. I told her I was sorry and that I had written it before I knew she was pregnant. I really felt bad. I meant every word when I wrote it, but I knew how deeply my words cut her already wounded soul.

Veronica had been sent to dorm 4 when she got to jail, while Kim was sent to dorm 3. Suddenly I saw on the Sheriff's website, that both of them were now in dorm 2, the rehab dorm. I asked her if they had purposely signed themselves into that dorm so they could be together. Veronica denied it and said she wanted nothing to do with Kim anymore, and that they were on opposite ends of the dorm and not even talking to each other anymore. She said she really didn't give a shit about Kim. When she ran away from my house, she just wanted to have a drug buddy she could get high with. It could have been anyone else, besides Kim.

Later I found out all that was a bunch of lies. They really did sign themselves into dorm 2 to be together, and Veronica and Kim were dating the whole time they were in jail together. Veronica cheated on me day after day, while telling me on the phone how much she supposedly loved me and how faithful she was to me. She went so far as to act all insulted that I hadn't noticed how much progress she had supposedly made in the rehab dorm. How much she had grown as a person. How much different she was now, compared to the last time she had been in jail.

But all that was just bullshit. Nothing had changed. She still was the same old lying cheater she had always been. While she told me that she wanted to have a future with me, get married and have a baby together, she told Kim that she wanted to have a future with her, and raise Kim's baby with her. Kim really was pregnant in jail, because she had sex with a dope boy in rehab. He called himself Lay-Z. In the past, Erin had sex with him, too. Kim was the 6th girl he got pregnant. Ahh, family values. It reminded me of the joke about Father's Day being the most confusing day in the hood.

But Veronica didn't just cheat on me with Kim. She also cheated on Kim with other people. She had absolutely no loyalty to anyone.

While Veronica had been in rehab, and her mother Rachel was hitting on me during those 2 weeks when Veronica and I weren't talking to each other, Rachel had told me that she felt her daughter was a sex addict. To me the term "sex addict" just seemed to be a lame excuse for being a slut. Hey, I can't help it. I have a problem: I like sex. Well, everyone likes sex. But that's no excuse to be a lying cheating whore. So cut that shit out, slut.

But then I read up on sex addiction. It often affects people who have been abused or abandoned. When a young woman's childhood lacks a healthy connection with a parent or she is sexually abused, she may develop a misunderstanding of the words love and sex. These girls will confuse sexual abuse, neglect or inappropriate sexual behavior for love and seek these destructive behaviors in relationships later on in life, because they never learned the correct meanings of love and intimacy. The abuse or abandonment they suffered in early childhood was deeply traumatic, and sex addiction is one of the ways they try to cope with their PTSD.

I read that therapists have noticed a significant link between sex addiction and sexual abuse. When sexual abuse occurs at a young age, the child often becomes dissociated between what healthy and non-healthy sexual relationships are.

Some people, who have been sexually abused during their childhood, reenact what has been done to them, to somehow gain control over it. I wondered if what Veronica did with the girls in all her fake relationships was a replay of what had been done to her by her mother's boyfriends. Did they finger her when she was a little girl? Is that why she was so obsessed with doing it to other girls now?

Other people use sex as a substitute for love.

Everything I read about sex addiction fit perfectly in Veronica's case. I came to the conclusion that Rachel was right. I sent some articles about this stuff to Veronica later, but she never wanted to talk about it.

Anyway, while she was in dorm 2 with Kim, a whole bunch of people tried to warn me that Veronica was cheating on me. I just didn't want it to be true.

Remember Nancy? She was Veronica's roommate in rehab. She had been holding Veronica's phone and read my text messages to Veronica, and they were both laughing at me, because I was so upset after finding out that Veronica was cheating on me with Dee.

Now Nancy was back in jail, too. She was in dorm 2 with Kim and Veronica. And she ended up writing me a letter, telling me that Veronica was lying to me the whole time, that she was fucking Kim almost every day, and that she was not really pregnant.

Nancy wrote she wished she had a guy like me in her life, because everyone in jail knew I was taking good care of Veronica, putting money on her books, talking to her on the phone every day, visiting her twice a week, and sending her funny postcards every day.

So Nancy decided to make a move on Veronica's man, and tried to get me on her team. What else is new? Like I said, drug addicts do that sort of thing all the time. There is no love or loyalty among them.

Altogether 14 different people reached out to me to warn me that Veronica was lying and cheating on me, and that she was not really pregnant. Several of them suggested that they would be a better girlfriend, if I gave them a chance. Not just Nancy. Another one of them was Veronica's ex-girlfriend Lola, who was now in prison. She wasn't gay, but she had dated Veronica for a few months, because she kept giving Lola drugs.

Lola wrote me dozens of long letters from prison. She had nobody else. Many of them were more than 10 pages long. One was even 17 pages. She wrote almost every day, even though I didn't even write her back at first. They became more and more intimate. At first she told me a bunch of horror stories about what a lowlife Veronica was. But then she started writing me love poems and explicit sex letters.

After I had found all of Veronica's love letters in my closet, she acted like it was no big deal. "So what? It's just letters," she scoffed. She obviously didn't grasp what a betrayal it is to send someone else love letters, when you're supposedly in a relationship.

So I decided to show her what it feels like, just like I had done when I invented Faith. I started writing Lola back. Almost all the drug addicts in Fort Myers know each other, and gossip travels fast. Even though Veronica was in jail and Lola was in prison, I figured it wouldn't be long, until Veronica found out that her ex-girlfriend and I were writing each other pretty steamy sex letters. But Veronica never did find out, so eventually I told her myself. She was really upset. Now all of a sudden she realized that writing letters to someone else was not nothing.

I told Veronica about each letter or phone call I had gotten from those 14 girls. And each time she claimed that they were only saying those things about her, because they were jealous of her, or they wanted to get with me, or they hated her, or they didn't want to see us happy together, or whatever.

Haley was happy when I told her I wanted to have lots of revenge sex with her, because I was done with Veronica after she ran off with Kim. But then, when I told her a week or two later that Veronica and I were talking again, because she was pregnant, Haley got really angry: "That's the oldest lie in the book! Veronica is just trying to manipulate you! She knows you had enough of her shit, and she thinks by pretending to be pregnant, she'll be able to make you stay with her. Don't fall for it!"

I told Haley that I was giving Veronica the benefit of a doubt, because I didn't want to leave her hanging, in case she really was pregnant.

A few days later, Haley called me and claimed that now she was pregnant, too. Supposedly I had gotten her pregnant when we had all that revenge sex. I didn't believe her for a second, but she insisted that it was true. Later, when I was back in Fort Myers, I made Haley pee on a pregnancy test right in front of me, so she couldn't fake it. It was negative. But she continued to pretend she was pregnant anyway: "The test must be broken! I know my body! I know I'm pregnant!"

I had anticipated that reaction, so I had bought 2 pregnancy tests, just in case. I made her take another one. That one was negative, too. She was definitely not pregnant.

Anyway, Veronica always had some kind of excuse, why what the other people were telling me about her supposedly wasn't true. And every single time I decided to give her the benefit of a doubt, because I didn't want to face the possibility that I had been wasting almost 2 years of my life with a worthless piece of shit who was really just playing me and using me.

I stuck with her through thick and thin, because I believed that's what you do when you love someone. I told myself a long time ago I wouldn't abandon Donna, even if she was in a wheelchair. And Veronica was crippled right now. Maybe not physically, but mentally and emotionally. I don't want to be the kind of person who leaves someone when they are most vulnerable. There's an old Swedish saying: "Love me when I least deserve it, because that's when I need it the most."

I told myself that all those other people didn't know Veronica like I knew her. I believed that they weren't lying, but that they were talking about the old Veronica. The grimey lowlife who had lived on the streets. But I believed she had changed. And they just couldn't see it, I told myself. Of course I was just lying to myself. They all lived with her in the same dorm. They were around her 24/7. They knew her a lot better than I did.

Several people told me that Veronica bragged about conning me. I knew they weren't all just making that up, but I told myself that Veronica was so damaged in the head, she thought it would make her look weak if she admitted to the other inmates that she had real feelings for me. She didn't want anyone to know that she was really just a little pile of misery, who depended on someone else's kindness for her survival.

So instead of telling people she appreciated that I was there for her, and risk looking like a charity case, she thought she would look cool if she told people she was conning me, like she was a hustler and a player. Just like during her conversation with Nancy at rehab, when I heard her pretend we never even had sex, and that I was just some dumb motherfucker that she was manipulating to buy her whatever she wanted. I think that was just her way of pretending to be in control of her life, when really she had no control over anything whatsoever. She wasn't even allowed to go to the bathroom without asking a corrections officer for permission first.

After more and more people told me that she wasn't really pregnant, I knew she had been lying all along. Erin and Lola both told me to ask her for the sticker on her food tray. Pregnant girls get double rations in jail, and the sticker on their tray says "pre-natal diet" and then their name. Lola told me if Veronica couldn't send me that sticker, she wasn't really pregnant.

So I asked her to send me the sticker. She claimed she did, but I never got it. She claimed her letter had gotten lost somehow. I asked her to send me another sticker. That's when she finally came clean. After months of pretending to be pregnant, she finally admitted that it was all a lie. She said she did it, because she was afraid I'd never talk to her again.

All this time, Veronica told me that she couldn't wait to come home to me, be sober, get married, have a baby and live happily ever after. But in her letter, Nancy wrote that that was all a lie, and that Veronica was telling people in jail that her dad was going to get her an apartment in Forestwood on Brantley Road, near College Parkway. It just so happened to be in walking distance of Pine Manor, one of the worst drug neighborhoods in Fort Myers.

Nancy wrote that Veronica was telling everyone she and Kim were going to live there and she would sell drugs and pimp out other girls. She was going to be the man, the provider, in her relationship with Kim.

A few days after Halloween, I drove back to Fort Myers. When I visited Veronica in jail, she acted arrogant and condescending. I could tell that she really was dating someone else, and that she was putting on a show for them. I was getting so tired of this shit. Why was I wasting my time with her, if she was really just conning me?

I had tried to show her unconditional love. I tried to show her that even after she fucked up repeatedly, I wasn't going to abandon her. But all I was doing was teaching her that it was ok to treat me like a doormat. Instead of learning what real love is, all she learned was that even if she cheats on me, I wasn't going to leave her. So to her, cheating on me was ok. I kept hoping that once she got out of jail, and we lived together, things would get better.

Veronica always tried to act tough, but she was so insecure, she mirrored the behavior of the people around her. She really didn't even know who she was, unless other people told her how to act. She was like a little high school girl who just wanted to fit in. If the people around her used certain phrases, she used them, too. If people talked black, she talked black, too. During one of our visos at the Salvation Army, she had asked me in a thick black accent: "What time it is?" She thought she sounded cool. She had no clue how retarded it looks when a little white girl from the suburbs tries to act like a black thug from the hood.

Virtually all the female inmates in LCJ are drug addicts who have prostituted themselves at some point or another to pay for their drug habit. And, like all drug addicts, they are used to lying and manipulating people, just like that guy had written in Sex, Drugs, and Taxi Cabs. No wonder Veronica was acting like a lying, cheating lowlife while she was in jail. She was trying to fit in.

I held on to the hope that once Veronica was released from jail, and came home to me, she would no longer be around manipulative con artists, and she'd take her behavioral cues from me instead. I figured if I show her nothing but kindness and love when she comes home, that's the kind of behavior she would learn to adopt.

But she never came home to me. Everything Nancy and the other 13 people had told me about Veronica was right.

A few days before her release, she told me that her

father was coming to town to pick her up. She said it would be rude if she didn't let him pick her up, because she hadn't seen him in ages. She told me not to worry, because she'd only spend a day or two with him at the most, and then she would be all mine. It sounded strangely familiar. Kayla had told me the same thing a few days before her release.

During my last viso with Veronica, one day before she was released from jail, I told her that I had a really bad feeling, and that my instincts told me I would never see her again.

"Don't be ridiculous," she said. "I love you. Of course I'm coming home to you. Watch, as soon as I get out, I'll call you from my dad's phone. I don't even really want to spend time with him. I'm just doing it because I have to, so he'll get off my back. He's only in town for two days, so the day after tomorrow, he'll drop me off at your house in the evening, and then I'm all yours."

There was no sense in arguing about it anymore, because her mind was made up. She told me that she had no choice but to have her dad pick her up, and she said it was really no big deal, because she would be home with me less than 48 hours later, so I shouldn't make such a big deal about it.

For the rest of the viso, we talked about something else. Somehow we ended up talking about Lucy. She had just been arrested again for drug related charges. Veronica told me she used to date Lucy, and asked: "Isn't Lucy hot?"

I didn't really know how to answer that. Was that a trick question? Would Veronica get pissed at me if I said another girl besides her was cute? Or was she going to tell me that she wanted Lucy to be her "female friend" when she gets out, and that I would have to share her with Lucy?

I told Veronica that I had never actually seen Lucy in person, but that I had known about her for over 3 years, because I used to date Lucy's stepmom Hussy when I moved to Florida, after Alice ran away from rehab in New York. Veronica was startled. "You used to date Lucy's mom? Wow! Small world," she said and grinned. "Why didn't you tell me that sooner?"

"I did tell you all about Hussy, but I didn't know you used to date Lucy," I replied. Then I told her that when Hussy and I used to hang out all day every day, she'd tell me about her young kids, or her abusive ex Dick. Veronica said she knew Dick. Of course. He sold drugs. They all know each other.

Hussy had told me a lot about Dick's teenage daughters Summer and Lucy, who was only a few years younger than Hussy. She had told me lots of stories about how badly Summer and Lucy were addicted to drugs, and all the trouble they kept getting into. So although I had never met Lucy, I actually knew her pretty well.

The next day was Veronica's last day in jail. It was the beginning of June, 2013. She called me one last time that night, only a few hours before her release early the next morning. She told me once again that she loved me and that she would be home soon, as soon as she got this annoying visit with her dad out of the way.

Her dad and Rachel had split up pretty much right after Veronica was born, and he had never really been a part of her life, except for sending her some money occasionally. He was a truck driver who drove all across the country, and she only saw him two or three times a year, for a day or two, if even that much.

She had told me that he owned a successful trucking company in Ohio. But when I met him in person during one of his short stays in Fort Myers while she was in jail last time, I found out that she had lied again. She always tried to make herself sound better than she really was. He didn't own a company. He didn't even own the truck he drove. It was a company truck. And he was homeless. He lived in the truck. He just used his brother's address in Ohio to receive mail.

Veronica rarely talked to him on the phone. Maybe once every two weeks. Meanwhile she called me several times a day every day. She had told me many times that she was estranged from both her parents, and didn't really want either one of them in her life once she came home. She said her mother was her biggest trigger for using drugs, and her father was a mentally ill dry alcoholic who heard voices. He thought he could talk to angels.

One time, when he and I were texting after Veronica got arrested again, he suddenly wrote, completely out of context: "The blue angel sees everything. The white angel laughs. And the red angel takes his revenge."

Aaalrighty then. Thanks for sharing.

MY BEST FRIEND GEORGE

"The most beautiful people we have known are those who have known defeat, known suffering, known struggle, known loss, and have found their way out of the depths. These persons have an appreciation, a sensitivity, and an understanding of life that fills them with compassion, gentleness, and a deep loving concern. Beautiful people do not just happen."
Elisabeth Kübler-Ross

I met George for the first time in August 2012. He was a heavyset guy in his late 50s, with white hair and glasses. He told me he hadn't been fishing since his dad had passed away, so I went fishing with him, even though I had never been, and I had no idea what I was doing. He enjoyed being able to teach me.

He also took me to a gun range for the first time in my life, and showed me how to shoot. I had been against guns my whole life, but now that I actually shot one, I was hooked. It was a whole lot of fun! I ended up buying an assault rifle and a hand gun. But then I felt the rifle was a bit much, so I ended up selling it again. I kept the pistol though.

George was old enough to be my dad. I guess that's why we got along so well. My parents lived in Germany, and Donna had been my only family in America. After the divorce, I had nobody. That's why the divorce and losing Alice later on had been extra hard on me.

When I met George in Bonita Springs, he was like a

father figure to me. I told him about all my crazy little stories with the girls I had met in Florida, and he'd always say: "Nobody has the right to abuse you." He agreed with me that cheating is a form of abuse, because emotional pain hurts so much worse than physical pain.

He was not a fan of Veronica. He already knew me when Veronica ran away from the Salvation Army rehab in September 2012. And I told him all about her running off with Kim 2 or 3 days later, instead of staying home with me. I talked to him every day, and he was familiar with the whole story. He knew that all she ever did was hurt me and cheat on me. He saw it much clearer than I did, because I kept holding on to the idea that she'd turn around eventually. He'd just sigh and say: "The heart wants what it wants."

I really loved Veronica, despite everything she did to me. Or, maybe I was just addicted to her. I had read an article about brain scans that showed that when someone goes through a painful break up, it activates the same part of the brain as cocaine withdrawal. In other words, these brain scans showed that missing a loved one was really not that much different from craving drugs.

It makes sense, if you think about it. Every pleasurable experience releases the feel-good chemical dopamine in the brain. So when you spend time with the person you love, it releases dopamine. Just like heroin or cocaine does. And when that person is suddenly gone, so is your source of dopamine. So the mental anguish you feel after a break up is not that different from an addict's cravings for cocaine. The article concluded that love is the original addiction all human beings share.

We all want to feel loved, and we are all miserable when we lose a loved one and it leaves a big emotional hole. And we all deal with it in our own way. Some people curl up on the couch and eat a tub of ice cream. Some get drunk at the bar down the street. Others smoke weed. Some smoke crack or shoot heroin. Others have a lot of sex, or become fitness fanatics. We all try to find a distraction that helps us get over the pain. But if the pain persists, we get addicted to whatever we're using to try to forget the pain.

In an interview with Vice magazine, Dr. Gabor Maté said about the current heroin epidemic in America: "Heroin is a painkiller. It's actually the strongest pain reliever that we have, and it relieves emotional pain as much as physical pain. So the real question is not why is there a heroin epidemic, but why is there so much pain amongst young people today? And that has to do with two factors: one is that a lot of young people are traumatized and abused in childhood, and another is that a lot of other people that are indirectly abused are still not getting their emotional needs met."

Dr. Gabor Maté said that today's rehab treatment is ineffective, because it sees the addiction as the problem. But addiction is not the problem. It's the addict's failed attempt to solve a problem.

I really don't like hanging out with American guys. I hate all that "bros before hoes" bullshit. I hate the way most of them talk about females, as if women are the opposite team in the battle of the sexes. I was raised to look at a girl as my partner, not my enemy. I was taught to respect girls, not use them and abuse them. I hate when some dumb brute goes on and on about chasing tail, or brags about getting into some girl's pants like he's expecting a trophy for it. I hate when guys holler at girls in the streets. It's so disrespectful. Maybe I'm old-fashioned. Or maybe I'm just the only guy with some class in a hundred mile radius. Just kidding.

Anyway, I liked hanging out with George, because he was different from most other American guys. I didn't have to put on some stupid macho act. I could be myself around him, and admit when I was hurt about something Veronica did, without him calling me a fag for having feelings.

He understood my pain, because he had been through some pretty traumatic stuff himself. He used to be an insurance adjuster, but when his father passed away, he was so grief-striken, he ended up losing his job. And when he lost his job, his wife left him. It was the perfect storm of emotional turmoil. It's a miracle he didn't kill himself. He just got drunk to get through the pain. He liked to joke that he's not an alcoholic, but a drunk: "Alcoholics go to meetings, drunks go to parties."

But now he hadn't touched alcohol in a long time, and he was completely sober ever since I had known him.

George knew I was counting down the days until Veronica came home. He kept telling me to brace myself for the worst, considering what had happened last time, when she ran away from the Salvation Army and then posted an ad on Backpage, cheating on me with God only knows how many people.

I told him that I was hoping for the best, but expecting the worst. I knew there was a good chance Veronica would do the same thing to me again this time around, even though she kept telling me over and over that she loved me, and how sorry she was about what she had done to me in the past, and that this time would be completely different. This time she would really come home to me and we'd live happily ever after.

But she didn't.

REVENGE SEX

*"Holding on to anger is like drinking poison
and expecting the other person to die."*
Gautama Buddha

During our last conversation, a few hours before her release at 4 am, Veronica had promised to call me from her dad's phone as soon as she got out of jail. But she didn't. Somehow I had known that she wouldn't. I didn't even wait up. I just went to sleep around midnight.

When I woke up the next morning around 9 am, I checked my phone to see if I had any missed calls. Nope. I spent the whole day waiting to hear from her, even though deep down I knew I wouldn't. My instincts told me I would never hear from her again after she gets out of jail, and I was right.

She had told me her dad would only be in town for 2 days, and he would drop her off at my condo on the evening of the second day. As part of her probation, Veronica had a 10 pm curfew. If she wasn't home by 10 pm, she could go back to jail.

So I waited until 10 pm on the second day. But I didn't hear a peep from her, and her dad didn't bring her to my place. She had done it to me again. Once again she had left me hanging and chose someone else over me, after I had waited for her for months. I had been faithful to her, had deleted every other girl from my Facebook page and from my phone. I had even changed my number, because she didn't want other girls to call me anymore. Meanwhile all she did was cheat on me, and now she just left me hanging like this. I was heartbroken. I couldn't believe anyone could be this low, this cruel, this selfish.

George had called me to find out whether Veronica came home or not. He knew all along that she wouldn't. He came over, because he didn't want me to be alone. He knew how upset I was. We waited for 10 pm together and watched some movies, even though I really couldn't concentrate. I was just counting the seconds until 10 pm, checking the time on my cell phone every few minutes.

At 10:01 pm, George stopped the movie, and said: "Well, that's it. I hope you're really done with Veronica now. She's no good for you. All she has ever done is make you miserable. She's toxic."

Then he grabbed the keyboard, went to Match.com and started creating an online dating profile for me. "I want you to meet a decent girl," he said. "Stop wasting your time with trash like Veronica."

I really was not in the mood to fill out an online dating profile right now. All I wanted to do was curl up in the fetal position, hide from the world and die. I was so fucking miserable. I just couldn't believe she would do this to me. Again. I just couldn't believe anyone could do that to anyone. What kind of a person lies to someone for months, tells them she wants to get married and have a baby, strings them along for months, gets their hopes up and then just abandons them like it's nothing? I hated her for doing this to me. I

HATED her so fucking MUCH right now.

I wanted revenge! I wanted to hurt her back, as badly as possible, any way I could. I had deleted her mother's phone number, along with every other girl's number. Otherwise I would have called Rachel right now and asked her to come over and suck my cock. Haley was in jail, but even if she was out, neither she nor Erin or Crystal would do the trick this time. I wanted to fuck the shit out of Veronica's mother. I knew that would get under her skin. I wanted to ram my big fat cock in Rachel's mouth and make her swallow my load. I wanted to fuck her in the ass. I knew Rachel hated it when Veronica's stepdad did that to her. I wanted to cum in Rachel's pussy and then brag about it, rub it in Veronica's face, and humiliate her. If that wasn't gonna hurt her, nothing would.

Obviously I wasn't thinking very clearly at that moment. While all these crazy revenge fantasies were going through my mind, I remembered my last viso with Veronica before she got out of jail. She had mentioned that she used to date Lucy, and that she thought Lucy was hot. For some reason, I figured it would really get under Veronica's skin if I fucked the shit out of Lucy.

And Lola, Veronica's ex-girlfriend who had sent me dozens of letters from prison, was released recently, and she was now back in Fort Myers. I had ignored her when she tried to contact me on Facebook, but now I decided to call her, and fuck the shit out of her, too.

Lola was staying at the Gulfview Motel on 41. She

shared a room with her mother, who was also a drug addict. In her letters, Lola had written over and over how miserable the drug lifestyle had made her, and that she was never gonna go back to that. Prison had given her time to think about her life, and she wanted to make a change. She wanted to live sober, and since I was the only sober person she knew, she fantasized about a future with me. That's why she started writing me those explicit sex letters and love poems.

I know she really meant it at the time, when she wrote me those letters from prison, and told me that she would never ever touch drugs again. But everything changes when you get out of prison, and you are faced with all that confusing freedom. You don't know what to do first. There are endless possibilities. Now you can do all the things you dreamed about doing, while you were in jail. You want to make the most of all that newfound freedom. And what was your favorite thing you used to do before you went to prison? Drugs. Despite all their best intentions, many, if not most, drug addicts relapse as soon as they get out of jail or prison. Many of them tell themselves that drinking is not the same as shooting heroin or smoking crack. But substance abuse is a slippery slope. Soon getting drunk just doesn't cut it anymore.

Veronica often joked that Lee County Jail had revolving doors. Most of the drug addicted girls were in and out of jail all the time. Girls like Snickers and Coconut were only half-kidding when they called LCJ their second home. Actually many of them were homeless on the outside, so they didn't even really have a first home. LCJ was it.

When I met Lola at the Gulfview Motel, her mother Betsy was there, too. Betsy looked like she had seen better days. She probably used to be a pretty girl at one time, but the years of drug use had not been kind to her. Her dark, leathery skin and toothless smile was undeniably the face of an old crackwhore, who had spent a lot of time walking the streets. But she was well-mannered and polite. She welcomed me and said: "You're right Lola, he is handsome."

Lola had told her mother about all the letters she had written me from prison, and her hopes to stay sober and live with me. Betsy was trying to be supportive, and to help her daughter have a better life than she did. That's why she was flattering me as soon as I walked into their run-down motel room.

There were two queen-size beds right next to each other. Lola and I sat on one of them, while Betsy sat on the other bed. We all chitchatted for a while. Girls usually gain a lot of weight while they are locked up, and Lola was no different. I had seen older pictures of her on her Facebook page. She used to be skinny and beautiful. Now she was chubby and had a big gut that hung over her tight jeans. Her face was still pretty though. She was 25, had beautiful eyes and long brown hair. But she never smiled, because she was ashamed of her crooked teeth.

She was nothing like I had pictured her from her letters. She had a harsh, masculine voice. To say that she was a bit rough around the edges would be an understatement. She couldn't hide the fact that she had grown up on the streets and never learned how to be a lady.

I wasn't attracted to her at all. But I still wanted to go through with my plan to have revenge sex with her, to get under Veronica's skin. Since we all knew why I was here, I figured Betsy would excuse herself after a few minutes, and give Lola and me some privacy. But she didn't. She sat right there on the bed across from us, chatting with me.

Lola was getting impatient. I guess I was supposed to make the first move, but I was too shy to bring up sex in front of her mother. So Lola decided to take matters into her own hands. Literally. She started playing with her shirt and adjusting her bra. I could see way too much of her beautiful breasts. They were covered in golden body glitter. It was impossible for me to ignore what she was doing. I told her that the way she kept playing with her breasts was really distracting. Obviously that was the whole point. She laughed and started massaging her breasts. Then she pulled her shirt and bra down, so that I could see her nipples. Her mother was sitting right there, laughing.

"You like my tits?" Lola asked. "They got big in prison. I'm still not used to how huge they are now. Wanna massage them? I bet you'd like it if I massaged your cock with my tits. Wanna titfuck me?"

I couldn't believe she was saying this stuff, while Betsy was sitting less than 4 feet away.

"You want me to fuck you with your mother sitting right here?" I asked in disbelief.

Betsy laughed and quickly interjected: "She's 25. She's a grown woman. I can't tell her what to do anymore. She can have sex with whoever she wants. So don't mind me. I won't bother you guys."

Lola could tell I was really uncomfortable with the idea of having sex with her, while her mother was lounging around on the bed next to us, watching TV. She said: "My mom can wait in the bathroom while we fuck."

This situation was so bizarre, it didn't even feel like the plot of a bad porno anymore. I felt like I was in the Twilight Zone.

"Nah, I can't have sex with you while your mother is right here in the room with us, even if she's in the bathroom. She's still right here. That's way too distracting."

"I can wait in the car outside, until you guys are done fucking," Betsy offered.

"Perfect," Lola agreed.

"Ugh, I guess," I replied. This was insane. But I had come all this way to have revenge sex with her, and I was only a few inches away from my goal. No point turning back now.

While Betsy walked out, she winked at me and said: "Don't take too long. It's hot out there and my friend doesn't have enough gas to keep the AC running in the car."

Lola took her clothes off and spread her legs, while massaging her breasts. I told her I needed her to suck my dick for a while first, because I wasn't hard.

"I hate sucking cock," she replied. Then she sat down between my legs and did it anyway. I was sooo not in the mood. This was just crazy. She kept complaining that her jaw hurt, and that she wanted me to fuck her instead. The more she complained, the longer it took. Finally she got me hard, and I got on top of her. After I came, I just wanted to get out of there. She asked me if I wanted to spend the day with her tomorrow. I said sure, and left.

She called me the next morning, but I didn't answer. I felt bad, but we just didn't click at all.

LUCY

"I have decided to stick with love.
Hate is too great a burden to bear."
Martin Luther King, Jr.

"A man reserves his true and deepest love not for the
species of woman in whose company he finds himself
electrified and enkindled, but for that one in whose
company he may feel tenderly drowsy."
George Jean Nathan

I knew from Hussy's old stories that Lucy posted escort
ads online. I went on Backpage to see if I could find
Lucy's ad. And sure enough, there she was. I called her
and we set up a date.

I never call girls on Backpage, because I really don't
like having sex with some random stranger. Especially
not after I have learned how miserable girls who trick
really are, how traumatizing it is for them to do this,
and that they all have severe emotional problems.
They're all on drugs, and they hate doing what they
have to do to make money for their next hit. I don't
want to be another one of those guys who hurts them
emotionally by using them for my own pleasure.

Another reason why I would never call some random
girl on Backpage is because I have read too many
articles about prostitution stings. Especially in Lee
county. I don't want to end up getting arrested by a
female undercover cop.

But I knew Lucy wasn't an undercover cop. And these were extenuating circumstances. I wasn't really calling Lucy to get off, I was calling her to get revenge on Veronica. Getting off was just a side effect. Well, it seemed to make sense at the time. Like I said, I wasn't really thinking all that clearly at the time. It didn't even occur to me at that moment, how inappropriate it was to have sex with Lucy, after I used to date her stepmom for a year.

Lucy was staying at the Holiday Inn. I knocked on her room door, and she let me in. She was beautiful. She was only 19, had long red hair, big beautiful eyes, and a warm smile. She had the sweetest little voice and an adorable laugh. She was like a Disney princess. She reminded me of Ariel, the little mermaid. I liked her from the first second I met her. Suddenly my revenge plot wasn't important anymore. I wanted to get to know Lucy, not just use her for my nefarious purposes.

She was really easy to talk to. She had such a sweet personality. But she seemed distracted. I knew why. She wanted to get high before we had sex. She told me she was going to freshen up in the bathroom, and I should take my clothes off and get comfortable on the bed. She switched the TV to some softcore porno on Showtime and told me to start rubbing myself, so I'd be ready for her when she got out of the bathroom.

I was masturbating for quite a while. The porno ended. She was in the bathroom forever. Finally I asked: "Can't find a vein?"

"What?! What did you just say?" she asked from inside

the bathroom. Then she came out with a surprised look on her face.

"I know you're shooting up in there. It's ok. You don't have to hide it from me. I used to date an addict. I know all about it," I explained.

"This is so weird. I go through all this trouble to hide my addiction from the guys I see. Nobody knows I do drugs. And you know all about it? And you're cool with it?" she asked.

"Well, I wish you didn't do drugs, because I know how miserable it makes you. But I know nothing I say is gonna make you stop, so just do your thing. I just figured it would be easier for you if you know you don't have to hide," I said.

She went back in the bathroom but left the door open this time. She asked me to stand by the door so we could talk. I felt a little silly, standing naked by the door, because my hard-on was pointing right at her face, while I kept rubbing myself so I wouldn't lose my erection. Then I stopped, because I felt like a perv.

"Keep rubbing your dick, baby, I'm almost finished," she said. She sat on the floor and tried to find a spot where she could shoot up. She said she was having a hard time, because all her veins were collapsed from years of use. I told her I knew. We talked and laughed for a while. Finally she was done, came out, and took her clothes off. Then she smoked some crack.

It was weird to see her naked, after I had heard stories

about her for 3 years. She had no idea who I was, but I knew everything about her. It didn't seem fair. I wanted to tell her. But at this point I had been masturbating for almost an hour, waiting for her to get ready. My dick was painfully hard, and I was so horny, I didn't want to have to explain stuff for hours right now. I really needed to fuck her first at this point.

When she sucked my dick, it was better than anyone had ever done it before. She was so tender and gentle. It didn't feel forced or mechanical. She was just so sweet and sensual. Then I asked her to lie down and spread her legs. She had the most beautiful little breasts. They were even more perfect than Veronica's. It didn't take long before I came inside of her.

Afterwards she went back in the bathroom to clean herself up and smoke more crack. She was still naked. I got dressed and stood by the bathroom door when I said: "I have to tell you something that might freak you out."

She gave me a suspicious look in the mirror and said: "What?"

"Even though this is the first time we met, I've actually known you for about 3 years," I said. As soon as I heard the words coming out of my mouth, I realized I sounded like a complete psycho. Like I had been stalking her for years or something. She probably pictured me lurking by her bedroom window, while wearing panties on my head and whispering, "my precioussss."

"What do you mean?" she said with a nervous giggle. She was getting uncomfortable. This was getting weird.

Then I told her about dating her stepmom Hussy, and that I knew it was weird, but that I hadn't seen her in a long time, because she had moved to Ocala.

"No way," Lucy said. Now I had her full attention. She completely forgot about her crack.

I told Lucy a bunch of private details about herself, about Hussy, her dad Dick, her sister Summer and their brother Little Dickey. I told her about her grandmother who had just passed away a few weeks earlier, and the trailer she had lived in. I told Lucy about her horses, her heart infection that had almost killed her a few months earlier, and that I had been Hussy's and Dick's landlord when they lived in my rental duplex in Lehigh Acres. Lucy knew right away which house I was talking about.

"This is crazy! So you've been fucking my dad's girlfriend every day for over a year?" she asked incredulously.

"Well, yeah, but I didn't know she was your dad's girlfriend. Hussy told me that she and your dad had been broken up for a long time, and that she wasn't even talking to him, because he's such an abusive asshole. I had no idea they were still together. And when I found out that she was lying to me about that, I broke up with her," I explained.

"Yeah, my dad is an asshole," Lucy admitted. "But Hussy is a psycho. She lies all the time."

"I know, her mom and her sister Ferrara told me the same thing," I said.

I told Lucy that Hussy had told me a bunch of times that she loved me and that we had even planned to move in together, but that I didn't want to sign a lease because I didn't trust her, and then she ended up moving to Ocala. I told her Hussy had stolen thousands of dollars from me and I had almost put her in jail.

"Oh my God, I remember all that! Someone called the cops on her and was gonna put her in jail. That was you?" Lucy asked, while laughing her adorable laugh.

When I told her about the letters Hussy wrote me, Lucy made me promise to bring them the next time we got together. I asked her if I could see her again the next day. She said yes.

Then I told her I had been dating Veronica for the past year and a half.

"What?! You were the guy who always visited her in jail?" Lucy asked. She told me Veronica was obnoxiously arrogant in jail and acted like she ran the place. She said Veronica bragged that her boyfriend was a millionaire and he would do anything for her, because she "got it like that."

I told Lucy that originally the only reason why I had called her was to have revenge sex with her, to get under Veronica's skin, because I knew they used to date. But now I actually liked hanging out with Lucy.

"Huh? No, Veronica and I never dated," Lucy said. "She was hitting on me in jail and tried to date me, but I wasn't interested. I'm not into girls like that. Besides, everyone in jail knows how Veronica is. She's a total whore. She hits on everybody."

Wow. So Veronica had lied about that, too.

The following day I visited Lucy at the Holiday Inn again. I gave her Hussy's love letters. She read them and laughed: "Oh my God, I gotta tell my aunt!"

She called her aunt and said: "You're not gonna believe this, but I'm with a guy right now who used to fuck Hussy every day for a year! Remember when she used to tell dad she had a job at a real estate firm? She was really going to this guy's house every day, and they had sex all the time!"

After she hung up, I asked her if that was her aunt Nicole. She said yes. Then I told her Hussy had said that Lucy's dad had been raping Lucy's aunt Nicole ever since she was 4 years old. I asked Lucy if that story was true.

"What the hell? My dad is an asshole, but he's not a child rapist," she said. "That's just one of Hussy's crazy lies again."

We had sex and then Lucy told me she needed to get more drugs. She felt so comfortable around me, that she told me that instead of her going downstairs and meeting her dope boy in the parking lot, she'd tell him to come up to her room. She said she didn't want me to leave, and I could hang out until he was gone, and then we could talk more.

Her dope boy called himself Las Vegas. He was a tall black kid with glasses. He tried to have swag and act like a thug, but he just looked like a dork. After he left, Lucy and I had sex again.

Afterwards we just lay on the bed and talked for a while. She told me that her grandma had been her whole world, before she past away recently. Lucy felt lost without her. Her grandma had raised her. It all sounded very familiar. Both, Alice and Veronica, also had been estranged from their parents and both of them had been raised by their grandmothers.

Then Lucy told me that Las Vegas was pimping her out. He rented the hotel room where she had sex with guys. She had to pay him a cut for the room each time she had sex, and pay him if he drove her to outcalls, and she gave him the rest of her money to buy drugs from him. So at the end of each day, after having sex with a bunch of guys, she had nothing to show for it, because Las Vegas got every last cent. And she owed him money on top of that, because she often did more drugs than she could afford with the money she had left.

My savior instinct kicked in, and I just wanted to take her away from all this. I felt so bad for her. She was such a sweetheart. She was just a kid, but she had already been through enough traumatic experiences for three lifetimes.

"If you want, you can stay with me tonight," she said while giving me a shy look.

"Sure," I replied. I knew she desperately wanted to feel loved. She craved affection. Especially now that her grandma was gone.

We spooned. She pressed herself as hard as she could against my body, grabbed my arm, put it around herself, placed my hand on her breast, and fell asleep cuddled up next to me, as if I was her blanket. I felt happy. I was so content, holding this sweet, beautiful girl in my arms while she was sleeping. There was no place in the world I'd rather be right now. I had completely forgotten about Veronica. And I think, for a little while, I helped Lucy forget about how much she missed her grandma.

Later I read an interesting article about hugging. Medical studies have shown that hugs and cuddling are important for your mental health. They kill depression, relieve anxiety and strengthen the immune system.

Hugs are healing. Cuddling is medicine. The heart rate slows, blood pressure stabilizes, and the immune system improves. Virginia Satir, a psychotherapist, wrote that we need four hugs a day for survival, eight hugs a day for maintenance, twelve hugs a day for growth. Hugging increases oxytocin, especially in women.

Studies have shown a link between oxytocin and the ability to achieve orgasm, positive social behavior, pair bonding, anxiety, and maternal behaviors. It is sometimes referred to as the "love hormone." A lack of oxytocin has been associated with maladaptive social traits such as depression, anxiety, aggressive behavior and drug use.

Hugging and cuddling have been proven to not only increase levels of the healing hormone oxytocin but also decrease the levels of the stress hormone cortisol.

Lucy and I started hanging out every day. At first I met her at her hotel rooms, but then after a few more days, she began coming to my apartment and sleeping over. She brought all her clothes to my place. She even cooked for me. I loved being around her. It seemed like she never stopped talking, and I never got tired of listening to her.

She was so lovable and affectionate. When we spent time together, her face just lit up with this big beautiful smile. She was like a little ray of sunshine. Whenever we went to Publix to buy groceries, she would hold my hand and pull me around the store, like a little girl. She probably used to do the same thing with her grandma.

But she was still a drug addict. Every day she asked me to drive her to these two trap houses in Pine Manor, or to some motel so she could buy drugs from Las Vegas. I was getting more and more uncomfortable. I really didn't want to keep doing that. The law of probability said that sooner or later we would get arrested on one of these drug runs.

One time we saw a police raid in progress at the trap house we were headed to. If we had gotten there 5 minutes earlier, we would have gotten arrested.

I wanted to help her get clean, and show her that a sober life is worth living, not drive her to trap houses and enable her to be a drug addict and watch her degrade herself on Backpage while she's slowly killing herself.

More and more often, she locked herself in my bathroom as soon as we came home, and she smoked crack for hours, until every last crumb was gone. Then, as soon as she got out of the bathroom, she wanted me to take her back to Pine Manor, to buy more crack. It all seemed so familiar again. Haley used to do exactly the same thing.

I told Lucy I didn't like that she kept locking herself in the bathroom for hours, and that I didn't want to keep driving her to these drug places. We started fighting, and she had Las Vegas pick her up at my place in the middle of the night.

Meanwhile she had violated her probation, because she never reported to her probation officer. He issued a warrant. The cops arrested her a day or two later, while she was staying at the La Quinta.

She called me from jail and told me she loved me. Her bond was $10,000, so the bondsman's fee was $1000. She asked me to bail her out. I told her I wouldn't, because she was totally off the chain and she really needed to get clean, and this was her chance to sober up.

She had called her aunt Nicole from my place a few times, and had given my number to Nicole and Nicole's number to me. We friended each other on Facebook. Nicole and I were the two most important people in her life at this point, so Lucy wanted us to be able to call each other, to let each other know how she was doing, once she went to jail. She had known that it was only a matter of time before her probation officer was going to issue a warrant, and she wanted to be prepared.

I called Nicole and told her Lucy was in jail, and that she had asked me to bail her out, but that I didn't want to.

I was so happy when I spent time with Lucy every day, but now that she was in jail, I started to get depressed again. And I started to think about Veronica again. Not because I wanted to get back with her. I hated her. I just remembered the pain she had caused me, and it still hurt. Thinking about Veronica was nothing but pain and misery. Thinking about Lucy made me happy. Without Lucy, there was nothing for me in Florida right now, so I went to New York again.

"Please don't bond Lucy out. She's going to end up dead if she keeps going the way she's going. She needs time to think about her life with a clear, sober mind," Nicole told me on the phone.

Nicole was a drug addict, too. She had been in prison for two years, and got out about 3 or 4 months before I met Lucy. She said prison saved her life, because it gave her a chance to sober up and think about her future. She had been clean since she got out and started her own little lawn care business. She went to church and AA meetings regularly.

Lucy called me a few times every day while I was in New York, and she told me she loved me and wanted to be my girlfriend. I told her I loved her, too. I really had been getting very attached to her when we spent all that time together. She was so lovable, I couldn't help but fall for her.

She told me she wanted me to come back from New York and get her out of jail. She said if I'd bond her out, she'd like to come live with me, because she was happy whenever we spent time together. I loved the idea of her coming to live with me. Spending time with her, cuddling with her, being led around by the hand, or getting one of her random little kisses made me so happy. It was impossible not to love this sweet little girl.

But I still wasn't going to bail her out, because I knew that no matter what she said right now, as soon as she got out, she'd be smoking crack nonstop again, and she'd be back in some cheap motel room, sucking some guy's dick, and then giving all her money to Las Vegas. I couldn't stand the thought of anyone else touching her. I was starting to feel possessive and protective of her. That's how I knew I was starting to have real feelings for her. I loved her, and I didn't want to share her with anyone else.

Nicole told me she was worried this guy Cho might bond Lucy out. Lucy had told me about some of her regular "clients." One guy paid her a lot of extra money so she would kiss him during sex. So she did, even though she really didn't want to. When he started running low on money, he couldn't afford to pay extra for kissing anymore, so she stopped. He got upset about that. I don't remember if that was Cho or someone else.

Anyway, Cho was one of her sugar daddies. He was a short, fat, bald Vietnamese guy in his early 50s, who was a pharmacist at one of the hospitals in Fort Myers. He was infatuated with Lucy, and when he realized that she was on drugs, he started to keep feeding her crack, so she would hang out with him. And he started to smoke crack too, to have something in common with her. What a fucking moron!

She told me Cho wanted to be in a relationship with her, but that she obviously wasn't really into him, and that she was just using him whenever she needed money, or a new phone, or clothes.

When she called me from jail, I asked her if she was still talking to Cho. She said no, that she had stopped talking to all other guys, and I was the only one in her life.

Afterwards I called Nicole and asked her if that was true. She said: "No, Lucy is lying. She's still talking to Cho, because she's hoping to con him into bailing her out."

When Lucy called me back later that day, I told her I didn't believe that she was no longer talking to Cho.

"It's true. I told him I want nothing to do with him

anymore, and that I'm with you now," Lucy said. "You can call him and ask him yourself."

"Ok," I called her bluff. "What's his number?"

She purposely gave me a wrong number. But I hacked her phone and got the right one. I called Cho and introduced myself. I told him what Lucy had said. As it turned out, she was telling him the same story she was telling me. She didn't tell him she wanted nothing to do with him anymore. Instead she told him she loved him and wanted to have a future with him, and come live at his house after he bailed her out.

Considering I wanted her to be sober when she was going to live with me, but Cho fed her crack, it was obvious to me where she would end up. She would choose drugs over me, just like Alice and Veronica did.

I was still talking to him, comparing stories, when Lucy called me back and asked me what I was doing. I told her I was still on the phone with Cho.

"No you're not," she said. She knew she had given me a wrong number, so she didn't think I was really able to talk to him. "Well, if you're talking to him, good. Then put him on a threeway, so I can tell him that I want nothing to do with him and that I'm with you. Right now, in front of you, so you can listen."

"Ok," I said, and called her bluff again. I merged the calls. Now Cho, Lucy and I were all on the phone together. She was startled and didn't know what to say for a second. She had to think quick.

Then she said: "I'm going to be with Cho, because he's going to bail me out."

I pretended to be shocked: "What? That's not what you said two minutes ago! What the fuck? Well, good luck with that. Never call me again!"

Then I hung up. Lucy called me right back and said: "I'm so sorry! I didn't mean it! I just had to say that because you put me on the spot. I love you and I want to come live with you. But I really want to get out of jail, and you said you won't bail me out, so I have to have Cho bail me out instead."

I guess in a drug addict's mind that makes sense. But if my parents ever argued over money, it would never ever occur to my mother to tell my stepdad: "Well, if you won't come up with the money I want, I guess I'll tell some other guy I love him and ask him for the money instead." Only sociopaths and drug addicts think it's ok to do that sort of thing.

Ever heard about the sociopath test? It's a little riddle that floats around the internet:

A girl attended the funeral of her own mother. There she met a guy whom she did not know. He was her dream guy. She fell in love with him at first sight. However, she never asked for his name or number and afterwards could not find anyone who knew who he was. A few days later the girl killed her own sister. Why did she do it?

259

Supposedly a sociopath will figure out the correct answer to this riddle pretty quickly, while a normal person will be stumped.

So, can you figure it out? No pressure. Nooo pressure. Take your time.

Alright, I'm not gonna keep torturing you. Well, if you're a sociopath, you already know the answer: she figured that if the guy showed up to her mother's funeral, then he might appear at another family member's funeral as well.

The point is that sociopaths don't care who they hurt to get what they want.

Anyway, I was really upset when Lucy acted like it was no big deal that she had been telling Cho and me the same story. To her it really wasn't a big deal. It was just business as usual. It's what all drug addicts do. She said that when she told me she loved me, it was the truth, but when she told Cho she loved him, it was only to con him into bailing her out.

How was I supposed to trust someone like that? This was the same kind of two-faced shit I hated about Veronica and every other drug addict I had met so far. I wanted nothing to do with her anymore. (How many times have I said that sentence so far?)

A few days later, Cho paid the $1000 to bail Lucy out. She went to his house with him. They smoked a bunch of crack together and had sex. That thought made my skin crawl. Then she wrote me a love letter, took a picture of it with her cell phone, and texted it to me. Cho found her letter to me at his house and kicked her out in the middle of the night.

She asked her aunt if she could stay with her until I got back from New York, but Nicole lived in a halfway house at the time and couldn't have Lucy there. The next morning, Cho pulled the bail, and the bondsman took Lucy back to jail.

When Lucy called me, she told me that now she was really done with Cho for good, and asked me to bail her out again. She said since Cho had already paid the $1000 the first time, all I had to do was sign some paperwork at the bondsman's office and they'd let her back out. I told her again that I didn't want to bail her out, at least not until I got back from New York. I told her she needed to sober up, because the drugs made her do really grimey things.

She swore once again that she wasn't talking to Cho anymore. I didn't believe her. I put Cho, Lucy and myself on a threeway call again, and it was a replay of the last time I had merged the calls. She sold me out again and said she'd be with Cho, because he'd bail her out.

Cho ended up having to pay another $1000, because the bondsman said he forfeited the first $1000. Lucy got out a second time, stayed with Cho, and smoked a bunch of crack with him. But as soon as his paycheck was used up, she ran off into the night. She had only been out for 3 or 4 days, when Cho pulled her bail again, and she went back to jail a third time.

I was really sick and tired of Lucy's shit at this point. She was no better than Veronica.

"Don't compare me to Veronica," Lucy said angrily. "I'm nothing like her! I would never hurt you like Veronica did."

Funny, Veronica used to tell me the same thing about Alice.

The sad part was that Lucy really didn't understand that she had already hurt me just like Veronica always did. The part of her brain that's responsible for empathy didn't work properly. It didn't really sink in that the things she does actually hurt other people. All she did was lie, cheat, and manipulate people to get what she wanted, like a typical sociopathic drug addict.

I wrote her a nasty postcard and told her to stop calling me.

BABY FEVER

"You know what the great thing about babies is?
They are like little bundles of hope.
Like the future in a basket."
Lish McBride

"The only creatures that are evolved enough to
convey pure love are dogs and infants."
Johnny Depp

Meanwhile I had run across Veronica's new Facebook page. Once her dad picked her up from jail in June 2013, he brought her to the 2 bedroom condo he had rented for her at Forestwood Apartments on Brantley Road.

Veronica posted pictures of herself, bragging about all the new clothes and shoes her dad had bought her. It made me sick, how shallow and materialistic she was. All she cared about was stuff. And what pissed me off even more was that there was not a single word about me on her Facebook page. It was like I never even existed. She didn't miss me at all. As soon as she didn't need me to take care of her in jail anymore, I became less than air. What a fucking lowlife she was.

I was so heartbroken when she just disappeared, I couldn't think about anything else, until I met Lucy. But Veronica couldn't care less about us breaking up. She was back on drugs already.

Later I found out that ever since Kim had been moved from Lee County Jail to the Lowell prison in Ocala in February 2013, Veronica had started dating another girl behind my back: Jasmine. Actually she had already been cheating on Kim with Jasmine, but once Kim was out of the picture, Veronica was officially dating Jasmine, while telling me that she was my loving, faithful girlfriend and future wife, and while still writing Kim letters at Lowell, and pretending that she was still with her. She wanted to get her hands on Kim's baby.

Kim was going to give birth in prison soon. Her parents knew the father was Lay-Z, that lowlife dope boy she fucked in rehab, so they wanted nothing to do with the baby, and it was going to be taken by DCF.

Veronica continued to tell Kim that she wanted to raise Kim's baby together with her, once she got out of jail. But she had really already moved on from Kim to Jasmine, and now she planned to adopt Kim's baby, cut Kim off altogether, and raise the baby as her own with Jasmine.

Veronica had endometriosis. It made her periods very painful, and it caused scarring in her fallopian tubes. There was a 50/50 chance she would never be able to get pregnant. And the state was never going to allow her to adopt a baby legally, because she had 3 strikes against her. She had a history of drug addiction, she had hepatitis C, and she was a convicted felon. So she figured her best bet to have a baby was to take someone else's.

I was being nosy and looked at her Facebook page ever other day or so. I could tell by the things she was posting that she was back on drugs. She brazenly posted pictures of herself making out with several drug addicted guys and girls, even though she supposedly was in a relationship with Jasmine. She was totally reckless and selfish. Veronica didn't care if anyone told Jasmine that she was cheating on her. She figured she could talk her way out of it. And the whole thing with Jasmine was really just another one in the endless list of her shallow, fake, meaningless relationships anyway.

A few months earlier, while she was still in dorm 2 in jail, she had sent me some of her rehab worksheets. One of them was about all the things a drug addict has to avoid to prevent a relapse. But now her Facebook posts showed that she was breaking every single one of the rules she needed to follow in order not to relapse. She was hanging out with all her old drug addict friends, she hung out with her mother Rachel who was her biggest trigger, she drank alcohol, and so on and so forth.

Then Veronica posted a picture of a new tattoo she got on her wrist, with Jasmine's name. In jail she had told so many different people that she was going to get a tattoo with their name, and now that she was out, she really got one. But instead of my name, it was Jasmine's.

I thought I was over and done with her, but seeing that tattoo really hurt. I lost it. I hated her sooo fucking much. I wrote her a nasty message on Facebook and cursed her out. I couldn't help myself. I needed to vent my utter contempt for her.

Veronica wrote back, but she really didn't make much sense. I could tell she was high. Some of what she wrote was arrogant like she didn't give a shit about me, and in other parts she wrote that she really did love me and she was sorry she ran off like that.

I found out later that some drug dealing thug, who called himself Urban, had written her a postcard two weeks before she was released from jail and told her he would "help her out" by giving her lots of drugs once she got out.

I realized that for most of her time in jail, she had been on the fence about whether she should really come home and live sober with me, like she told me, or move into the empty apartment her dad got her and live there unsupervised, so she could do whatever she wanted, without anyone giving her a hard time about doing drugs. Once she got the postcard from Urban, her mind was made up. That's when she first told me that I shouldn't pick her up from jail, because her dad was coming to town to pick her up.

As soon as she got out, and hung out with her mother, she relapsed. She was taking Xanax and drinking, just like Rachel. Then she started dating Urban and had sex with him to get crack and heroin, while still pretending to be dating Jasmine, because she didn't want any of her so-called friends to know that she wasn't really making money selling drugs, but sucking a dope boy's dick for drugs. She wanted to appear like a successful hustler, not like a loser crackwhore.

Officially Urban was just her "best friend." But they had sex every day, and she told him that she loved him and wanted to have a baby with him. She got his name tattooed on her ankle. She told me later that she was high as a kite when she got the tattoos with Jasmine's and Urban's names and she couldn't believe she'd do something so stupid, because she didn't really care about either one of them. I guess she just fell into the same old rut of dating a dope boy and a crackwhore at the same time, like she always had in the past.

But while she was supposedly dating them, she was having sex with a bunch of other people. She was tricking with at least half a dozen guys and had sex with a couple of girls in exchange for giving them drugs. It was sad and pathetic, but she thought she was pimpin'.

At some point I guess she really did start to miss me, and she kept trying to find excuses to write me text messages to ask me pointless questions. Then she told me that she really loved me and wanted to prove it to me by paying me back all the money I had put on her books while she was in jail.

She said she'd start paying me back at least $30 every week and that all I had to do was come to her apartment and pick it up in person. I knew it was really just her way of trying to have me back in her life. She wanted to see me so badly, she was willing to pay me to come see her, just like she was paying the girls she had sex with by feeding them drugs she had gotten from Urban for sucking his dick.

But she had hurt me so badly, I hated her guts. I never wanted to see her again. I told her I appreciated the gesture, but that there was no need for me to pick up the money in person. She could send it by Western Union, or mail me a check, or send it via Paypal, or load it on a Green Dot card for me. But she kept telling me that all that was too difficult, and I should just come to her place and get it in person. Finally I told her that I wasn't even in Florida. I had been in New York for the past few weeks, ever since Lucy went to jail. I didn't tell Veronica about Lucy yet though.

I started to feel bad for Veronica, because I knew that under her fake front, she was miserable with her life. I knew she regretted her decision to run off like that after she got out of jail. And she was ashamed that she had relapsed so quickly. I told her a few times that I could tell by the way she sounded on the phone, and by her Facebook messages, and the odd pauses between her text messages, that she was using drugs again. But she kept denying it and pretended that everything was great, and she was clean. We started talking to each other more and more again.

Then one day she posted on Facebook that she really really wanted to have a baby. It made me pretty emotional to read that, because we had talked about having a baby together for the past year and a half. That thought doesn't just go away from one minute to the next. So I asked her if she still wanted to have a baby together.

She was really happy and said yes. But she was also scared, because she was afraid it was some sort of trap, and I was going to get her hopes up, and then hurt her really badly somehow to get revenge for what she did to me. I promised her that I wasn't playing any games, and that I was just as serious about having a baby with her as she was. We made plans for me to return to Fort Myers as soon as possible, and stay with her at her apartment on Brantley Road. We would have sex every day, until she was pregnant.

I asked her what she was going to tell her so-called girlfriend Jasmine. She told me she'd figure something out. I could tell she really wasn't all that worried about Jasmine, because the whole relationship really was just fake bullshit, even though Veronica didn't want to admit it. But it was really just her excuse for why she didn't come home to live sober with me. As long as she supposedly was in a relationship with someone else, she had an excuse to keep living on Brantley Road, and do drugs.

Later I found out that Veronica had 2 roommates: Anita and Kathleen. Kathleen was very very pregnant, and Veronica had been hitting on her, had sex with her while she was pregnant, and told her she wanted to have a relationship with her and raise her baby with her.

And Veronica had sex with one of her old girlfriends, Shelly, who was also about to give birth in a few weeks. Veronica also told her that she loved her, wanted to have a future with her, and raise her baby with her. She was fishing again, hoping to get her hands on at least one of all these babies that were about to be born.

LOTS OF BABY MAKING

"I'm addicted and I don't know why
Guess I've always been this way
All these roads steer me wrong
But I still drive them all night long, all night long
All you young wild girls
You make a mess of me
Yeah, you young wild girls
You'll be the death of me, the death of me"
Bruno Mars

Kathleen had a warrant and was hiding from the police. The U.S. Marshals raided Veronica's apartment and arrested Kathleen. She was in jail before I got back to Fort Myers.

When I arrived at Veronica's apartment, she opened the door with a shy smile. She was white as a ghost, had dark rings under her eyes and scabs all over her face. She looked like shit.

I gave her a hug and said: "Let's just get this out of the way... I know you're using again, so don't even bother pretending you're clean."

First she tried to deny it. Then she admitted she had been smoking crack "here and there, but not all the time, and not in a couple of days." I knew she was lying, because her scabs were so fresh, some of them were still bleeding. She probably took a hit of crack right before she opened the door for me.

It had been two months since she got out of jail. Now that she stood in front of me, I realized how much I had missed her. I couldn't help it. When I get attached to someone, I get really really attached. It is almost impossible for me to let go. And even after everything that had happened, after everything she did, I still loved her.

I quickly realized that her apartment was now a trap house. People were coming and going 24/7 to buy or sell drugs. People were smoking crack around the clock. Hookers used the bedrooms to trick. Her roommate Anita was also a drug addicted hooker, and she had guys over and had sex with them right there in the apartment. Veronica told me that she wasn't doing anything like that. She claimed she was making money selling drugs. But later I found out that was all bullshit. She had sex with a bunch of guys, even while I was staying with her. She tried to hide it from me, but it was only a matter of time before I realized what was going on. It broke my heart all over again.

While she was hiding the fact that she was having sex with other guys behind my back, she was open about having sex with several girls. She was so badly on drugs, her brain was not working right. She couldn't even feel her own feelings, never mind empathize with someone else's. It simply didn't register in her brain, how badly she was hurting me whenever she told me that she wanted to have sex with this girl or that girl. She thought as long as we had sex every day, I would be ok with her sleeping around. She just wasn't used to someone really caring about her and about what she did.

It was exhausting for me to be around all these crackheads, because they never went to sleep. Before I got there, I thought Veronica and I would have some private time at night, to cuddle up and watch movies in bed, but she and the others smoked crack all night, until the sun came up. They stayed up for days at a time. Veronica and I usually had to sneak into the bedroom for a few minutes at some point during the day, to try to make a baby, while people were in the other rooms, smoking crack.

Every time Veronica promised that we'd have a night to ourselves, she'd just end up smoking crack with a bunch of people. I got pissed, and went home. I needed some sleep. But the next day I came back to her place. This went on for a couple of days.

One day, after Veronica and I finished having sex, she was lying in bed next to me as usual, with her knees pulled up to her chest, because resting in that position for a few minutes afterwards was supposed to make it easier for my sperm to travel through her cervix, and help her conceive. Then she asked me if I'd like to watch her fuck her roommate Anita. Anita was a pretty 27 year old blonde. Under any other circumstances I probably would have liked to see her naked. But the thought of watching Veronica cheat on me wasn't appealing at all.

"I don't know," I said. "I'd probably get really jealous if I watched you have sex with someone else. I'd feel really left out."

"After I fuck her, you can fuck me," Veronica said. "Or you can fuck her if you want to."

"You'd be ok with me having sex with Anita?" I asked.

"Yeah, as long as I get to fuck her too," she laughed. "I had sex with Anita two weeks ago, before you got back to Fort Myers. It was amazing. We fucked for like 2 hours. You're gonna like fucking her."

Two hours? She had probably been rolling on ecstasy or something, I figured.

Then Veronica pulled a bag out of her closet, and poured out the contents onto the bed next to me. It was at least half a dozen large dildos and vibrators.

"What the hell?! Where did you get all these?" I asked. I regretted that question as soon as it came out of my mouth. I really didn't want to hear that Urban or some other guy bought them, because he liked to fuck her with these sex toys. I couldn't handle that thought. And I didn't want to hear about her fucking some other girl with a dildo.

"They're my mom's," Veronica replied with a giggle.

"WHAT?!? Why do you have your mom's dildos?!?" I asked. After everything I had heard about Veronica's and Rachel's sick mother-daughter relationship, I honestly expected her to tell me that she and her mother had played with the dildos together while having sex with each other, or some guy. I wouldn't put it past them that maybe they had a threesome together with a dope boy or something.

"My mom stayed with me for a few days," she explained, while closely examining each one of the dildos, sliding her hand along the shaft, and checking the batteries. They were all dead. I guess having sex for two hours with Anita will do that.

Veronica explained that Rachel had been cheating on Veronica's stepdad with her new boyfriend, Ted, an engineer from Toronto, Canada. That's why Rachel needed the dildos, while she was staying at Veronica's apartment. And now she and her mom were sharing the dildos. Lovely. No wonder Veronica was so screwed up in the head.

"If you like watching me fuck Anita, the three of us could have sex together all the time," Veronica suggested. "Or maybe we could even be in a threeway relationship together. That way I get to fuck a girl whenever I feel like it, and you get to fuck both of us."

That was not my idea of a relationship. I didn't want to share Veronica with anyone. I didn't want it to be ok for us to sleep with other people. I knew it would just lead to problems and heartache. Sometimes I really wished I could not care. Life would be so much simpler.

But the more Veronica talked about us having a threesome with Anita, the more tempting the idea became. Finally she persuaded me. I was going to give it a try at least once. Hey, how bad could it be to have sex with two beautiful girls? And if it would make

Veronica happy...

I started to get excited about the idea. I couldn't wait to try it. Now I was actually looking forward to having sex with Veronica and Anita. And then Veronica passed out. She hadn't slept in a few days, and NOW she was gonna go to sleep? What the fuck?!

I couldn't sleep. I went in the living room to watch some TV. Anita was sitting on the couch. We ended up talking for hours. She was really nice. Then she took a shower and walked around naked in front of me, like it was no big deal, while we continued talking.

I pretended not to notice how pretty she looked naked. Eventually I asked her if Veronica had mentioned anything about a threesome, or a threeway relationship. Anita said yes, they had talked about it last night. I asked her how she felt about it. She said: "I think you're really cool, and yeah, I'd like to date you. And if Veronica is ok with it, hey, let's all be one big happy family!"

We both smiled. I mentioned that Veronica told me that they had sex two weeks ago. Anita replied: "Two weeks ago? No, we had sex last night, when you went home to get some sleep."

What the FUCK?!? Veronica had lied to me and cheated on me again. This shit with her was just never gonna stop. I just couldn't trust anything she said. Anita could tell I was upset, and said she was sorry. "But once you and I had sex too, you'll feel better," she said. "You wanna try to wake up Veronica, so you can fuck both of us?"

I figured if we try to wake Veronica now, who knows if she'll be in the mood to have sex, or if she's just gonna want to smoke crack for hours again, and then we'd have to wait forever.

"Nah, let's do it without her," I said. I really wanted to have sex with Anita now. While she had been walking around naked in front of me, combing her hair and pretending not to be able to find anything to wear, all I could think about was what it would feel like to be inside of her. I didn't care if Veronica would be mad about it, because she did whatever the hell she wanted, and she didn't care at all if I would be upset about it. It was obvious that my feelings never made one bit of difference in Veronica's decision making process.

That night I found out that Anita used to be a gymnast. She did all sorts of acrobatics while we had sex. She did a legitimate split on my dick. Then she rode me while facing me, and then she rotated on my dick until she faced the opposite way and she let me watch her ass while she was twerking with my dick inside of her.

When I got on top of her, she pulled her legs all the way back, until her knees were next to her ears, and her feet were behind her head. Her wet lips glistened, and her pussy looked so plump and juicy from this angle. I loved it. She could tell that I couldn't hold it in anymore, and said: "Don't pull out, baby. I wanna feel you cum in my pussy."

Yeah, I could definitely get used to that. When Veronica

276

woke up the next morning, she asked me what I did last night, while she was sleeping. I told her Anita and I had been talking all night. Veronica gave me a suspicious look, but I didn't tell her yet that Anita and I had sex.

The next day, this girl Nina came over. I knew from Veronica's Facebook page, that she had been cheating on Jasmine with Nina. I really didn't want her here, because I didn't want Veronica to tell me she wanted to go in the bedroom with Nina and have sex with her. I would have flipped out. Nina brought her friend Dallas along. He was a young skinny gay guy. And this girl Miriam tagged along with them as well. Miriam was one of Veronica's ex-girlfriends.

We all sat on Veronica's bed and talked, while they smoked crack. The only one missing was Anita. Apparently she wasn't invited to our little slumber party. She was alone in the other bedroom.

Veronica was high as fuck, and she started kissing Miriam right in front of me. It really bothered me, but I didn't say anything.

Later everyone went on the porch for a cigarette break. Veronica told me she needed to talk to me alone in the bedroom. We locked the door. I asked her what was up. She said: "Nothing. I just wanted to have a little time alone with you. You've been so patient while we all smoked crack. I just wanted to make love to you."

When the others were done smoking, they tried to come back in the bedroom, but the door was locked. I was on top of Veronica, about to cum, and she yelled at them through the door to give us a minute and to wait in the living room.

After we finished, Veronica told me that she'd like to be in a threeway relationship with me and Miriam. "You'll like fucking her," she said.

"What about Anita?" I asked.

"Forget about Anita. You'll like Miriam better," she replied.

You'd think I would have been used to this crazy shit by now, but I wasn't. When we walked out of the bedroom, I was still out of breath, and I felt self-conscious, because I felt like the others were all staring at Veronica and me, because they knew we just had sex. And they probably did, but nobody said anything.

Veronica, Miriam and Nina went back out on the porch and talked. As it turned out, Veronica had been talking to this guy Warren, a black dope boy and pimp, who was looking for some hookers he could send on calls. The three of them had obviously been discussing this stuff the whole time behind my back.

Now Miriam had to get ready to go on her first call. Warren was about to be here, to pick her up. For some reason Veronica was fixing her make-up, too.

"What are you doing?" I asked.

"Miriam is going on a date. But she's never done that sort of thing, so I'll go with her," she replied.

"Bullshit! You're not going anywhere with Miriam to fuck some guy. What the hell is wrong with you?" I replied angrily.

"I'm not gonna let her go alone. I'll just sit in the living room while she fucks him in the bedroom," Veronica said.

Yeah, right. I didn't believe a word she said. I knew she was going to go on a "double" with Miriam and go fuck someone, and use the opportunity to have sex with Miriam.

"You know what? Fuck this shit! I am so done with you. Go do whatever the fuck you want, you piece of shit! I'm outta here," I scoffed.

Obviously she didn't just ask me into the bedroom earlier to make a baby, but because she figured it would shut me up, and I wouldn't say anything if she was going to go off with Miriam now.

When she realized her plan didn't work, she frantically begged me not to leave: "Please don't go! PLEASE! PLEASE DON'T GO!!!"

She was screaming at me with tears in her eyes. She didn't care how this looked in front of the others. For just a minute, she was unguarded, and let her true self shine through. She really did care about me. She was a totally selfish, inconsiderate, manipulative, fucked-up-in-the-head person, but she really did have feelings for me, and she really didn't want me to leave her. And for that short moment, I felt closer to her than I had ever felt.

She told Nina to go instead.

Over the next few days, Veronica and I had sex every day, and argued every day, because she kept acting like a psycho on all that crack she was smoking.

Anita hated Miriam, because she knew she had been replaced, and she was no longer going to be part of our happy little threesome family. She started to dislike Veronica more and more as well, and whenever Veronica wasn't looking, Anita would be affectionate towards me, give me a kiss or hug me.

At one point Veronica claimed her mother was going to come pick her up, and that I couldn't be there for that, for some strange reason. She told me I would have to leave, and come back at 10 pm, after her mother dropped her off again.

When I got back at 10:30 pm, Veronica still wasn't home, despite her 10 pm curfew. I asked Anita if Veronica was really at her mother's house in Naples. Anita said "Uh, yeah," but she didn't sound very convincing. I told her I was so tired of not being able to trust Veronica at all, for even a second.

Anita replied: "You know how Veronica is. She's never going to change. Why do you put up with it? Why are you wasting your time with her? I'm looking for a good man like you. I want to settle down and start a family."

I had lost count how many times one of Veronica's so-called friends had tried to make a move on me by now. But Anita was right. Ever since I had known Veronica, all she had ever done was lie to me and make me miserable. Even in the very beginning, when her leg hurt and she told me I was the only one she wanted to have sex with, and then someone else's cum slowly dripped out of her pussy.

Even after she had lost me for a few months, and then begged me in tears not to leave her again a few nights ago, she was still cheating on me now.

"Let's have sex," I told Anita. We went in her bedroom, and she sucked my dick for a while, before I got on top of her. It was after midnight by now. Veronica still wasn't home, but I was kinda hoping she'd walk in on us. The thought actually turned me on.

But she didn't come home in time. Anita and I didn't get caught in the act. It was past 1 am, when Veronica finally got home. She was so high, she couldn't even stand up straight or talk. She obviously had not been with her mother. She probably fucked that dope boy Urban and he gave her a bunch of drugs for it. I asked her where she was. She acted all snooty and said she didn't owe me any explanation. I got pissed, so I went home.

The next day she called me and asked me to come back. I got there around noon. A couple of different people were there, smoking crack. Some of them left eventually, but a short latin girl stayed. She had just been released from jail and had nowhere else to go.

Veronica told me that Kathleen used to have this sugar daddy Tim before she went to jail, and that Tim was still coming to the house. She claimed he was fucking Anita, and that when he showed up unexpectedly at the door this morning, Veronica didn't let him in and told him to leave, because Anita wasn't home.

Coincidentally, Veronica suddenly had a bunch of new clothes from Victoria's Secret, and she had money and drugs. Hmmm.

Then my prescription sunglasses went missing. I was sure the short latin girl had stolen them. She was totally fucked up from smoking so much crack. I kept telling her that the glasses won't do anyone any good, because of the prescription. She acted like she didn't have them. We all started to search the whole house for my glasses. And I ended up finding a freshly used condom in Veronica's nightstand. She obviously had fucked Tim earlier that day, and then quickly hid the condom in the drawer, before I got there. I was so disgusted with her.

Later that day, she told me her friend Shelly was going to come over, and that she wanted to fuck her. I stuck around for a little while, and met Shelly. But once they kept whispering to each other in the bathroom together, I left. I couldn't bear to be around this psychotic shit any longer. Veronica really didn't give a fuck how her behavior affected me. She was too high, too brain-damaged, to consider anyone's feelings. I went home that night. Shelly messaged me on Facebook. She told me it was nice to meet me, and asked me why I left so suddenly. I told her I just couldn't take this shit with

Veronica anymore.

LUCY AND VERONICA

"Jealousy is the fear of comparison."
Max Frisch

The next morning I got a call from Lucy. She had been released from jail a day or two earlier. Perfect timing!

She was staying at the Super 8 on Colonial Boulevard, with her newest pimp, G-Force. He was a black kid with short dreadlocks. He had taken the place of Las Vegas. He pimped Lucy out, sold her drugs, had sex with her, and took all her money. These scumbags were the kinds of people Lucy thought were her "friends." It made me sick.

She thought that as long as they didn't hit her, they weren't really her pimps. I guess she had never heard the saying "you catch more flies with honey than with vinegar." These lowlives knew they didn't have to hit her to convince her to sell her body. All they had to do was dangle some crack in front of her face. They were manipulating her with drugs, and she didn't even know it. Or maybe she just didn't care.

I met up with her that afternoon. After all the crazy shit at Veronica's house, I had forgotten how pissed I was at Lucy for throwing me under the bus during those two threeway phonecalls with Cho a few weeks ago. And compared to the shit Veronica had been doing to me these past few days, Lucy's transgressions really didn't seem like such a big deal anymore.

Veronica didn't know I was with Lucy, when she called me later that night. I didn't answer the phone. Veronica left a message and asked me to come back. She told me she asked Miriam to come back over and that she was going to fuck her. She said I shouldn't flip out about it.

I was so sick of this crap with Veronica. Things had been bad when she was in jail. But now that she was out, things were much, much worse. I liked being around Lucy so much better. It seemed so peaceful, compared to the frantic insanity that surrounded Veronica every minute of every day.

I had been with Veronica for almost 2 years now, but in the few short months since I had met Lucy, I had spent a lot more quality time with her, than with Veronica.

George was right, Veronica was a toxic person. I was really just miserable the whole time I was with her. She had never gone out of her way to do even a single nice thing for me. She was the most selfish person I ever met. Nothing she ever did was a selfless act of kindness. Absolutely every moment of every day was about her, her wants and her needs, and how she could get them. And any time she appeared to do something nice for someone else, it was calculated, with an ulterior motive, to benefit herself somehow.

For me, the most important thing in a relationship is loyalty. But Veronica had no loyalty whatsoever, to me or anyone else. If my special someone ever ended up in a wheelchair, I would not abandon her. Even when there was a chance that Veronica might lose her leg to MRSA, I wouldn't have left her. But I knew that if I ever ended up in a wheelchair, Veronica would abandon me in a heartbeat.

She simply was not the kind of person you can build a life with. The sad thing is that most of the fucked up things she did to me, she did while she was sober. She didn't even have the excuse of being high.

Like I said, drug addicts remind me of actresses who all audition for the same role in a horror movie. They all start to think and act alike. So Lucy displayed a lot of the same bad qualities I hated about Veronica. But I knew that deep down she was not as rotten to the core as Veronica was.

When Lucy had left her clothes at my house, she also left her diary. I was nosy, so I read it. These were her most intimate thoughts. And a lot of the things she wrote were prayers. She begged God to give her the strength to overcome her addiction. She begged him to take away her mental anguish. A lot of the things she wrote were brutally honest, and they showed how much pain she was hiding behind her beautiful smile.

Although she and Veronica acted the same in a lot of ways, because they both had the same substance abuse problems, and the same mental and emotional issues, Lucy had a beautiful soul. Veronica didn't.

Lucy and I spent the night together. We slept late the next morning, cuddled up in each other's arms. Veronica called me again. This time I answered the phone. She asked me why I hadn't come back yet. I told her I was spending time with Lucy. Veronica was PISSED!

While I had been staying at her apartment, I told her that I had met Lucy and that I spent a lot of time with her before going to New York. I was always honest with Veronica about everything. I tried to lead by example. I wanted her to learn to stop lying and be honest with me, and I needed to practice what I preached.

When Veronica tried to act like I had betrayed her, I reminded her of the fact that she had cheated on me every day since I had known her, and that the only reason I even met Lucy was because Veronica ran off with Kim, and then got tattoos with Jasmine's and Urban's names, instead of mine, like she had always promised. So she had no room whatsoever to act like I was the one who betrayed her.

"Do you love Lucy?" Veronica asked me. She knew to me the word love carries a lot more weight than to Americans. German is a much more precise language than English. Americans throw the word love around for everything: I love my wife! I love all my friends! I love rock music! I love the rain! I love comic books! I love peanut butter!

The word you use to describe your feelings for your wife should not be the same word you use to describe your feelings for peanut butter. In German, there are a dozen different words that decribe varying degrees of liking something a lot. Germans almost never use the word love, unless they mean a deep romantic love. I have never told my parents I love them, because it would sound melodramatic, inappropriate, and almost incestuous. In German, you tell your mother that you hold her very dear, not that you are in love with her.

"Yeah, I love her," I replied.

"Did you ever TELL Lucy you love her?" Veronica asked.

"Well, yeah, of course I did."

I could tell that hurt Veronica's feelings. Then I asked her: "And how many times have you told Kim or Jasmine or all those other people you have cheated on me with, that you love them?"

She didn't answer.

Later that day, Veronica texted me: "You should bring Lucy here. We could all hang out together."

That seemed like a trap. I couldn't see how anything good would come from that. I told Lucy what Veronica wrote.

"Does she have drugs at her house?" Lucy asked.

"Of course," I replied.

"Ok, let's go! But will you take me home if I feel uncomfortable? I don't want to be stuck at her place."

When we arrived at her apartment on Brantley Road, the three of us hung out on Veronica's bed. We chitchatted for a while. After they did some drugs together, Lucy whispered to me that she wanted to leave, so I took her back to the Super 8 on Colonial.

"Well that was kinda awkward," Lucy said and laughed.

Veronica had asked me to come right back to her apartment after I dropped Lucy off. On our way to the Super 8, Veronica texted me: "I want to fuck Lucy too."

I just shook my head in disbelief. What the hell was wrong with that girl?

When Lucy and I arrived at the motel, I parked the car and we talked for a while. She played around with her phone, checked her make-up, fidgeted around with her purse, and smoked a cigarette. But she wouldn't get out of the car. When you're on drugs, and you're stuck in your own head, time just flies by.

"I'm not sure if you realize this," I said, "but we've been sitting here in the parking lot for about half an hour now. What do you wanna do? Do you want me to come up to your room? Or do you want to come home with me to Bonita Springs? Or what's going on?"

Then Lucy gave me a mischievous look and asked me to take her to Yogurt Mountain at the Edison Mall.

She showed me her favorite toppings and we had a little competition, to see who could conjure up the most delicious yogurt creation. Then she said she wanted to eat it outside, by the little fountain.

While we sat on the bench, she spoonfed me some of her yogurt. We had a lot of fun, talked and laughed.

Then Veronica called me: "Where the hell are you? You've been gone for over an hour. It doesn't take that long to drop Lucy off at the Super 8."

I told her we were at Yogurt Mountain. Lucy was giggling in the background. Veronica got really upset and hung up on me.

"I love our little date," Lucy said. "Do you think you could ever have a moment like this with Veronica?"

"Probably not," I replied.

She was satisfied, and asked me to take her back to the Super 8.

When I got back to Veronica's apartment, she was livid: "What the FUCK were you doing with Lucy at Yogurt Mountain? This shit gotta STOP RIGHT NOW! I don't want you hanging out with her anymore! I'm putting a stop to this right NOW! You're MY man!"

"Are you kidding me?" I yelled back. "All you have been doing these past few days is tell me you want to fuck this person and that person. You kept making out with some of them right in front of me, and left me messages that you were going to fuck them, and I shouldn't flip out about it. And you've been fucking all these other guys behind my back. And now you're gonna act like I'm doing something wrong when I hang out with Lucy? I wouldn't even know her at all, if you acted like a decent human being and not like such a total slut. You gotta make up your mind if we're boyfriend and girlfriend or not. I'm sick of this crazy shit with you. You can't have it both ways. You can't have your cake and eat it too."

After a few minutes, she calmed down and told me some dope boy called Norbert was going to come over in a little while. She said she needed to talk to him about a business deal. He was going to front her some drugs, and she would sell them for a profit.

When Norbert got there, she told me she'd have to talk to him in the bedroom.

"No fucking way!" I said.

"It's not what you think. I just gotta talk to him. Don't worry, I'll leave the bedroom door open."

You couldn't really see the bedroom door from the living room couch, so I got up every few minutes and walked around the corner into the dining area, to peek through the open door. I pretended to do something at the dining room table for a minute, and then returned to the couch. I did that a few times. I felt like an idiot. Then suddenly I saw that the bedroom door was locked.

"What the FUCK?" I yelled and rattled on the door knob. Veronica opened. "I fucking had it with this shit. I'm outta here. Have a nice life," I said angrily.

"No, don't leave! Norbert is going right now," she said.

After Norbert left, Veronica and I started fighting with each other. We were both yelling.

"What the fuck are you doing with some thug in your bedroom?"

"I only called him to make you jealous, because I was so jealous about you spending all that time with Lucy. I just wanted to piss you off," she replied.

"Well, you did a good job," I said and left.

The next morning she texted me at 8 am: "I'm sorry. Will you please come back? I don't want to fight."

I replied that I was gonna head over to her place right now. But she already fell back asleep and didn't see my response. When I got to her apartment, Anita opened the door.

"Where's Veronica?"

Anita just pointed at Veronica's closed bedroom door with a stoic look on her face. She didn't say anything.

I opened the door, and found Veronica and Norbert naked in bed together. They were both sleeping. Obviously she had called him back after I left last night. They did drugs together, had sex, and then passed out.

I flipped the fuck out! First I was speechless. Then I started screaming at them at the top of my lungs. But they were in a coma-like sleep. Nothing was going to wake them up right now.

This is the kind of situation where people get killed.

There are dozens of movies, books, and sad country songs about a guy walking in on his girl, in bed with some other guy, and going on a shooting rampage, killing them both in the heat of passion.

For a minute there, I seriously thought about bashing their heads in with a blunt object. But then I figured they weren't worth it. I wasn't going to spend the rest of my life in prison for killing some ghetto dope boy and a lowlife piece of shit whore.

But I had to let my aggression out somehow, so I kicked the door while storming out of the bedroom. I destroyyyed that door.

I was beside myself with hatred for Veronica. I was going to lose my mind. I felt like Veronica purposely looked for ways to inflict emotional pain on other people. She was a monster. It was as if she was actually trying as hard as she could to be the worst person on the planet. Every time I thought she couldn't stoop any lower, and the things she did to hurt me couldn't get any worse, she found a new way to hurt me even more.

On the drive home, I called Veronica's probation officer and told him that she had been doing drugs the whole time, and that the only reason she had been passing her mandatory drug tests was because she hid a little 5 Hour Energy bottle with someone else's clean pee inside her vagina. He thanked me for the heads up and told me he would call her in for a drug test right now.

When Veronica showed up at his office later that day, he told her that he knew she was hiding a bottle of clean pee, and that if she used it, she'd be tampering with evidence and she'd be committing a new felony. Instead of peeing, she ran away. Usually it takes a week or so for the probation violation paperwork to go through, but he issued her warrants the very same day. Veronica was going to be back in jail soon. Karma is a bitch!

BACK TO JAIL

"Whoever fights monsters should see to it that in the process he does not become a monster. And if you gaze long enough into an abyss, the abyss will gaze back into you."
Friedrich Nietzsche

Later that day, Veronica texted me: "Why did u do that? I love u! I thought we were going to have a baby together. Why would u send me back to jail?"

I texted back: "Don't gimme that love bullshit. U fuck everything that has a pulse. U don't give a fuck about anyone but yourself. What the fuck did u think was gonna happen when I find u in bed with some nigger? U r lucky I didn't kill u, u cunt."

I never really use slurs like nigger or cunt. I really don't curse a lot, unless I'm very upset. Unfortunately being very upset was the new normal, whenever I was around Veronica.

The first time I had told Patty about Veronica, Patty had made snide remarks: "Oh, you found yourself another drug addict to replace Alice. Nice. I guess you like to torture yourself."

"Veronica is different," I defended her. "She really wants to get clean. When she gets out of jail, she's going to the Salation Army rehab program. And after that she's going to live with me, and get her old job back as a medical insurance biller at her stepdad's doctor's office just down the street from my apartment."

"No she won't," Patty replied. "I'm a drug counselor, remember? I've been dealing with these people for years. They're all the same. They are broken. And you can't fix them. Their brains don't work like your or my brain. They have criminal minds. You can never ever trust them. They always lie. They always try to con you. Even if she gets a job, she'll only use the time away from you to cheat on you. You will never be happy with her. Loving a drug addict is like hugging someone who has no arms. They can never hug you back. And Veronica will never love you back the way you love her. She can't. She's in love with her drugs."

At the time, I thought Patty was just being mean, because she was jealous that I'd rather be with Alice or Veronica, than with her.

But now it was like everything Veronica had done, since Patty told me that stuff, was an attempt to prove Patty right. It was a horrible feeling to love Veronica, and never be able to trust her for even a second. It was a given, that she would never do the right thing, whenever she was faced with any kind of decision. I got used to the fact that she would betray me every chance she got. How sad is it that that was normal to me?

Actually finding Veronica in bed with someone else, seeing it with my own eyes, really drove it home. I was wounded to the core when I kicked that bedroom door and stormed out. I felt like I had reached the lowest point of my life.

In a way, it almost felt like a good thing. Things could only get better from this point on, I told myself. Nothing and nobody could ever hurt me worse than this. I had been to the abyss, and survived. What doesn't kill you makes you stronger. From now on, I was never going to allow another person to hurt me like this and get away with it. I promised myself if anyone hurt me, I would not forgive them, and I would not give them a second chance to hurt me again. Instead, I would punish them. My vengeance would be swift and fierce.

All that sounded really impressive in my head. But then I forgave Veronica anyway. I know, I know, it was stupid. But the heart wants what the heart wants, as George always said, whenever I defied all common sense and forgave Veronica yet again.

We talked on the phone and she cried so much, it melted my heart.

"Do you still wanna have a baby with me?" I asked.

"Yes, of course," she cried. "I love you."

"I love you, too. How about we do what we planned to do in case you run away from the Salvation Army? You can come hide at my place until you're pregnant and showing, and then we hire a lawyer and get you house arrest instead of jail time," I suggested.

I picked her up at her apartment a little while later. She packed her clothes and grabbed her little chihuahua, Venus. Veronica had named her dog after the goddess of love, because she had a heart-shaped spot on her forehead.

On our way to my apartment, Veronica asked me to stop at Warren's house, to get drugs. She disappeared in there for about half an hour. I was really uncomfortable, and when she got out, I asked her if she had sex with him. "No, of course not! I don't have sex with Warren," she replied with an indignant tone of voice, as if I had just accused her of the craziest thing ever. For my sanity's sake, I chose to believe her. But a few weeks later, Anita told me that Veronica had sex with Warren all the time.

When we got home, Veronica shot up some Ds and smoked crack. Then we made love.

The next morning, Veronica's phone was ringing off the hook. It was her mother Rachel: "Where the hell is Venus? I want Venus back right now!"

Venus was Veronica's chihuahua, but because she spent so much time in jail over the past 2 years, her mother had been taking care of the dog. A week or two after Veronica got out of jail, and she and Rachel hung out together at her new apartment on Brantley Road, her mother gave her the dog back. But now that Veronica had a warrant, and she was about to go back to jail, Rachel wanted Venus back.

Veronica told some of her so-called friends, that she was hiding in Port Charlotte. She told her mother the same story. She didn't want anyone to know she was staying with me, so the police wouldn't find her here. But at the same time she was taking pictures of me cuddling with Venus on my couch, and texted them to her mother, to show her that Venus was ok. She was too high to realize that she was giving away her location.

Then Rachel called me and asked: "Do you know where Venus is? I don't care where Veronica is. I don't give a shit if she is with you or anyone else. She can go fuck a truckload of Haitians for all I care. I just want Venus back!"

I pretended not to know: "I have no idea where that stupid dog is. I found Veronica in bed with some guy, and I haven't talked to her since. I want nothing to do with her anymore. She's dead to me. The last I heard was that she's hiding in Port Charlotte somewhere."

Of course Rachel knew I was lying, because Veronica had just texted her pictures of me and Venus five minutes ago. But I didn't know that yet.

Rachel continued to call Veronica's phone. They kept arguing. Veronica told Rachel she would meet her at Starbucks at the Coconut Point Mall, and give her the dog.

Then Veronica hung up and told me: "Venus is my dog! I have all the vet papers to prove she's my dog! I don't want to give her back. My mother is a crazy drunk. Venus is so much better off here with you and me."

"Well, if she's your dog, then don't give her back," I said. "You don't have to give her back, if you don't want to."

"I have to. My mom is psycho. She's not gonna stop. She's gonna keep causing problems for me. She's gonna make my life miserable, until I give her Venus," Veronica replied.

"It's up to you, sweetie. Whatever you want to do," I said.

She called her mother back and told her she would meet her at Starbucks with Venus. Then she changed her mind again. Then she smoked some crack. Then she argued with her mother again. This went on for hours.

Then she finally told me to call her mother and tell her that I would meet her at the McDonald's on 41 near San Carlos Park.

"If I call her and say that, your mom will know you're staying with me," I said.

"Well, I've been sending her pictures of you and Venus all day long," Veronica replied.

"What?!? Now she knows you're here and not in Port Charlotte. Why would you do that?"

"I don't know. I wasn't really thinking about it. I just wanted to send her some pictures to show her that Venus is ok."

"Geez! Great. Now she's probably gonna call the cops on you."

"Nah, my mom is crazy, but she's not gonna do that."

I called Rachel and said: "When I was staying at Veronica's place, I brought my Xbox. I left it there. I told her I want it back. She said that she'll give me my Xbox back, if I do her a favor and meet up with you and give you Venus. I just met up with Veronica, and she gave me the dog. So now I have Venus. Do you want me to meet you at the McDonald's in San Carlos?"

Rachel was startled. This did not go as she had planned. Then she said: "You want to meet me alone? Without Veronica? Uhhm... no... I don't trust you... I don't want the dog from you... I want Veronica to bring me the dog."

I hung up and told Veronica that I had a bad feeling about this. My instincts told me that Rachel was setting a trap for Veronica. She was probably going to have the police waiting at that McDonald's. I told her again that we should just keep the dog. Screw her mom.

A few minutes later, Rachel called me back: "Ok, fine, I'll meet you at McDonald's."

Veronica said good bye to Venus and handed her to me. I told Veronica to lock the door behind me, just to be safe. I got into the car and Veronica waved good bye. Venus stared at her through the car window and barked. I felt so bad, because I knew Veronica really loved that little dog. And I had gotten attached to her, too. Venus was shy at first, but then she warmed up to me and was all over me, cuddling with me and kissing my face. She was an awesome little dog.

As soon as I pulled out of the gate of my community, there was already a police cruiser behind me. I got nervous. Was this just a coincidence, or had this cop been waiting for me inside of the community?

As soon as I passed the gate, I made a left turn. The cruiser followed me and turned on his flashing lights. I pulled over. The cop got out of his car and walked up to my window. "Where's the female?" he demanded to know.

I was shocked. Of course I knew he meant Veronica, but I tried to play stupid and slowly pointed at the female dog sitting next to me. "You mean her?"

"Don't bullshit me. You know who I'm talking about. If you don't tell me right now where she is, I'll arrest you for aiding and abetting a fugitive," the cop said.

Oh my God, I'm going to jail, I thought. It's finally gonna happen! After driving to trap houses a hundred times, I'm gonna end up getting arrested right in front of my own house. I was scared. "She's in my house," I said quietly. I tried to look calm, like I didn't have a care in the world, but my heart was pounding.

By now three other police cruisers had pulled up behind us. This was turning into a major production. I felt like I was gonna be on the evening news, in handcuffs.

"Give me your cell phone and the car keys," the cop demanded. Then he talked to the other cops. They took my keys and drove back into the community to arrest Veronica, while he waited with me.

He asked me if there are any weapons in my apartment. I told him about my gun, but I stressed the fact that Veronica didn't know that I had one, or where it was. He warned the other cops that she may be armed and dangerous. I told him again that she didn't know about the gun. I was sweating bullets, because when a felon lives in a house with a gun, she is technically in possession of the gun. That's another felony right there. And they could have charged me with a felony for giving a gun to a felon.

The cops went into my apartment and looked for Veronica, but they couldn't find her. They radioed the officer who was waiting with me. He asked me where she was hiding and if I had warned her. I told him no I didn't, I couldn't, because he had my cell phone.

Then he looked at my phone and said that she was texting me. He read me her message: "Why would u do this to me? I love u! I thought u love me too."

I felt so bad. I didn't want her to think I turned her in. Not now. We were finally getting along. We had been having a good time together for the past two days, while we were staying at my place with Venus. Things were finally starting to be the way I had always pictured them in my head. Veronica and me at home, spending some quality time together, without all these other crazy crackheads or dope boys.

The other officers couldn't find Veronica, because she was hiding behind a closet door in my guest bathroom. When she texted me that message that the cop read to me, she also texted her mother, and told her that I had called the cops on her, that she was hiding in my bathroom, and that Rachel should come rescue her. But instead, Rachel told the cops where her daughter was hiding in my house.

The other officers returned to my car and handed me my gun. They didn't charge Veronica or me with it. That was really nice of them. Then they told me: "We saw her crack pipe on your dining room table. If we don't find her, we will charge you with that pipe and take you in." Terrific! I knew it. I was going to jail today.

Then their police radios crackled. The cops stepped away and talked on their radios and then to each other. They had gotten a call from their dispatcher, with new information from Rachel. That's when I realized what was going on: Rachel had told the cops hours ago that she would meet up with Veronica, and told them to arrest her, because she had a warrant. So for the past few hours, the cops had been waiting at Starbucks, and then later at McDonald's, to arrest Veronica, just like I had thought. But when I told Rachel I was going to meet her alone, the cops came to my house and waited for me.

We all went back to my place. The cops told me to go get Veronica out of the bathroom. She cried and told me to go away. I felt terrible. I just wanted to give her a hug, and make it all better somehow, but the cops followed me into the bathroom and arrested her.

"Will you please tell her it wasn't me?" I begged the officer who grabbed her.

"It really wasn't him," the cop assured Veronica and then took her outside. All the officers left. It still didn't really sink in yet what just happened.

I went into the living room. Venus was hiding under the table. One of the cops came back and said Rachel was on her way here to pick up the dog.

"I don't want her here," I told him. "I can't stand that woman. She's the reason why Veronica is an addict. And I can't believe she would do THIS to her."

"If you don't give her the dog, she might press charges for theft," the officer replied.

I wasn't in the mood to argue. I was stressed out enough already. "Alright fine. But you give her the dog. I don't even want to look at that woman right now."

The cop tried to help me catch Venus, but she was too quick. She kept hiding under the dining room table, then squirreled her way behind the couch, then around the living room table back under the dining room table. "Ah, fuck it. Ok, tell Rachel she can come get the dog," I said. The officer left. Venus calmed down a bit, and I was able to catch her. I had her in my arms, when Rachel came knocking. I opened the door and handed her the dog.

"Ohhh hiii Oliver," she said in this fake friendly tone of voice that made me want to kick her in the ovaries. "Thank you sooo muuuch for taking care of Venus for me!"

I didn't say anything. God, I hated that cunt. The officer who accompanied Rachel said: "Veronica left her crack pipe and needle lying around your house. We didn't charge you with it this time, but you better get rid of that stuff right away."

A few minutes later, Rachel knocked on my door again: "Oh, can I have Veronica's phone pleaseee?"

I really didn't want to give it to her, but it was lying right there on the kitchen counter, in plain sight of the officer who accompanied her again. I handed it to her without saying a word.

"Thank you sooo muuuch, Oliver."

I shoulda kicked her in the vagina, but then I probably woulda lost my shoe. Just kidding.

About 3 or 4 weeks later, Rachel moved in right next door from me. Riiiight... next... door! Jesus H Christ! What... the... Fuck?!? What kind of a crazy psycho does that? I guess she figured now that her daughter was going to be out of commission for a while, I was fair game, and she was probably planning to make a move on me again, like she had done last year, while Veronica was at the Salvation Army.

LCJ SOAP OPERA

"Life is like Friday on a soap opera. It gives you the illusion that everything is going to wrap up, and then the same old shit starts up on Monday."
Stephen King

A few hours later, Veronica called me from jail: "I can't believe my mother did this to me. I HATE HER! I never want to talk to her again. I was just getting used to living at our condo, with you and Venus. I was looking forward to our life together. Honestly, while I was in jail last time, I was worried that I wouldn't be able to be sober and live up to your expectations. I felt like I was gonna let you down, and that I would be really uncomfortable. I thought I would feel like I'm under a microscope all the time. But I really liked living with you. I was comfortable. And happy. I fell in love with you all over again. I feel like my mother ripped me out of our life together. I will NEVER forgive her for this!"

I felt the same way. While she was staying with me for those two days, I finally felt like things could actually work out. I felt like my sobriety would rub off on her. And because she was such a personality mirror, who always took her behavioral cues from the people around her, I thought that, while living with me, she would learn to be kind, lovable, humble, charitable, honest and loyal, because I'd like to think that those are my most dominant character traits.

"I want to put that bitch in jail," Veronica said. "My mother is a junkie, just like me, but she's always on her high horse, like she's better than me, because she has never been arrested. I want to knock that halo off her head. I want her to go to jail and know what it's like! Let's think of a way to get her locked up! Maybe we can have her arrested for stealing Venus. She's my dog, and if you go get my paperwork from the vet, we can prove it."

When Veronica called me back the next morning, she asked me what I was doing. She was worried that I would start hanging out with other girls again: "I know I have hurt you really bad, and I really have no right to ask you not to hang out with other girls while I'm in jail. But I just want you to know that I really love you, and it would hurt me a lot if you start seeing other girls."

I promised her that I wouldn't. I had waited for her this long, a few more months wouldn't make much of a difference at this point, as long as she promised not to run off again next time she gets out, and not to cheat on me any more while she's in jail. No jailhouse romance, no "special friends," no sex with someone else, no love letters. I wanted her to be 100% faithful and loyal to me, just like I would be to her. I wanted to have a normal relationship with her. Love is a deep bond between 2 people. Not 3 or more.

She swore she would be good this time: "Trust me, I have learned my lesson. I am never going to hurt you again. I am so sick of these grimey people in jail. I can't stand any of them. I have no interest in dating them, or even talking to them. I just want to come home to you, make love to you, and live with you. I want to have a baby with you. I'm not going to it fuck up again."

Then she told me that she knew she couldn't ask me to sit home alone for months again. She said: "If you're going to hang out with anyone else, I'd be least hurt, if it was with Lucy. I don't want you hanging out with any other girls at all, but if you are gonna hang out with one, I'd rather it be with Lucy than someone else."

I figured that was her way of saying: "I know you're going to want to have sex, and I can't expect you to be celibate for yet another year, just because I fucked things up between us again. I know this was all my fault. I owe you one. So go have sex with Lucy, you have my blessing." I don't know if that's really what she meant, but that's how I took it.

Lucy called me a little while later. She was staying at the Suburban on Metro and Colonial, with her latest pimp, Wigger. He was a white nigger. He sagged his ghetto chic pants, spoke in incomprehensible ebonic gibberish, like he had been dropped on his head as a baby, and walked with a bounce in his step, because he thought he had swag. Man, I hated that little douchebag.

It was the same deal as always: He pimped Lucy out, took her money for the hotel room, took her money if he drove her to outcalls, had sex with her, fed her drugs, and took whatever money she had left. She degraded herself on Backpage all day long, and then had not a penny to show for it at the end of each day. I hated all these fucking lowlives who took advantage of her. But she thought these guys were her "friends."

I told Lucy that Veronica's mother had her arrested while she was staying with me. Lucy was glad that Veronica was out of the picture, and she had me all to herself. I told her that Veronica said that if I was going to hang out with any other girl, she wanted it to be Lucy. Lucy thought that was funny. "Does Veronica know we're having sex?" she asked.

"Yeah, of course," I replied. "Well, she knows we used to hang out every day when she ran off after getting out of jail and getting Jasmine's name tattooed on her wrist. I haven't really told her yet that you and I are hanging out right now, or that we're still having sex."

Veronica called me later that day, and I asked Lucy to be quiet, because I didn't want to rub things in Veronica's face and hurt her feelings. Lucy didn't listen. Instead, she tickled me, grabbed my phone and started laughing into it. She thought it was hilarious. Luckily Veronica didn't hear Lucy, because the Global Tel collect call message was still playing, and Lucy hadn't pressed zero to accept the call yet. I wrestled the phone away from her, gave her a dirty look, and walked out of the room, so I could talk to Veronica in private.

Every time Veronica called, Lucy tried to make noise or grab the phone. She wanted Veronica to know that I was spending every day with her.

I saw on her aunt Nicole's Facebook page, that Lucy's younger sister Summer was in Cape Coral Hospital with liver failure. She had a serious drinking problem. I told Lucy about her sister's condition. She asked me if I could drive her to the hospital to see her. I agreed. Then she asked me if we could go buy some little presents for Summer first. We went to the CVS on the corner of 41 and Edison Avenue and she bought some crayons and paper for Summer.

It was getting later and later. Instead of going straight to the hospital, Lucy wanted to stop here and there, to meet up with different dope boys and get more drugs. Then she asked me to take her back to her room at the Suburban. She had cooked dinner for me, but we didn't get a chance to eat, because we were in a hurry to go see Summer before the visiting hours at the hospital were over. That was hours ago.

She told me she wanted to do some more drugs in her room, before we headed to the hospital. She shot up and then started smoking crack. This was taking forever. She knew I was getting annoyed, because I had offered to take her to go see her sister in Cape Coral, and all she did was waste hour after hour with this drug bullshit.

She said she wanted to have sex before we were going to go see Summer. She told me to take my clothes off and get my dick hard for her, so I'd be ready for her by the time she's done smoking crack. I masturbated for an hour, while she paced around the room smoking crack, or sat down on the bed next to me, occasionally rubbing my dick with one hand, while playing with the phone in her other hand, or sucking the head of my painfully hard dick for a few seconds with a little smirk on her face, because she knew she was teasing me and it was driving me crazy.

Then Wigger called her and said that he needed the

room. He was on his way up. Great. I was so frustrated.

"I can tell him to wait in the hallway while we fuck," Lucy said.

"Nah, thanks. I don't like having sex while people are waiting for me to finish on the other side of the door. That's fucking creepy," I replied.

Lucy let Wigger and some other girl into the room. She asked me not to leave, because she still wanted to go see her sister. She said she just needed to talk to Wigger for a minute first. They disappeared in the bathroom together. They were in there for half an hour, while the other girl and I were sitting in the room, waiting. I was getting so disgusted.

I really didn't want to think about Lucy fucking that douchebag in the bathroom, but a few days earlier, she and I had taken a shower together in her room at the Super 8, and when her pimp G-Force unexpectedly came back to the room, she gave me a blowjob in the shower, while G-Force was sitting on the bed, watching TV.

I tried to convince myself that she wasn't doing the same damn thing with Wigger right now, and that they were probably just talking in the bathroom. Negotiating about drugs or something.

Finally they came out of the bathroom. I asked Lucy if she was ready to go see her sister now. She said no, she wanted to smoke more crack now. I was so fed up, I left. It was midnight.

Around 3 am, she called me and asked me if I would drive her to the hospital the next morning. I said yes. At 8 am she called me and told me that Wigger would drive her instead. I said: "Fine. Whatever," and went back to sleep.

Later that day I was in the mall. Lucy called me, but there was a lot of noise, so I didn't answer. About half an hour later, after I left the mall, I called her back. Wigger answered her phone. He told me she had called me while getting arrested for drug possession, and she was on her way to jail now.

It had barely been a week since Veronica had been arrested at my house, and now Lucy was in jail, too. And Haley had been in jail for months already. Haley and Lucy were in dorm 1, the trustee dorm. Trustees are inmates who work in the laundry room, or the kitchen. Or they clean. They get preferential treatment and double food rations. Veronica was in dorm 4.

I hadn't talked to Haley in a few months, after I changed my number for Veronica, so other girls couldn't call me anymore. But after Veronica ran off, and I started seeing Lucy, I had sent a thank you note to some of the 14 girls who had warned me about Veronica. Snitching is frowned upon in jail, even though pretty much all of them have turned each other in at some point or another to collect the Crimestoppers reward.

Anyway, I wanted them to know that they did the right thing, because telling a guy his girl is cheating on him and that she's only pretending to be pregnant is not snitching, but looking out for someone. It's a good thing. It's an act of kindness. It should be rewarded. So I felt the least I could do is write them a thank you note. I had also written Haley, and given her my new number.

Now I had Haley, Veronica, and Lucy call me from jail every day. This was getting crazy. And all these Global Tel collect calls were getting expensive.

Veronica really didn't like that I talked to Haley occasionally. But she hated that I was talking to Lucy now, too. She said it made her look bad in jail, that her man was talking to other girls in there.

Yupp... I was dating a crackwhore who never passed up a chance to cheat on me, and then she told me I was making HER look bad. Alrighty then. Suffer from cognitive dissonance much?

I told her that she shouldn't worry about their opinions. Who cares what the other inmates think? Their opinion was of no consequence. She was never going to see any of them again, once she got out and lived a sober life with me in Bonita Springs, far away from the cheap motels on 41 and Palm Beach.

Veronica and Lucy ended up going to court on the same day, so they sat in the holding cell together for a few hours. They talked and got along. Afterwards Veronica told me she would like to be in a threeway relationship with me and Lucy. She said she'd still like to fuck her, and that way I could fuck both of them. I didn't like that idea at all at this point, because they were both in jail, and I was out here. So this would end up being Veronica and Lucy dating each other in jail, and having sex together, while I sat out here with my thumb up my ass. No thank you.

When Lucy called me, I asked her about that whole threeway relationship business. She laughed and said: "Veronica is crazy. I don't want to date her. And I don't want to share you with her or anyone else. I love you and I want you all to myself."

Inmates in Lee County Jail have to make a visitor list. They can put up to five people on their list, and then only these five people can visit them. But during their first week in jail, they are allowed to see visitors without making a list, because it takes the jail a while to process the paperwork. Lucy asked me to come see her for her first visit, and to set up the second visit for her aunt Nicole. She told me to put my own name down for the second visit as well, just in case Nicole didn't show up. She never did in the past, so Lucy figured she wouldn't show up this time either. She was right.

When I told Veronica that Lucy wanted me to come see her, I figured she'd be ok with it, since she wanted all three of us to be in a relationship together anyway. But Veronica flipped out. She was very jealous and said it would really hurt her feelings, if I went to visit Lucy. Veronica said I was the only person who came to visit her, and I was not allowed to visit anyone else.

So I didn't go to my viso with Lucy. She called me up afterwards and she was crying: "Why didn't you come see me? I thought you love me. I have nobody else."

I felt terribly guilty. I didn't realize it would hurt her this much if I didn't show up. I told her I was sorry, and that I didn't expect Veronica to get so upset about me visiting Lucy. I told her I would come see her the next day, with her aunt Nicole.

Later that night some latin lady called me from jail. She told me Lucy had asked her to call me, to convince me to come see her. The lady said Lucy was crying because I didn't come to the viso, and I was all she talked about. I promised the lady that I wouldn't let Lucy down again.

Then Haley called me and asked me what all the fuss was about, and why Lucy was crying all the time. Haley and Lucy used to be friends when they had met each other in jail a year or two earlier. But now they didn't talk to each other anymore, because neither one of them wanted the other to call me. Haley and her friends hated Lucy, because they felt she was making a move on Haley's man: me.

This was all getting way too complicated.

Gossip travels fast in jail. Everyone knows everyone else's business. So it didn't take long until everyone in dorm 1 and dorm 4 knew that Haley, Lucy and Veronica were all calling me every day. Apparently the other inmates started to think I was the most eligible bachelor in LCJ or something. And more and more female inmates tried to contact me or pretended to know me, to make themselves sound important. Girls I had never even met, never even knew they existed, claimed to know me. They were telling elaborate stories about having sex with me, or getting arrested at my house, or whatever. It was bizarre. Suddenly I was a jailhouse celebrity. Everyone knew the name Oliver.

Nicole and I made plans for me to pick her up the next day, but then she blew me off, just like Lucy had anticipated. Nicole said she might stop by at some point during the viso and say hello. She didn't. The only people I know, who are this unreliable, are addicts. So I had a feeling that Nicole had relapsed.

Lucy was so happy to see me, she cried again. She was just the sweetest little thing. I loved her so much. She cried and smiled, cried and smiled, because I came to see her. It almost made me cry. I wanted to give her a hug so badly. I wanted her to know how much I cared about her. She told me she didn't want me to talk to Haley or Veronica anymore. She wanted me to be all hers.

When I talked to Veronica later, I was honest and told her that I had visited Lucy, because she was so upset. Veronica got really angry and told me she wanted me to change my number again and not talk to Lucy, Haley or any other girl anymore.

Then Lucy told me that everyone in jail knew that Veronica was cheating on me the whole time again. As soon as Veronica got back to jail, she started writing letters to Jasmine in dorm 3 and told her she loved her and wanted to have a future with her. And she was also writing love letters to Kathleen, her pregnant roommate, who had been arrested by the U.S. Marshals.

I couldn't believe it. Not after Veronica had told me all that stuff about how upset she was over being ripped out of our life together, and that she had fallen in love with me all over again, that she had learned her lesson, and she would never write love letters to someone else or cheat on me again.

And Lucy told me there were rumors that Veronica was dating her bunkie Wendy. She used to be friends with Jasmine in dorm 3, but then she was moved to dorm 4 and was now sleeping in the bunk next to Veronica's. Wendy was an ugly, freckle-faced, red-haired little troll. Veronica had mentioned her to me on the phone a few times in the past few days, and asked me to make calls for Wendy, because she couldn't get in touch with her father, and her boyfriend wouldn't answer the phone or come to viso.

In the past, when I was in New York, and Veronica was supposedly dating Jasmine while living on Brantley Road, but she had sex with a bunch of other people, I had written 2 or 3 postcards to Jasmine, to warn her about Veronica.

I told Jasmine that 14 people had warned me about what a lying lowlife Veronica was, and that I was glad they did. And I figured Jasmine had the right to know that Veronica had not only been cheating on me and her jail girlfriend Kim with Jasmine, but she was now cheating on Jasime with a bunch of other people, including Kim, Kathleen, Anita, Nina, Shelly, Miriam, Urban, and a few others. Veronica was still writing Kim love letters in prison, to try to get her hands on her baby.

Veronica had called Crimestoppers on Nina to collect the money, and Nina ended up in dorm 3 with Jasmine, and told her that she had sex with Veronica. That's how Jasmine found out that everything I had been telling her about Veronica was really true. Jasmine wrote me back and told me that she was done with her, and that she and I both deserved someone better than Veronica. Jasmine said she was getting out of jail soon, and that she was going to move to Key West with her mother 3 days later. She said we should hook up during those 3 days, while she's still in Fort Myers.

When Lucy told me that Veronica had been writing love letters to Jasmine and Kathleen again ever since she got arrested at my house, I just didn't want to believe it. I decided to find out the truth for myself. I sent Jasmine a letter and asked her if Veronica was writing her again. I figured she owed me a favor, and she would tell me the truth. But Jasmine never wrote me back.

Lucy asked: "If I can prove to you that Veronica is really cheating on you again, and she's really writing love letters to Jasmine and Kathleen, will you stop talking to her? Will you break up with her for good this time and will you be my boyfriend?"

I told her: "Yeah, if you can prove that, then I want nothing to do with her anymore, and then I would love to be your boyfriend."

The next day I was having lunch with George at Cici's Pizza, when Lucy called and put some girl named Shondra on the phone. She said she was a trustee who moves from dorm to dorm, and she had passed a love letter from Veronica to Jasmine. I told Lucy that I hoped she didn't make Shondra lie for her, because that's the kind of grimey lowlife shit Veronica had done to me several times in the past. Lucy swore that she didn't put Shondra up to it, and that it was the truth.

The next morning I got a call from Jasmine. She had been released from jail a few hours earlier. She said she wanted to meet up with me, and she had something for me: a bunch of love letters from Veronica.

A bunch? What the FUCK?!?

I met Jasmine at the Days Inn on 41, where she was staying with her mother. We sat in the car and talked for a while. She handed me Veronica's letters. I gave her the letters Veronica had written me recently. We compared notes. Veronica was telling each of us the same thing: I love you so much, I want to have a future with you, you're all I think about, I've never felt about anyone the way I feel about you, bla bla bla. Same old, same old.

I told Jasmine I had to leave, because I was about to have a viso with Veronica. Jasmine and I made plans to spend the next day together.

When I went to see Veronica, the video screens were broken. We couldn't see each other, but we could hear each other. I held her love letters to Jasmine in my hands when I asked her: "So have you written any letters to Jasmine or Kathleen since you were arrested at my house?"

"No, absolutely not," she replied. "And if anyone says that I did, they are lying!"

"You dumb cunt! I have your fucking letters in my hand right now!! FUCK YOUUU! I'm so done with this shit," I yelled and left.

Veronica called me later that night and acted indignant: "At least you could have finished the viso with me and let me explain. Ok, fine, yeah I wrote some letters to Jasmine. But it's not like they were love letters. I was just talking to her about some stuff, but I never wrote I love her or I still want to be with her."

"Are you fucking RETARDED?" I screamed. "That's EXACTLY what you wrote. You fucking wrote that you love her and you still want to be with her!!! Seriously, what the fuck is WRONG with you, you PSYCHO?"

Then I hung up the phone. She tried to call back, but I didn't answer.

The next morning, when Lucy called, I told her I had officially broken up with Veronica, and I was now all hers. She was really happy and said: "I love you, I love you, I love you sooo much!" That made me feel really good. I had the biggest smile on my face. Finally this crazy love triangle nonsense was done and over with, and I could just concentrate on one girl. I was glad it was Lucy.

She told me that I was going to be the only person on her visitation list. She didn't want anyone else to come visit her. Only me. And she said that she wasn't going to talk to any other guys anymore. She promised she would be nothing like Veronica. She would show me that she's a much better girlfriend. She would be 100% faithful to me.

And I promised that I would not talk to any other girls anymore either, and I wouldn't have sex with anyone but her from now on. And I meant it. I was going to wait for her to get out of jail. I really didn't want to be with anyone else. I was really happy whenever I was around Lucy. She was my little ray of sunshine.

When Lucy called me back a little while later, she sounded depressed.

"What's wrong?" I asked.

She said: "I told some people in dorm 1 that you are my boyfriend now, and they just laughed at me. They said you don't really care about me. Everyone in jail knows you, because you talk to a whole bunch of girls in jail. And everyone knows that you're Veronica's man."

"What? No, I don't talk to a bunch of girls. I don't know why all these girls pretend to know me. I talk to Haley, because I have known her for 4 years now. We are really good friends. And I talked to Veronica, because she was my girlfriend. And I talk to you, because I love you, and you're my new girlfriend. That's it. I don't talk to anyone else. I wrote a few people some thank you notes a while ago, because they warned me about Veronica. I really appreciated that they told me she was cheating on me with Kim, and that she wasn't really pregnant. But I don't talk to a bunch of girls in jail. And you know that I don't like to have sex with girls I don't know, and I don't call girls on Backpage. I really do love you," I replied.

I asked her when our next viso was, so we could talk about this in person. She said her list hadn't been processed yet.

The next day, I suddenly got a call from Wigger: "Yo, don't fall for Lucy's games. Don't be a duck!"

I had talked to him a few times since Lucy got arrested, because a bunch of her new clothes were in the hotel room they shared, and she wanted me to get all her things from Wigger and keep them at my house, until she'd come home to me. I could barely understand a damn thing he said, because he slurred his words so badly.

But from what I understood, he was telling me that Lucy didn't really care about me, and she was just using me, just like she had used him and a bunch of other guys. I had the feeling he was mad, because she wanted me to get her things from him, but he had thought they were going to be together, although he had a girlfriend, Abby, who was also in jail right now. In dorm 1 with Lucy and Haley. He had been cheating on Abby with Lucy and a bunch of other girls.

When Lucy called me back, I told her about Wigger's strange call. I asked her what he meant by that. She said she didn't know. But something about the tone of her voice made me suspicious. I did a little research, and found out that her visitation list had been approved, and I was not the only person on her list. There were 4 other guys besides me, and she had scheduled her two visits for next week with two other guys: her old pimp G-Force, and her sugar daddy Cho. She was playing the same sick games as Veronica.

I was really hurt and disappointed. I felt so betrayed. I really thought she was different.

Once again I sent her a nasty postcard and told her not to call me again.

Veronica kept calling me, so I finally answered the phone, and we started talking again. She told me she didn't know why she wrote those letters to Jasmine and Kathleen. She said she really didn't want to be with any of them, that she loved me, and that she wanted to come home to me. She asked me to come see her so we could talk.

I went to viso the next day, and she told me that she knew she had some sort of mental problem that compelled her to keep telling all these people that she supposedly loves them. She said: "I keep selling them dreams, and then I treat them like shit. I don't know why I do it. I'm not even interested in them, but it's like a sick game or something. I guess I just wanna see if I can get them. I feel bad sometimes, because I really shit all over Snickers and Shelly, Kathleen, and Jasmine."

"And what about me?" I asked. "Do you feel bad that you keep hurting me with your behavior?"

"Of course," she said. "I really do love you."

To me it seemed like Veronica had some sort of obsessive compulsive disorder that made her act this way. I knew she really did have OCD. When I stayed with her at her apartment, I had seen her comb her hair for over an hour.

I love when a girl has long, flowing hair. It's so feminine. But Veronica always tied her hair back into a really tight ponytail. It was a shame, because she had beautiful hair.

I had seen her stand in front of the mirror and just get lost in a trance-like state, while she combed the tightly pulled back hair on her head over and over and over with a toothbrush. Each individual hair had to be exactly where she wanted it to be. Later some of the other inmates told me that she did the same thing in jail.

While she told me during that viso that she supposedly felt bad for selling dreams to all these different people and for hurting me, I noticed that she had a hard time hiding a smirk. She really didn't feel any remorse. She was actually proud of herself. She wasn't really apologizing for cheating on me, she was bragging to me about her conquests.

"Man, I fucked so many girls while I was living on Brantley," she said and laughed. "I totally shit all over Jasmine!"

"Yeah, and you tricked with a bunch of guys too," I said calmly.

"No, no, that's not true! I didn't post on Backpage. I didn't trick," she objected.

In her sick mind, she wasn't really a whore, if she didn't post an ad on Backpage and had sex with hundreds of guys, and she just had sex with dozens of "regulars" and dope boys instead.

"Really? You seriously think fucking Urban, and Tim, and all those other guys wasn't tricking? I found a freshly used condom in your nightstand. I found you in bed with Norbert," I said. I was getting disgusted with her all over again.

She started laughing: "Yeah, I can't believe we didn't wake up when you kicked the door in!" She thought it was hilarious. She had no sense of empathy whatsoever. She couldn't put herself in my shoes and consider how that situation felt on my end. She really did not comprehend how terribly she hurt me when she cheated on me.

"You really think the stuff you did to me is funny?" I asked. "How would you feel if I sat here and laughed about having sex with Anita?"

"That was crazy, when I fucked Anita," Veronica laughed. "We fucked for like two hours!"

"Do you understand how badly you're hurting me when you say shit like that?" I asked. "Seriously, let's turn the tables. How would you feel if I told you I fucked Anita twice, and it was awesome?"

She stopped laughing and got a suspicious look on her face: "DID you have sex with Anita?"

"Yeah. Twice. And it was awesome. She did all sorts of acrobatics, and she let me cum inside her pussy," I replied calmly.

"What? What the fuck are you talking about?" Veronica asked angrily. "Is this supposed to be a joke? Like when you made up Faith? Or did you really fuck Anita?"

"I really fucked her. And I really liked it," I replied with a cold, cruel superiority in my voice.

Veronica got so pissed! She started ranting: "Imma kill that bitch! That fucking hoe! I knew something was up when you guys stayed up all night and talked! I knew I couldn't trust her! Imma beat the shit out of her if I ever see her again." Then she got quiet. She was in her own head, plotting her revenge against Anita.

"Did you use a condom?" she asked.

"No. We were going to be in a relationship together, remember? So Anita let me cum inside of her without a condom," I said. I started to enjoy seeing Veronica this upset. Karma is a bitch.

"That's DISGUSTING! What if she got pregnant?" she asked.

"Why is it disgusting if I fuck other girls and cum inside of them without a condom, but it's ok for you to fuck all these girls, and other guys, and you let them cum inside of you?" I asked.

"I don't ever fuck anyone without a condom! You're the only one I let cum inside of me. I always use a condom with other guys! You even found one of them in my nightstand," she yelled.

"Bullshit! I saw your text messages when you were talking to Urban about having him get you pregnant. You let that dirty lowlife thug cum inside of you without a condom all the time! And I'm sure he wasn't the only one. And remember when we first met, and your leg was hurting and you told me I was the only one you wanted to have sex with? There was someone else's cum dripping out of your pussy while you said that. Ever since I've known you, all you have ever done is lie and cheat. And you think it's cool. You're actually proud of yourself, like some sort of sick sociopath. You don't give a shit if you hurt other people, but when someone does it back to you, you act all upset," I replied.

She got quiet and said: "I don't want to argue anymore. I'm sorry for all the shit I've done. I really do love you."

I didn't feel like arguing either. I was so sick and tired of feeling like shit. It was so emotionally draining. I was exhausted.

"Why can't things between us ever just be easy?" I asked sadly. "I'm so sick of all this drama."

We stopped arguing and everything went back to the

way it used to be. She called several times a day every day, and I visited her twice a week. We were back together. She told me she really wanted to have a future with me and she wasn't going to fuck it up again. She swore that from now on, she would be 100% faithful to me and not play any of her sick games anymore, not cheat anymore, not write any more love letters to anyone else or do anything else she shouldn't be doing as my girlfriend.

Then Haley called me and told me that everyone in jail knew about Veronica dating her bunkie Wendy. She said they were fucking each other pretty much every day, and they almost got caught a few times. The corrections officers got so sick of always seeing Veronica and Wendy together in dark corners, or taking showers together, they separated them and sent Wendy back to dorm 3.

I didn't want to believe it. But Haley had never really lied to me. Well, except when she stole my hard drives, and when she pretended that I got her pregnant. But since she had been in jail, everything she told me about Veronica was always true.

I looked on the Sheriff's website, and I saw that Wendy really had been moved to dorm 3.

When Veronica called me back, I asked her what was going on in jail, and if there was any interesting new gossip. I gave her a chance to tell me that her "best friend" Wendy was no longer in the same dorm with her. But she didn't bring it up. I had noticed that in the past few weeks, there had been complete radio silence about Wendy. Veronica used to mention her all the time in the beginning, because they were friends and they were hanging out together. But lately Veronica never mentioned Wendy at all anymore. I knew what that meant.

When people withhold seemingly harmless information, it's usually because it's not harmless after all, and they are afraid if they reveal that bit of information, it will get them into trouble. So I knew that the only reason why Veronica wasn't mentioning Wendy's name anymore was because there was something going on between them.

And now the fact that they had been separated and Wendy was sent to another dorm, and Veronica didn't even mention that, when I casually asked her for the latest gossip, was proof that she was hiding her relationship with Wendy from me. Veronica told me a while ago that Wendy had given birth to a baby boy right before going to jail. So I figured now Veronica was going to try to get her hands on Wendy's baby, in case she couldn't get Kim's or Shelly's or Kathleen's baby.

I told Veronica that I knew she was cheating on me again, that she was dating Wendy behind my back, that they had sex all the time, and that they had been separated now.

"What? No! That's crazy! There is absolutely nothing going on between Wendy and me. Her being sent to dorm 3 had nothing to do with me. She got caught in the wrong bunk area. That had NOTHING to do with me," Veronica claimed.

But then, a few minutes later, she slipped and said: "Wendy and I used to be in the same bunk area, but she got moved to another one. She has this stupid high school girl crush on me, so she kept coming over to my bunk area, and then she got caught."

Like always when Veronica was in one of her shallow fake relationships with some girl, she claimed that the other girl was madly in love with her, she was stalking her, she was obsessed with her, but Veronica wasn't into her at all. It was the same story every time. She had told me the same thing about Miriam, Lola, Shelly, Theresa, Snickers, Nancy, Kim, Nina, Jasmine and Kathleen.

She always pretended they were chasing after her, because they were supposedly madly in love with her, but she didn't want anything from them.

But I, and everyone in jail, knew that it was really the other way around. She was constantly chasing after several people at the same time, trying to sell them dreams, writing them love letters, trying to make out with them, trying to make them believe that she was in love with them and that she had never felt that way about anyone else before, while cheating on them the whole time and telling other people the same thing, often word for word. It was like she was some sort of escaped mental patient.

I actually felt bad for her, because I knew she really did have severe mental problems from the abuse and abandonment she had to endure as a child, and the years of traumatizing sex with guys who just used her but didn't care about her as a human being. She was starving for affection. She desperately wanted to feel loved, truly loved, but really didn't know how to accomplish that. So she tried to improve her odds by throwing herself at a bunch of people at the same time. She really didn't understand that that behavior ruined her chances of ever finding real love, and ever having a deep, meaningful bond with another human being.

Now this latest replay of the same old story, this time with Wendy, just seemed sad and pathetic. I was really hurt, but at the same time I couldn't stop thinking about how much pain Veronica was really in. She had never even known what it's like to have a normal mother and father. All she had ever known was people using her to either get sex from her, or drugs, or snacks in jail. Her sense of selfworth was nonexistent. She felt she had no value, had nothing to offer, besides sex, drugs or snacks. So she used those three things to bribe people into "loving" her.

The more I thought about this stuff, the more I just wanted to give her a hug and tell her I love her. She had been cheating on me, and instead of feeling bad for myself, I felt bad for her. How sick is that?

But it couldn't go on, because her cheating on me was tearing me apart inside. So I told her: "This shit with Wendy needs to end RIGHT NOW. I'm serious. This is your last chance. If you don't stop this shit behind my back, I'm done with you for good."

She replied that there was nothing going on with

Wendy, and she swore she would be good. She said it was unfair that I was acting like she was being bad again, because this time she was really innocent, she was really being good, and she was really being faithful to me.

The next day Haley called me back and told me that everyone in jail was talking about how Wendy in dorm 3 was screaming across the hall at Veronica in dorm 4. Haley said, Wendy had been calling Veronica a lying piece of shit whore, or something along those lines. Apparently Wendy had found out that as soon as she was moved to dorm 3, Veronica was already cheating on her. She was calling Jasmine in Key West and sending more love letters to Kathleen.

When Veronica called me, I asked her why Wendy had been screaming at her across the hall. Obviously that clearly indicated that they were in a relationship, and Wendy was jealous, because Veronica was cheating on her.

"No, it's not like that at all. Wendy is just some silly little girl who is totally in love with me. But I don't feel that way about her at all. I only want to be with you. I love you," Veronica said.

Haley wasn't the only one who told me that everyone in jail knew that Veronica and Wendy were dating. More and more inmates contacted me to tell me what Veronica was doing behind my back.

When she had been cheating on me with Kim, 14 people had reached out to me to warn me. Now 9 people told me that she was cheating on me with Wendy. I told her what each and every one of those 9 people said. And every time Veronica claimed they were lying about her, because they supposedly had ulterior motives. Meanwhile she was bragging in jail that no matter what any of the other inmates told me about her, I would never leave her, because she had me wrapped around her little finger.

Then a few people told me Veronica and Wendy went to court together and were making out in the holding cell. They were so blatant and over-the-top, some of the other girls in the cell were offended by it, and when they got back to jail after court, they told the other inmates how obnoxious Veronica and Wendy were.

I had a viso with Veronica later that same day. I asked her again if there was anything going on between her and Wendy. She swore there wasn't. But I just wouldn't drop it. I asked her again and again. Finally she gave in and said: "Alright, fine. Yeah, Wendy and I have been flirting a little. But it's no big deal."

"I fucking hate you," I said, got up, and left.

I had it with her. She was obviously never ever going to change. I was so sick of feeling hurt and betrayed all the time. I remembered how she reacted when I told her that I had sex with Anita. I figured the only way to make her understand how destructive her behavior is, is to do it back to her. I decided to call a bunch of girls I hadn't talked to in a while.

I hadn't talked to Anita in months, ever since Veronica

had been arrested. Anita was now living with her grandmother in Cape Coral. I told her about all the crazy stuff that happened with Veronica since the last time we talked.

Anita replied: "I told you a long time ago, Veronica will never change. She's a piece of shit. She even stole money out of my purse when we were roommates. And she's lying about not tricking. She fucked a bunch of guys before you got there, and even when you were living with us. Why would you want to waste any more of your time with a stupid little girl like Veronica, when you could have a woman like me? I am ready to settle down. I want to have a normal life and a family. I would love to have a good man like you in my life."

I picked her up at her grandmother's house and she spent the night at my place. We had sex a few times. But I knew I couldn't be in a relationship with her, because she was still tricking, and doing drugs. She would just be a clone of Veronica.

The next day, after I dropped Anita off, I picked up Erin. I hadn't seen her in a few months either. She just got out of Collier County Jail again. She stayed with me for a couple of days and we had sex a few times. Then I dropped her off at her friend Josie's house, because Erin wanted Josie to help her dye her dark hair blond. I was supposed to pick Erin up afterwards, because she wanted to live with me and be in a real relationship.

But since she also used to have a drug problem in the past, and she asked me to buy her a $50 bag of weed before she went to Josie's house, I was afraid things with her would end up being no different than with Veronica or Lucy.

I probably should have given Erin more of a chance, because even after I ditched her at Josie's house, she kept calling me every day, to try to get together. She really was serious about settling down and having a serious, monogamous relationship. A week or two later, she moved in with some guy in Port Charlotte, and she has been with him ever since. As far as I know, she's still clean. Good for her. I regret not picking her up from Josie's house. But I was still too hung up on Veronica, and paying her back for all the pain she had caused me for the past 2 years.

A bunch of girls from LCJ, who had heard my name in jail, contacted me on Facebook once they got out. I'm really not a player or a pimp. I don't want to have a bunch of trophy girls. I don't want a girl just for sex. I want one girl in my life who I can trust and build a future with. So I usually ignored all these girls who were trying to get with me, just because they knew I had taken good care of Veronica.

But one girl was very persistent. Her name was Daisy. She wrote me on Facebook almost every day. She was only 19, and black. I hate gangsta rap and that whole illiterate ghetto mentality. But Daisy was not ghetto. She was a polite, articulate, intelligent, hard-working girl. I had been ignoring her advances for the past few weeks, but now I told her I wanted to meet her. I picked her up after work. She was a waitress at Culvers in Naples. We ended up meeting a bunch of times and had sex. She had been in dorm 2 with Veronica, so she told me how much Veronica had been cheating on me the whole time, and that she was always bragging about playing me like a fiddle.

Hussy had moved back from Ocala a few weeks ago. She lived in LaBelle with her new boyfriend Brian now. He worked at a bamboo plantation. She told me she'd like to start seeing me again, because things with her and Brian weren't working out. She caught him cheating on her. So I met up with her a bunch of times. We usually had sex at least twice a day, like we used to.

I told her about meeting Lucy, and everything that had happened since then. Hussy was not happy at all about that, and told me to be careful. She said Lucy was a con artist who had hurt a lot of people. Look who's talking!

Veronica and I weren't talking to each other since I found out she had been making out with Wendy in court, and she admitted that there was something going on between them, but tried to trivialize it.

After I had a whole lot of sex with a bunch of different girls, I sent Veronica a letter and bragged about it. I told her how good they were, and how much I enjoyed fucking each of them. I told her I had so much sex every day, some days with more than one girl, I was exhausted. I hoped my letter would really get under her skin, and show her what it's like to be on the receiving end of that kind of grimey behavior.

She called me and cried: "Why would you do that to me? Why would you hurt me like that? I hate you!"

"Are you fucking kidding me?" I asked. "That's the kind of shit you've been doing to me for years. Now I did it to you for a week or two, and you act like I'm a monster. All I did was give you a taste of your own medicine for a few days."

After a while we both calmed down again. She told me she loved me and still wanted to come home to me, have a baby and be together. We made up. I told her that this was really, really her last chance. If she cheated on me with Wendy or anyone else again, I would be done with her for good. I told her if I hear one more rumor about her and another girl, I was done. She said that wasn't fair, because even if she didn't do anything, people would still accuse her of being with this girl or that girl.

When Haley called me and I told her what Veronica said, she replied: "Bullshit. Veronica is such a drama queen. Nobody gives a shit about her. People have better things to do than to make up stories about her. The only reason people talk about her is because she's a hot mess. I have a lot of friends in jail, but you don't ever hear any rumors about me being in a relationship with some other girl in jail."

After Veronica and Wendy made out in the court holding cell, they had themselves moved into dorm 2 together. Just like Veronica had done with Kim the last time she was in jail. And just like with Kim, Veronica claimed that she and Wendy weren't even talking to each other anymore, and they were on opposite ends of the dorm.

"I swear there is nothing going on between us anymore now," Veronica said. "The corrections officers watch us like hawks, because they know there used to be something between Wendy and me, and we were separated into two different dorms. They're not going to allow us to even talk to each other in the rehab dorm now."

Later I found out that was all just a bunch of lies again. They never stopped dating. They were a couple the whole time they were in dorm 2 together. Veronica never stopped cheating on me for even one day.

Remember Wigger's girlfriend Abby? He had been cheating on her with Lucy and a couple of other girls, while she was in jail. Abby had a sister, Tabby. Both of them were drug addicted hookers, and occasionally they had threesomes together with a "client." Nice.

One of the girls Wigger was fucking behind Abby's back while she was in jail was her own sister, Tabby. Yupp, Abby's boyfriend was cheating on her with her own sister. Classy. What a guy, what a guy.

Then Tabby got arrested and ended up being Veronica's new bunkie in dorm 4, after Wendy had been moved from dorm 4 back to dorm 3. Veronica started cheating on me, and on Wendy, with Tabby. Once Veronica was moved to dorm 2, she continued to write Tabby love letters behind Wendy's back. And she continued to write love letters to Kathleen, who was in dorm 2 with Veronica and Wendy. Are you getting a headache yet?

Haley kept telling me that Veronica was still lying to

me. Veronica denied it. Other people told me Haley was telling me the truth. Veronica claimed they were all just a bunch of haters. She said if I wanted to know the truth about what she was doing in dorm 2, I should ask the girls she was hanging out with, like her friend Cassidy. She would tell me that Veronica was being good, and that she told everyone she was my girlfriend, nobody else's, and that she wasn't seeing anyone else behind my back anymore.

After Veronica had made several other girls lie to me in the past, I had no intention of asking the people she told me to ask. I figured if I asked Cassidy anything, Veronica would bribe her with some snacks to tell me whatever Veronica told her to say.

I decided to pick my own two girls in dorm 2 and ask them what was really going on between Veronica and Wendy now. One of them was Morgan, the girl who used to be Kayla's best friend. I hadn't talked to her in two years, ever since I had dropped a garbage bag with her things off, after she had cheated on me with her baby daddy for some heroin.

Morgan had violated her probation a few months ago and was now also in jail. Even though I hadn't talked to her in ages, I hoped she still cared about me enough not to let Veronica keep hurting me like that, and that she would tell me what was really going on behind my back.

Then there was Greta. She was one of Haley's best friends. Since she knew Haley and I were very close, I believed she would tell me the truth as well.

I wrote both of them a letter, asking them to please be honest with me and not let Veronica play games with my heart anymore. I told them how much she had hurt me for the past two years, and that enough was enough. Neither one of them wrote me back. Instead they gave my letters to Veronica. Traitors! She called me up and bragged about it.

A day or two later, Greta was released from jail. I contacted her on Facebook, and now she told me that Veronica was cheating on me with Wendy the whole time.

Then, a few days later, Wendy screamed at Kathleen, because she found out that Veronica was still writing her love letters. The officers sent Wendy to D pod. It's the jail within jail. Usually the inmates are allowed to roam around in a large dorm, but if they break the rules, they get locked up in small cells in D pod.

I just couldn't lie to myself anymore. Veronica was still the same old lowlife, still lying and cheating on me. She really was never going to change, no matter how many times she swore she was going to be faithful to me from now on.

I sent Veronica one final letter. I told her what a pathetic lowlife piece of shit she was. And then I decided to give her a taste of her own medicine one last time.

I had sex with a couple of different girls over the next few days, and I took a picture of each one of them sitting on my bed. Then I printed each picture as a postcard, and mailed them all to Veronica. On the back of each postcard, I wrote a spiteful little comment, about how much sexier this girl was than Veronica, or how much better that girl was at making me feel good. And behind each comment, I drew a carefree little smiley face. I wanted her to picture us laughing at her, because we were.

Veronica had written me a while ago, that if she ever found another girl in "our" bed, she would kill me and the other girl. So I figured it would get under her skin to see all these girls on "our" bed.

And while looking at each picture, she would know that each of these beautiful girls had been naked in "our" bed and spread her legs for me.

Each of the girls I asked was happy to participate in my little revenge plot, because none of them liked Veronica, and they all knew what a lying, cheating lowlife she was, and how much she had hurt me and many other people with her psychotic games.

Later some girl called me from dorm 2, and told me that the whole dorm was laughing about Veronica behind her back, because she had been bragging that she was a master manipulator and that she controlled me like a mindless little puppy who would do whatever she said. So those postcards kinda cramped her jailhouse swag a bit.

And every time another one of my postcards arrived, and the officer yelled Veronica's name across the dorm during mail call, her face got beat red with embarrassment on her walk of shame, to go get the card. Everyone knew it was another picture of another girl I fucked, while thumbing my nose at Veronica.

I had learned during my hacking days, how to really get under someone's skin, if I wanted to. And it worked. I heard from other inmates that Veronica's jaw dropped to the floor when she started getting those cards from her "obedient puppy."

I heard that she was ripping them up in a fit of rage, as soon as she got them, and then pieced them back together afterwards, to get another look. When I sent her a picture of Lucy, she couldn't rip it up fast enough with her hands, because the glossy photo paper was too strong, so she tore it to pieces with her teeth.

I heard that even inmates who usually didn't get involved in petty jail house drama thought it was great that I put Veronica in her place with my entertaining little stunt.

How ya like me now, bitch?

Veronica continued to throw herself at Wendy, Kathleen, a girl called Moira and a bunch of other girls in several different dorms, telling each of them that she supposedly loved them oh so much. It was just sad. She was making a spectacle of herself. But that wasn't my problem anymore.

I was done with her. Really, really, really done this time.

NICOLE

"We accept the love we think we deserve."
Stephen Chbosky

*"A woman has got to love a bad man once or twice
in her life to be thankful for a good one."*
Mae West

*"Everyone says that love hurts. But that's not true.
Loneliness hurts, rejection hurts, losing someone
hurts. Everyone confuses these with love, but in
reality love is the only thing in this world that covers
up all the pain and makes us feel wonderful again."*
Unknown

When Lucy's aunt Nicole was released from prison in April 2013, she swore she would never touch drugs again. She moved into a halfway house, started her own little lawn care business, did tattoos on the side, and went to church and NA meetings regularly. She was determined to never go back to her old life.

When I met Lucy in June 2013, she had told me to keep in touch with her aunt, because she knew she was headed for jail soon. She wanted me and Nicole to be able to update each other about her situation.

Lucy's mother was a drug addict, who had abandoned her as a baby, and her dad Dick was a drug dealing scumbag. It was Nicole who raised Lucy, almost like her own daughter. Nicole was the one holding Lucy in all her baby pictures. She taught her how to walk, how to talk, and how to take drugs. Later Lucy's grandma Gloria took over for Nicole.

Nicole and I friended each other on Facebook, and while Lucy was in jail, Nicole and I started chatting with each other at night. I told her I loved Lucy, and that I was hoping to be able to show her that a sober life was worth living.

Nicole and I became pretty close, and we often chatted all night long. She started telling me about herself. She said she had tried to kill herself many times, because she had been through some really traumatic stuff in her childhood.

She told me her brother, Lucy's dad Dick, had raped her ever since she was 4 years old. They weren't related by blood. Nicole's father had married Dick's mother Gloria.

While Dick raped Nicole night after night, his brother raped Nicole's younger sister. Nicole often heard her sister cry and choke in the bathroom, while Dick's brother shoved his dick in her mouth.

Dick was more than 10 years older than Nicole, so he was a teenager when she was still a toddler. He raped her for years, until she was 15. He was in the car with her, and tried to force her to have sex with him again. She floored the gas pedal and headed straight for a tree. She wanted to kill him and herself. The car hit the tree at 80 mph. He was lucky and didn't get all that hurt. But her right leg was shattered. She wasn't able to walk from the age of 15 until she was 18. That's when he finally stopped raping her. But he continued to make nasty remarks to her all the time, saying things like: "What color panties are you wearing?" or "Remember, I was the first to fuck the shit out of you." She hated Dick, but never told Lucy what her father had done to her.

I felt really bad for Nicole, because she seemed like a nice person, but all her life she had been used and abused by guys. Her brother Dick wasn't the only one to rape her. And all her boyfriends were the same type of guy: some drug-using, violent redneck who treated her like shit and frequently beat her. That's all she had ever known. She thought that's all she deserved. No wonder she tried to kill herself so many times, and was addicted to drugs. To her, life was pain.

At the NA meetings, Nicole met Johnny. He was the same type of guy as all the other guys she had dated before him. He was some drug addicted lowlife with a long criminal record, who had spent his entire adult life in prison. He just got out.

They hit it off and started dating. It didn't take long before he relapsed. Of course that made her use drugs again, too. She stopped going to the NA meetings, because her sponsor and the other people she had met there and looked to for help, had all relapsed as well. Now they were calling her for drugs.

That didn't really come as a surprise to me. The more I read about the AA/NA 12-step program, the less impressed I was. Ask any drug counselor, and they will tell you that the relapse rate for drugs like crack or heroin is about 98%. That means the current gold standard of addiction treatment, the 12-step-program, fails almost 100% of the time to keep people off drugs. In other words, it's clearly not working. Ask any addict, and they will tell you a dozen stories about their addict friends who went to a rehab program, and relapsed as soon as they got out.

But imagine if any other medication or medical treatment had an almost 100% failure rate. That medication would not only be taken off the market, the makers would be sued for medical malpractice or land in jail. And now imagine if the patients who didn't get any better after the treatment were being blamed for the treatment's failure. That's exactly what happens when an addict fails to recover after being in a 12-step-based rehab program.

The AA program was originally based on God as a cure for addiction. Only after people complained that this was akin to faith healing (Which also doesn't work. Nobody in their right mind would choose prayer instead of Penicillin when they get a bad infection.) was the word God replaced with the term "Higher Power." But it's still a thinly disguised religious program with religious terminology throughout. And since I don't believe God exists, to me it's no surprise that a treatment program that is based on something that doesn't exist is doomed to fail every time.

At one point I spoke to a lady who had been running a halfway house for 17 years. She told me how strict her house rules were, and that the girls in her house had a curfew, had to attend an AA/NA meeting every day, etc.

A little while later in the conversation, she told me that in those 17 years, she had only seen one single addict come through her halfway house, who truly got clean and did not relapse anymore afterwards. I thought it was funny that somehow she didn't connect the dots in her head, that what she was doing was clearly not working. But of course she blamed the addicts for their failure to get better. They just didn't want to get better bad enough. Imagine if you had an infected appendix, and instead of surgery or antibiotics, the doctor told you to attend prayer meetings every day, and when your appendix ruptures and kills you anyway, the doctor says: "Well, I guess you didn't want to get better badly enough."

The magazine Free Inquiry published a very thorough article about AA, written by Steven Mohr, called "Exposing the Myth of Alcoholics Anonymous." Mohr characterizes AA as nothing more than a religious cult.

Bankole A. Johnson, chairman of the Department of Psychiatry and Neurobehavioral Sciences at the University of Virginia, wrote in an article for the Washington Post: "For decades, Americans have clung to a near-religious conviction that rehab - and the 12-step model pioneered by Alcoholics Anonymous that almost all facilities rely upon - offers effective treatment for alcoholism and other addictions. Here's the problem: We have little indication that this treatment is effective. When an alcoholic goes to rehab but does not recover, it is he who is said to have failed. But it is rehab that is failing addicts. The therapies offered in most U.S. alcohol and drug treatment centers are so divorced from state-of-the-art medical knowledge that we might dismiss them as merely quaint - if it weren't for the fact that addiction is a deadly and devastating disease."

He concludes: "There is little compelling evidence that the AA method works, inside or outside a rehab facility. Although AA's emphasis on anonymity makes it difficult for outside researchers to determine its success rates, some have tried. What they have found doesn't inspire much confidence in AA's approach. A recent review by the Cochrane Library, a health-care research group, of studies on alcohol treatment conducted between 1966 and 2005 states its results plainly: "No experimental studies unequivocally demonstrated the effectiveness of AA or TSF [12-step facilitation] approaches for reducing alcohol or drug dependence."

But some addicts do get better. So there is hope. The Harvard Medical School did a study, and asked a whole bunch of people, who really truly got clean, how they did it. 80% of them answered that they did not do it with the AA program, but on their own, at home, by staying away from other addicts, with the love and support of their loved ones. And I think that is the key: don't hang out with other addicts. Not even at meetings. Not even when they're in recovery, because virtually all of them will relapse sooner or later. So stay as far away from other addicts as possible. Surround yourself with truly sober people who love you.

As I mentioned earlier, I believe drug addiction is a substitute for love. So it seems only logical to me that love is what can help an addict overcome their drug addiction. And there are rehab programs out there that are not based on the 12-step program, but on actual medical science, and on building strong, loving relationships.

Anyway, let's get back to Nicole:

The guy she met at an AA meeting relapsed, and she followed soon after. At first she used just a little bit, occasionally. She lied to herself and pretended that she could do drugs recreationally, here and there, without letting it get out of hand. But slowly it got worse. It always does. Eventually she and Johnny couldn't afford the amount of drugs they required, so Johnny tried to talk her into stripping, and then wanted her to escort on Backpage.

Take my word for it: if a guy is ok with you stripping or escorting, he doesn't really love you. He cares more about money or drugs, than about you. He's not your friend, and he's not your lover. He's using you as his meal ticket. He's pimping you out, even if he manages to make you think it's your idea. A real man would rather go scrub toilets to earn a living, than watch his girl degrade herself in a strip club or as a whore.

One day Nicole told me she needed money, and asked me if there was anything she could do for me to earn some quick cash. I told her she could clean my house, if she wanted to. I figured $40 for 4 hours of cleaning would be fair. But she was only there for about an hour and a half, and she was texting all the time. The only people I knew, who text with such hectic urgency and frequency, are drug addicts. So my instincts told me she was using drugs again, even if she was still at a stage where her addiction seemed manageable.

A few weeks went by. Lucy had been in and out of jail a few times. Now she was back in, and she told me that I was the only person on her visitation list. She told me she loved me and that she wasn't talking to any other guys anymore. I was the only one. But then Wigger warned me not to trust her, and I found out she was playing me and a bunch of other guys. She had scheduled a viso with her pimp G-Force and her sugar daddy Cho.

I felt really hurt and betrayed, because this was the same kind of grimey shit that Veronica had done to me so many times, and Lucy had promised never to hurt me like that. And then she did it anyway. So I was done with her. I wanted nothing to do with her anymore. I told Nicole that Lucy did nothing but lie and cheat, just like Veronica, and I was sick of it. Nicole replied that I was right not to put up with Lucy's games. She said I deserved to be treated better than that.

A few weeks later, Nicole messaged me on Facebook and told me that she was going to start dancing as a stripper at Lookers. She asked me if I would come see her. I told her I don't like strip clubs. She offered to come to my house and strip for me there. I told her that probably wasn't a good idea, because I would get turned on, and then I'd probably want to have sex with her. She replied that that was the whole point of taking her clothes off in front me. Wow. So after Veronica's mother had hit on me, and Lola's mother told me it was ok to fuck her daughter right in front of her, now Lucy's aunt told me I could fuck her if I wanted to.

Nicole was a gorgeous 30 year old natural blonde, with steel blue eyes and large breasts. In prison, the other inmates had called her Barbarian Barbie, because she was beautiful and athletic.

Lucy obviously didn't give a shit about me. By now I had found out that she not only had been talking to a bunch of guys besides me, but she was doing exactly the same thing that Veronica always did: Lucy was writing love letters to a bunch of different people. I was by no means the only one in her life, like she claimed. She had even written a letter to Veronica, asking her to have herself moved from dorm 4 to dorm 1, where Lucy was, so they could fuck.

But at this point Veronica wanted nothing to do with Lucy anymore, because Lucy had told me that Veronica was dating Wendy behind my back. So Veronica ended up sending me the letter Lucy wrote her, to show me that I couldn't trust Lucy and she was just playing me. Veronica trash-talked Lucy all the time and said things like: "Lucy got really fat in jail. And did you ever notice her head is too big for her body? I'm so much hotter than her."

Lucy had also written a letter to her sugar daddy Cho, that said she loved him and wanted to be with him. He ended up texting me a photo of her letter, to rub it in my face, and he told me that he had also intercepted one of her love letters to some other guy.

She was writing several different dope boys on the

outside, male inmates in other parts of the jail, and female inmates, including Snickers. She was throwing herself at a dozen different people at once, telling each of them the same thing. Just like Veronica. It was bizarre. It was like Lucy was a slightly younger clone of Veronica.

Lucy was just as desperate to feel loved, and she thought she would accomplish that by casting the widest possible net, instead of putting all her eggs in one basket with just one person. She was just as selfish as Veronica, and didn't consider my feelings even for one second while she was doing all that stuff. I didn't exist while she chased after all these other people.

Fuck her, I thought. Karma is a bitch.

I told Nicole that I was in New York, but that I would like to watch her strip for me, once I get back to Fort Myers. She told me to hurry back.

I arrived in Fort Myers in early November, 2013. One day before Lucy was about to be released again. So I could have picked her up from jail, like she asked me to two weeks earlier. But then she decided to go smoke crack with Cho and fuck him instead. The thought of that guy, or any other guy, touching her made me sick.

She obviously had no loyalty to me whatsoever, even though she always told me she loved me oh so much. So why should I have any loyalty to her? Why should I consider her feelings for even a second while I pursue other people?

I picked up Nicole at Lucy's grandfather's house. We went back to my place. She was really nervous. I told her she didn't really have to strip if she didn't want to, and that I'd be perfectly happy just having sex with her. She was relieved. She told me she couldn't bring herself to strip at Lookers, because she was way too shy. It hadn't been her idea anyway. It was Johnny's.

He had also tried to force her to trick on Backpage, but she said she couldn't bring herself to have sex with all these random guys. She had a full blown panic attack, when Johnny drove her to some guy's house to fuck him. That's why she had messaged me on Facebook a few days ago, hoping I'd like what I see once she stripped for me, and maybe we'd click, and then I'd agree to see her every day, and take care of her, the way I used to take care of Lucy's stepmom Hussy.

Inbetween the day she had messaged me, and the day I returned to Fort Myers and picked her up, Johnny had gotten arrested. Nicole had tried to break up with him. He got violent and started beating her at the Hess gas station on Palm Beach Boulevard. He threw her on the ground. Other people stopped him, to help her get away from him. But she had to get her belongings out of his pickup truck first. He ran over her foot with the truck. She hobbled away, into the gas station.

He rammed the glass front and tried to drive the truck through the store to run her over. The cops arrested him and he was charged with assault with a deadly weapon, among other things. He was still on probation. Now he was going to head back to prison for a long time. Good. I fucking hate lowlives like him.

It's never ok to hit a girl. Never. Not even if she cheats on you. A girl is not your property. She's a human being. She is just as important as you. She is your equal. And her wishes and feelings are just as valid as yours. All you can do is treat her nice, and hope she wants to be with you. If she chooses to be with you, great! If not, or if she chooses to leave you at some point, you have to let her go. You have no right to stop her. You don't own her, and you don't have the right to tell her what to do. She's your partner. Not your servant, not your sex slave, and not your punching bag.

But you're not her punching bag either. You don't have to let her hurt you. If she treats you like garbage, if she shows you nothing but disrespect, then walk away from her. Find someone who treats you better. Nobody has the right to abuse you, as my friend George always said.

Anyway, Nicole and I went into the bedroom, and she took her clothes off. She was really shy. She thought she wasn't as pretty as the girls I was used to, and she didn't measure up. She apologized for the scars on her leg. I hadn't even noticed them. She was beautiful. Once she was naked, she covered her breasts and pussy with her hands and giggled nervously. Then she jumped under the covers next to me. I knew this was really scary and stressful for her. I gently asked her, if she still wanted to go through with this. She said yes, with a timid smile.

I asked her to suck me, and she did. I felt like I didn't have sex in months. She made me feel really good, and I would have cum in her mouth soon, but I wasn't sure if that was ok, and I didn't want to gross her out. And I really wanted to know what her pussy felt like, so I asked her to lie down. I got on top of her, and we kissed while I slowly pushed myself inside of her. I concentrated on how I felt while being inside of her. I felt really content and happy. I could have stayed like this with her forever. She was so warm and soft. We didn't just have sex. We cuddled, while I was inside of her.

Haley had been in jail for almost a year already. And Veronica and Lucy had been in jail for months at this point. Nicole was the first girl with whom I felt a real, emotional connection in a long time. We had been chatting for months, and we liked each other. And now, finally, we had sex. After I came inside of her, she smiled. I handed her a towel so she wouldn't leak all over the bed.

"Are you still nervous?" I asked.

"No," she said and smiled. "I'm glad we finally did it."

We cuddled up next to each other and talked for a while. Of course Lucy came up.

"What are we gonna tell her?" I asked.

"I think it's better if we don't tell her anything right now," Nicole replied.

"Yeah, you're right. And I'm not even talking to her anymore anyway. I was done with her, after I found out she was fucking around with all these other guys, while she told me I was the only one. I'm so sick of this two-faced shit. And she really has no right to be upset. It's not like she cared how I felt when she was messing around with all these other guys. She's fucking God only knows how many people on Backpage. And a bunch of dope boys. And Ziggy, G-Force, Cho and who knows who else. So if I like having sex with you, what's the big deal? It's not like she really cares about me anyway. She hasn't been faithful to me, so why would I be faithful to her?"

I was trying to make myself feel better, because deep down I did feel really guilty. I knew that Lucy would be hurt if she found out, because despite all her grimey shit, and although she was throwing herself at dozens of people, telling all of them that she loved them or wanted to be with them, or she had sex with them, I believed that some part of her really did love me. But it didn't matter, because she and I weren't together. We weren't even talking to each other. Lucy was with someone else. I didn't know who, because it was someone else every day. All that mattered was that it wasn't me.

After we got dressed, I took Nicole to my new favorite little restaurant: Cheng's on 41. It's nothing fancy. Just a little Chinese restaurant with a large buffet. It's almost like Golden Corral, but much closer to my condo. We ate, talked and laughed. I really liked her a lot, and I think Nicole felt the same way. She looked so happy. She had the biggest smile on her face. I took a picture of her and posted it on Facebook. Her friends commented that this was the happiest she had looked in forever.

Nicole and I met up a lot after that first time, and she started sleeping over at my place. I loved falling asleep with her next to me, because she was the most affectionate person I had ever met. She always felt the need to touch me somehow. While we slept, either her head was on my chest, or her arms or legs where intertwined with mine in some way. Her touch felt so comforting.

Many times Lucy texted or called her, and Nicole had to pretend to be somewhere else, so Lucy wouldn't know that we were seeing each other.

A few days after Lucy got out of jail, she asked me to come get her, so we could spend some time together, before she went to rehab. Nicole had slept over the night before, and she was still at my house. While Lucy was texting me, she was also texting Nicole, asking her where she was. Nicole lied. She told Nicole that I was going to come pick Lucy up in a little while, and she asked Nicole if she would like to get something to eat with us.

Nicole and I looked at each other and giggled. We both felt bad for lying to Lucy. Then Nicole texted Lucy, that she should ask me if I wouldn't mind if Nicole tagged along with us. Lucy relayed the question to me, and I replied that I didn't want Nicole to come along, because I wanted to spend time alone with Lucy, since I hadn't seen her in months. That was the truth.

Nicole and I didn't want the three of us to hang out together for now, because it would be weird to have to pretend not to know each other in front of Lucy.

Nicole said that she knew Lucy really did have feelings for me, and it would break Lucy's heart to know that we were seeing each other. She said Lucy was so fragile right now, one more painful disappointment might push her over the edge, and she might kill herself. I felt really really bad when Nicole told me that. I really didn't want to hurt Lucy, even though she hurt me all the time.

But then Nicole said we shouldn't feel guilty, considering how Lucy had been treating me. And Lucy had slept with Nicole's boyfriend Antonio in the past. Before Nicole went to prison, Lucy had nowhere else to go, so she stayed with Nicole for a while. Lucy was only 17 at the time. When Antonio came over, Lucy had sex with him. It devastated Nicole, and she tried to kill herself with a drug overdose. That's why going to prison ended up saving her life.

We agreed not to tell Lucy that we were seeing each other, and that I would drop Nicole off down the street from Lucy's grandfather's house, so that Lucy wouldn't see my car, and Nicole could pretend that she was at a neighbor's house. Then, a few minutes later, I would pull up in front of the house and pick up Lucy.

But we never got that far, because after I dropped Nicole off, Lucy was nowhere to be found. She was probably fucking someone on Backpage again, or sucking some dope boy's dick. She didn't waste a single thought on how badly that hurt me.

It still bothered me a lot that Lucy tricked 24/7, but every day I cared a little bit less, because I was coming to terms with the fact that Lucy was not my girl. She was way too busy fucking every guy in town and smoking crack around the clock. I tried to convince her to get clean, but there was no talking to her. I simply was not as important to her, as she was to me.

Nicole slept over at my place a lot, and we were getting closer and closer. One night I drew her a hot bath in my jetted tub, lit some candles, played some soft music, and brought her a piece of cake while she was enjoying a bubble bath.

She was really touched and said: "You are the nicest guy I've ever met. I'm not used to guys treating me like this. I feel like a princess. This is the most romantic thing anyone has ever done for me." Then she teared up.

She told me about her previous boyfriends and how they had raped and beaten her, and how they always talked down to her like she was stupid and worthless. She wasn't used to a guy talking to her with respect, and actually really listening to her when she talked, like she was important.

These dumb lowlives she used to date set the bar pretty low. I looked like Casanova compared to these douchebags, without even trying. I really wasn't going out of my way to do anything that was out of the ordinary. I was just being my normal self. I was used to treating a nice girl nice. It's not like I skywrote her name with a plane, or posted a giant billboard with a big heart, or covered the bed with a hundred roses. She was really sweet, and I liked her a lot, so of course I treated her nice. I wanted to make her happy. I wanted her to enjoy being around me. Isn't that what you're supposed to do when you like someone?

After she got out of the tub, I told her that she had been making me feel really good these past few days, and I'd like to return the favor. I asked her if she would like me to give her a massage, or maybe go down on her, or maybe both.

"Really? You'd go down on me?" Her face lit up. It was like she couldn't believe someone actually cared enough about her, to give her an orgasm.

"Sure," I said. "I'd love to make you feel good."

"I would love that," she said with a shy giggle.

She lay down on the bed and spread her legs. I kissed my way up her inner thighs, until I reached her beautiful pussy, and then I slowly started licking her lips, and gently sucked her clit. I was in no rush. I knew she needed time to forget her nervousness. I was going to give her all the time in the world. This was all about her, so I would have sucked her clit for hours, if she wanted me to.

After a few minutes she moaned: "Oh my God, this feels really amazing!" I could tell she was really getting into it. She forgot the rest of the world for a little while, and all she could think about was my tongue circling her clit, teasing her relentlessly.

Then she asked me to put a finger inside of her while I was sucking her clit. She asked me if she could take pictures of me while I was licking her. Like this was a special occasion, and she always wanted to remember this moment. She took about 15 pictures, while moaning and pushing her pussy into my mouth. I loved making her feel this good. I would do it for her every day, if she wanted me to. I wanted her to know that she deserved to be treated nice, and to be happy and to feel good.

Patty used to tell me that she was so hung up on me, because I was the only guy who could make her cum, because apparently I was pretty good at going down on a girl. Maybe she just said that to make me feel special. I don't know. But every girl I've ever gone down on said I'm pretty good at it. Maybe that's my hidden superpower.

Afterwards Nicole asked me to fuck her. I told her I would like to take pictures of her, too. She got on top of me and rode my dick while posing for the camera. Then I got on top of her and took pictures of my dick inside of her. I loved having sex with her.

One day she told me she wanted to show me what she had learned from some black girls in prison. She stood on her hands, with her head facing the floor and her feet in the air. Then she leaned her feet against the wall, and she started twerking her butt like that. We both cracked up.

I asked her to do that again, but naked, and let me video

tape her. She did. She was leaning on her hands, upside down, while wiggling her perfect ass and pussy in my face.

She was just awesome! I loved hanging out with her. Not just because of the sex. She just had a really great personality. I felt so comfortable around her, like we had known each other forever. And she was so down to earth. We always made each other laugh with stupid jokes and funny voices. She was a silly little dork in a pretty girl's body. The perfect combination.

They always say in romantic comedies that beautiful girls usually have shitty personalities, and ugly girls have beautiful personalities. And then there's the Holy Grail that's really hard to find: a beautiful girl with an ugly girl's beautiful personality. Nicole was it. She was every guy's dream girl.

LUCY AND NICOLE

"Prostitutes have very improperly been styled women of pleasure; they are women of pain, of sorrow, of grief, of bitter and continual repentance, without any hope of obtaining a pardon."
Unknown

"Be kind. Everyone you meet is fighting a hard battle."
Plato

"To know even one life has breathed easier because you have lived. This is to have succeeded."
Ralph Waldo Emerson

Nicole had slept at my house again the previous night, when Lucy called me to give her a ride to the Greyhound station, so she could visit her mother in Georgia and go to rehab. Nicole and I had sex that morning, and then I dropped her off at Lucy's grandfather's house. Later I returned to pick up Lucy and take her to the bus. It was the first time I had seen her in months. She felt self-conscious, because she had gained a lot of weight in jail. She asked me if I thought she was ugly now.

I said: "No, you'll never be ugly in my eyes, sweetie. Everyone gains weight in jail, and you should know by now that you will always be beautiful in my eyes, whether you're a skinny minnie, or you're 300 pounds."

That made Lucy smile, and she gave me a kiss. Then

she said Nicole would like to come along for the ride. I said ok. Nicole got into my car, and for Lucy's benefit, we pretended not to have seen each other ever since she cleaned my house months ago. It was weird and awkward. Nicole and I kept giving each other looks in the rear view mirror.

We arrived late at the Greyhound station, and the bus was about to leave without Lucy. She and I jumped out of the car, and she grabbed my hand and led me around the building, to the bus. I knew right away that she really had no intention of getting on the bus and go to rehab, because she didn't grab her bags. She left them in my car. She asked the bus driver, if she could postpone her trip for a few days. He said no, her ticket was only valid for today.

The bus was actually going to drive from Fort Myers to Fort Lauderdale, and then from there to Orlando, and then from Orlando to Atlanda, Georgia.

Lucy asked the driver, if she could get on the bus in Orlando at 4 am, instead of boarding now in Fort Myers at 8 pm. He said yes.

I tried to tell Lucy to get on the bus now and not postpone the trip, or she would never go to rehab. She completely ignored me while talking to the bus driver. Afterwards she said she postponed the ride, so she and I could spend more time together, and then I could drive her to catch the bus in Orlando.

I kept looking at Nicole, hoping she'd say something, to convince Lucy to get on the bus, but she didn't. I could see in Nicole's eyes that she was high as a kite. Ever since Lucy got out of jail, she and Nicole were hanging out and doing more and more drugs together. It reminded me of the way Veronica and her mother Rachel were getting high together, when she got out of jail last time.

After we left the Greyhound station, I thought Lucy and I would spend some time together, because she said that was her reason for not getting on the bus. But once we arrived at her grandpa's house, to drop Nicole off, Lucy said she would go back in the house with her. I asked her why. She said she wanted to spend some more time with Nicole, before she went to rehab.

"You spent the last few days getting high with Nicole. But you and I haven't seen each other in months. I can't believe you'd rather go smoke more crack with her, than spend time with me," I said. It reminded me of what Veronica did with Kim after I picked her up from the Salvation Army.

First she denied that that was her reason for going back into the house with Nicole. But then she finally admitted it. She told me to go home. I was crushed.

I never did drive her to Orlando that night. The bus ticket expired the next morning, and Lucy never went to rehab.

Before, Nicole's drug habit had still been manageable. But now, being around Lucy, her habit was getting worse and worse. She was shooting up Ds, heroin, snorting coke, smoking crack and taking mollys.

Slowly but surely, Nicole was getting just as bad as Lucy.

It really started to bother me, because I knew where she was headed: sucking dick and spreading her legs for a hundred guys on Backpage. That thought made my stomach turn. I didn't want to keep losing one girl after another to drugs and Backpage. I couldn't take it anymore.

I tried to talk to Nicole about it, but she said she was fine. She said she really wasn't doing that many drugs, and she was making enough money with tattoos to pay for her habit. She said she would never hurt me like Lucy did. Déjà vu. How many times did a drug addict tell me she wasn't going to treat me like the previous drug addict? How many times did a drug addict tell me she wasn't like the others?

But Nicole was getting flakier and flakier. She had told me she would cook me dinner on my birthday. She made a list of all the things I needed to buy so she could cook her special sweet and sour chicken. But then she just went ghost on my birthday and left me hanging. That really really hurt. That was when I knew this was the beginning of the end.

A day or two later, she told me she was really sorry for abandoning me on my birthday, and she said she would make it up to me tonight. But then she just disappeared again.

Another day or two later, she asked me to pick her up after work. She was holding a sign at the car wash next to the Red Roof Inn in North Fort Myers. But when I asked her later that day when I should come get her, she disappeared again.

One of the nights she slept over, she walked out of the house in the middle of the night and disappeared for a few hours. When she got back at 4 am, she said she had met up with a dope boy at the Coconut Point Mall, to get some drugs. I asked who it was, and what took so long, but she was being evasive. Something wasn't right.

She was texting all the time. She told me she had some tattoo jobs. I drove her there, and then she disappeared again for many hours. She claimed she was working on the tattoo the whole time. But when she asked me to pick her up, she was somewhere completely different.

I had a feeling she was tricking, so I asked her about it. She started to cry and said: "I'm not that kind of girl! Ask anyone! I don't sleep around like that. I'm not like Lucy and those other girls."

But I could tell she was hiding something from me, and she wasn't being honest about where she was going or what she was doing, and who she was with. And since I already knew about her drug use, the only other thing worth hiding from me was having sex with someone else. So I was sure she was tricking. But she continued to deny it and got really emotional and defensive every time I questioned her about anything.

I told her that if she wanted to just be friends with benefits, fine, just say so. But since she and I had been talking about being in a real relationship together, and she had told me she loved me, it wasn't fair to lie to me, if she was still seeing other people.

"I swear I'm not seeing anyone else. I just want to be with you. You are the nicest guy I've ever met. I SWEAR I'm not having sex with anyone else," she said. She was in tears again.

She told me she loved me and gave me a kiss. I smiled and told her I loved her, too.

Later Lucy called me and told me she wanted to hang out. Nicole had disappeared again, doing who knows what with who knows who, so I had no reason not to hang out with Lucy. I took her home with me, and we talked all night. She told me she was sorry for writing the letter to Veronica and the one to Cho. She said she felt bad for the way things ended between us, when I found out she lied to me about me being the only one on her viso list.

Suddenly Jasmine called Lucy. Jasmine had returned from Key West a few weeks ago, and had been back in Fort Myers. She had already relapsed on her first day out, before she handed me the letters Veronica had written her in jail. Jasmine's mother was an alcoholic, and they both got drunk to celebrate her freedom. She shot up Ds just a few hours later.

She had pretended to be clean in Key West, but I could tell by her posts on her Facebook page, that she was behaving like every other addict who was in the process of relapsing after getting out of jail.

Veronica had cheated on me with Jasmine, and gotten her name tattooed on her wrist. But Jasmine had also dated Snickers at some point in the past, like everyone else in jail. And she was Abby's best friend. But ever since she returned from Key West, she was living with Wigger at Abby's house, sleeping with Wigger in Abby's bed. Abby's boyfriend Wigger had not only cheated on her with her own sister Tabby. Now he was cheating on Abby with her best friend Jasmine. What a guy, what a guy.

Jasmine and Wigger got into a fight, because he'd been cheating on her with some other girl. Jasmine had enough and wanted to get away from him, She called Lucy to see if she could stay with her. They had been in the same dorm in jail for a while. Lucy told Jasmine that she was staying at my house and offered that we could come get her.

A few weeks ago, Veronica had told me that someone really needed to tell Abby what a lowlife Wigger was, because he was cheating on Abby the whole time while she was in jail.

Take a moment to fully appreciate the irony in that. Go ahead, I'll wait.

Veronica felt bad that Wigger was cheating on Abby! Meanwhile she was cheating on me the whole damn time! She understood that Wigger was a fucking lowlife for doing that to Abby, but somehow it didn't sink in, that she was a fucking lowlife too, for doing exactly the same thing to me.

When Lucy got out of jail and we started hanging out again, she told me the same thing: someone needed to tell Abby what Wigger was doing being her back.

So I ended up writing Abby a letter. I didn't even know her, but I knew what she was going through, and I wanted to warn her about Wigger, just like people had warned me about Veronica. It was a simple act of kindness. She deserved to know. A real friend would have told her. But she had no real friends. All her so-called friends were drug addicts, who had no loyalty to anyone, and who would hit on Abby's man in a heartbeat, if there was drugs or money in it for them. Even her own sister Tabby betrayed her. And now her best friend Jasmine did, too.

After Abby got my letter, she asked Wigger if what I wrote was true. Of course he denied it, but he was really pissed at me.

So now there was a possibility that Jasmine's fight with Wigger in the middle of the night was just a trick, to get me to go there. Maybe he and his homeboyzzz were waiting for me. Well, I wasn't gonna let some little ghetto thugs intimidate me. After all, I had a gun now! What it do, homeslice? Holla!

I hid my gun on me and felt like James Bond. Lucy and I were on a mission! It was 3 am by the time we got to Abby's house. Jasmine got into the car and told Lucy that she was upset, because Wigger had been cheating on her. She was sick and tired of the way he was treating her, so she was done with him. On her way out, she stole some crack from him.

When we got home, Lucy hid in the bathroom and smoked Jasmine's crack for hours. She just wouldn't stop. She left the door unlocked, so Jasmine and I tried to get her to come out. But she was busy rearranging the towels. Over and over again, with the twitchy motions of a tweaking crackhead.

Lucy said that she wanted to watch Beautiful Creatures, so Jasmine and I were waiting for her on the living room couch. We kept calling her, but she wouldn't come. Then Lucy called me into the bathroom.

I went inside. She was still rearranging the towels. Then she said: "I just wanted to let you know that I'm a very jealous person, and it really bothers me that you are sitting in the living room with Jasmine."

Jasmine and I had been sitting on opposite ends of the couch. We really weren't doing anything, just talking, and we had been calling Lucy over and over, so we could finally start the movie. But to make her happy, now I sat in the bathroom with her, so she wouldn't feel jealous anymore. I was getting really tired. It was 6 am by now.

Suddenly Lucy decided to make dinner for all of us. At 6 am!

She had made a nice dinner for me a few days ago, right after Thanksgiving. We had wanted to spend the holiday together, but then she had been smoking crack around the clock instead, and tricking. So we decided to make up for it a few days later instead. She was proud of herself and sent pictures of the dinner she prepared for me to her grandpa and Nicole. I thought that was really sweet.

She decided to impress Jasmine with her cooking skills, and made a little bit of everything she could find in my fridge and freezer. She made a ton of food. Jasmine and I kept telling her that we really weren't hungry, but Lucy wouldn't take no for an answer. So we ate something to humor her. Jasmine was already nauseous from the Ds she had shot up, but eating dinner at 6:30 am pushed her over the edge and she started throwing up. I told her she could lie down in the guest room, but she said she didn't feel comfortable sleeping in a bed. She preferred sleeping on the couch. So I brought her some blankets and a little bucket, in case she had to throw up again.

Then I went to sleep. It was 7 am. Lucy kissed me good night and told me she would join me in bed in a minute. At 8 am I woke up, because Lucy sent me a text, telling me she'd be right in. She did that a lot, sending me texts while we were in the same house, but she was in one room, and I was in the other. I went back to sleep.

At 10 am my phone rang. It was a Global Tel call from jail. I hadn't heard from Veronica since before Thanksgiving, ever since Wendy was sent to D pod for screaming at Kathleen, because Wendy found out that Veronica was still sending love letters to Kathleen. I was done with her. I wasn't even thinking about her, while I had been spending time with Nicole and Lucy.

But the call wasn't from Veronica. It was her friend Cassidy. The girl she had told me to ask about what she was doing in dorm 2 with Wendy. The one who would tell me that Veronica was being 100% faithful to me and that there was nothing going on between her and Wendy.

Cassidy said she was being released from jail the following night or early morning, and she had nowhere else to go. Could I come pick her up, and could she come stay with me for a few days, until she figured things out. I didn't know this girl at all, but she said she had something for me: a love letter that Veronica had written to Wendy in D pod. Wow.

Veronica had given the letter to Morgan, the girl who used to be Kayla's best friend, and who had given my letter to Veronica, after I asked her to tell me the truth about what Veronica was doing behind my back. But now Morgan really did come through for me after all, and instead of giving Veronica's letter to Wendy, she decided to give it to me instead. Morgan knew that Cassidy was about to be released, and she gave the letter to her, so she could pass it on to me, once she got out. Thank you, Morgan. I owe you one.

I told Cassidy on the phone that I really appreciated that she was going to give me the letter, instead of passing it to Wendy, and I promised that I'd be there to pick her up.

I really wanted that letter! I knew that once I saw it with my own eyes, I would be over Veronica for good. I really hadn't missed her at all since Thanksgiving, because I was so busy with Nicole and Lucy.

Then I told Cassidy that Lucy and Jasmine were staying with me right now, and to spread the word in jail, before she got out. I figured it would get under Veronica's skin. Then I got up to go find Lucy and tell her about Cassidy's call.

Lucy wasn't in her spot in my bed. And she wasn't in the bathroom. And Jasmine was no longer on the couch. I figured maybe they're on the porch, smoking. Nope. Not there either.

So I texted her: "Where r u?"

Lucy texted me right back: "I'll call u later."

I figured maybe they were meeting a dope boy at the mall or something. Who the hell knows? But then my instincts told me to check the guest bedroom. When I walked in, I found Lucy and Jasmine in bed together! The same bed where I had found Veronica cheating on me with Kim a year earlier!

I was speechless. I just walked back out.

How the fuck could Lucy do this to me? Last night, when we had picked up Jasmine at Abby's house, we went to Walmart afterwards, because they both wanted to dye their hair bright red. While we were walking around the store in the middle of the night, Jasmine was arguing with Wigger on the phone and told him she wasn't coming back. Lucy took my hand, and said: "I hope we will never argue like that. I want things to always be ok between us. I love you." Then we kissed.

And now this fucking psycho was in my guest bed with Jasmine! The same damn girl Veronica had cheated on me with, after Kim.

I really was living in the Twilight Zone. And Lucy was an eerie copy of Veronica. It seemed like she was determined to do everything to me that Veronica had done before her. Or like she was auditioning for the same role in a crazy horror movie.

I said loudly, but calmly: "Get up and pack your stuff. I'm going to drop you guys off wherever you want to go. But you can't stay here."

Lucy came out. She was still high, and said: "What do you mean?"

"What do you think I mean? I want you to get out," I replied.

"NO! Where the fuck am I supposed to go? I have nowhere else to go! I'M NOT LEAVING!" she yelled.

I didn't give a shit at this point. She could go to her grandfather's house, or stay with Cho or G-Force or Wigger or whoever else. But I wanted nothing to do with her anymore. I was not gonna let her betray me the same way Veronica did, because I already knew what happens next in this movie. I had seen it all before. I felt like Bill Murray in Groundhog Day. I was reliving the same situations over and over. Only the names changed.

Meanwhile Jasmine pretended to be sleeping. Or maybe she was really just as comatose as Veronica and Norbert had been, when I had caught them in bed together, and they didn't wake up, no matter how loud I yelled.

"I'm not going ANYWHERE!" Lucy continued to scream. I started to feel bad for her. She really really didn't want to go. She knew she had fucked up again, and she didn't want it to end like this. We had just made up last night. She had just told me last night how sorry she was for fucking things up between us when she was in jail and she had other guys visit her. And now she fucked it all up again already.

"If you don't leave, I will call the cops and you'll get arrested for trespassing," I said calmly.

"I don't care! CALL THE COPS! I'm not leaving! I'M NOT LEAVING!!!" Lucy screamed.

"Don't test me," I replied calmly. "I don't make empty threats. I really will call the cops if you don't leave. And you will be in jail two hours later. Is that really what you want?"

I grabbed my phone and pretended to start dialing.

"Fine, I'll go. I can't believe you! We didn't do anything! We were just lying there."

Veronica said the same thing when I found her in bed with Kim. And then again when I found her in bed with Norbert.

"I didn't do anything wrong! But I'm not gonna explain myself!" Lucy yelled.

"I'm not asking you to explain yourself. Just pack your stuff and go. We're done," I replied with the same unshakable calmness. This whole situation didn't even feel real. I was totally detached from what was going on. I felt absolutely nothing. Like I was watching a movie, and this stuff wasn't really happening to me.

I woke Jasmine up and told her to get dressed and pack her stuff. She pretended not to know what was going on, so I explained to her that she had to leave, because I found her in bed with Lucy.

"This is so petty," she scoffed under her breath.

Funny. She didn't think it was petty when Veronica or Wigger were cheating on her. Then her anger felt perfectly justified. But now I was being petty, because I wasn't ok with Lucy fucking someone else in my guest bed, after we had just made up last night?

Then Lucy came over to me with big puppy dog eyes, and asked me like a little kid: "Am I allowed to come back at some point? Or am I never allowed to come back?"

She was so adorable at that moment, I just wanted to squeeze her and let her know how much I love her.

You know that feeling, when you have to punish a puppy for peeing on the rug, but it breaks your heart to spank him, because all you really want to do is cuddle him? That's exactly how I felt right now.

"Yeah, you can come back some day," I said.

Her face lit up. It made her feel a little bit better that this was not really going to be the end between us. Now she knew I still loved her, even if I was mad at her right now.

On our way out the door, she showed me a notebook she had stolen out of one of my office drawers. She said: "I'm gonna make a scrapbook! Of all our meals together! I'm gonna cook for you every day, and we'll take pictures and then we'll put all the pictures in this book, so we can always remember it!"

It took everything I had not to hug her and kiss her and tell her I love her, and that I really didn't want her to leave. It was breaking my heart. She was just the sweetest little girl in the world. All she wanted was to feel loved. But I had to take a stand. I couldn't keep letting her treat me like this and let her cheat on me like it's no big deal. Either she was going to learn that the only way to be with me was to be faithful to me, or she was going to have to go fuck dope boys and Backpage pervs again.

In the car she started texting some guy who called himself Fatso. He was supposed to pick them up at the Edison Mall. When we were almost there, she said: "Great, now Fatso isn't answering his phone. I think we're gonna be stranded."

I dropped them off in front of the main entrance.

"Are you really gonna make me get out of the car?" Lucy asked. "You have no sympathy. You are so cold." Then she slammed the door. I left. I didn't even get out of the parking lot, when Lucy already called me back: "Please don't leave me here! Please turn around and take me home with you."

I felt so bad. But she needed to learn that her actions have consequences. You can't just fuck someone in my guest bed and then act like nothing happened and everything is ok with the world. I hung up the phone. Then I texted Nicole. I hadn't heard from her in a day or two, ever since she had disappeared again. I knew she was getting really bad on drugs, and at this point she was probably no better than Lucy.

Nicole texted me right back: "Hey sugar. I'm at the Days Inn in North Fort Myers, please come get me."

When I arrived at the hotel, she was sitting in the parking lot. She told me she had been staying in a room at the hotel with someone else, and he ditched her.

I figured it was most likely a dope boy, and either she had been fucking him for drugs, or she had been tricking. Like I said, girls don't live in hotel rooms, unless they're tricking. I couldn't stand thinking about it. I just gave her a hug. She looked sad and exhausted. She was so worn down.

I took her home to my place, and we cuddled and talked. I told her what had happened with Lucy and

Jasmine, and Cassidy's call.

Nicole told me she had a new probation officer, and that he called her in that day, out of the blue. She was supposed to report to his office at 4:30 pm. But by the time we got there, it was 4:58 pm. He was really pissed and screamed at her. He felt disrespected. He told her this wasn't a game, and she better be at his office tomorrow, at 8:30 am sharp. If she was there at 8:31 am, he'd violate her and send her back to jail. And she'd better be ready for a drug test.

She was hysterically crying when she came out of his office. I tried to calm her down. She had a full blown panic attack. She couldn't breathe or stand up straight. I gave her a hug and just held her tight, while gently telling her that everything would be ok. Finally she calmed down a bit. She said she would obviously fail the drug test tomorrow.

We made plans for her to get a plastic cigar tube and smuggle clean pee in her vagina. She was supposed to practice that night, because she had never done it before, but then she started texting frantically again, and suddenly told me she had to go do a tattoo for an hour at night. She disappeared all night. When I finally picked her up, it was midnight. Now we had to go searching for a cigar tube, go home, and practice. We went to bed at 4 am. Then we got up at 6 am. I checked the Sheriff's website and saw that Cassidy had been released, but she didn't call me. I messaged her on Facebook and asked her what happened.

Then I took Nicole to her probation officer. We stopped

at the same CVS where Lucy and I had bought presents for Summer when she was in the hospital. We went in the bathroom together and she prepared herself for the drug test by placing the plastic tube inside of her vagina. It was really uncomfortable, and she had a hard time walking.

Once we got to the office, she went inside and I waited for her in the lobby. After half an hour she texted me: "You might as well go home. I'm getting arrested. I'm going to jail."

"What?!?! What the hell happened?" I texted back.

She told me later that they were watching her so closely while she was peeing, she wouldn't have been able to use the tube, so she just admitted that she had drugs in her system. She removed the tube and peed dirty. Her probation officer was really nasty to her. She started crying and yelled at him that he had no idea what she had been through in her life. Then she told him about Lucy's dad Dick raping her ever since she was a little girl, all her suicide attempts, and that Johnny had tried to run her over with a truck just a few days ago.

The officer felt bad for her and told her he'd give her another chance, but as part of her probation, from now on she would have to go to mental health counselling at Salus Care on Ortiz Ave at least once a week, and to NA meetings at least twice a week.

I had already gone home, when she texted me about three hours later: "I didn't get arrested after all."

"Huh? What? Well, that's great! Do u want me to come get u?" I texted back.

"No, I already got a ride. I'm gonna do a tattoo and then u can pick me up at 1 pm," she texted back.

My spider senses were tingling again. I had been right in the middle of this. I was part of the story. I had driven her to probation, waited for her there, and we were going to spend the day together and celebrate that she passed the test. For her not to call me right away and tell me that she wasn't going to jail after all, and to call someone else for a ride, meant only one thing: she was fucking someone else.

I didn't hear from her until 4 pm. Then she asked me to come get her. We went home, and she started getting dressed up in the bathroom.

I sat down on the edge of the tub and tried to have a talk with her: "You've been acting really shady lately. You keep telling me you want to be with me, but I get the feeling you're seeing someone else."

"No, I'm not! I swear!" she replied while putting on her make-up.

"Well, if you are, just be honest about it, so that we are both on the same page. Don't make me think there is something between us if there's not. If you just want to be friends with benefits, just say so. It's ok, as long as we're on the same page," I explained.

"No, I swear, there is nobody else. I'm not the kind of

girl who sleeps around," she reassured me, while straightening her hair.

She was obviously getting all dressed up to go somewhere. When she was done, she said: "Oh, my friend Jeanie just texted me. I have to babysit her kids. She is visiting her baby daddy in jail."

I was suspicious. Why the hell would she get all dressed up to babysit? And why was she getting dressed up BEFORE she got the text to go babysit?

She was frantically texting in the car, and then told me she would meet Jeanie at Walmart on Colonial and Ortiz.

"Huh? Why would you meet Jeanie at Ortiz instead of at her house? If she's going to visit someone at the jail on Ortiz, she would have to drive you all the way back to her house first, and then drive all the way back to Ortiz Avenue for the viso. That doesn't make any sense."

"Uhmm, she's buying some food stamps from me, so we're going shopping at Walmart first, and then I'll babysit while she's at the viso," Nicole replied.

I knew Nicole didn't have any food stamps anymore. Lucy had told me just the other day, that she was mad at Nicole, because she had sold all her food stamps this month, and now they had nothing to eat. So Nicole was definitely lying about what she was doing at Walmart, and who she was meeting, and why. If she had simply met a drug dealer, she would have told me. So again, the only possible answer was that she was about to go have sex with someone.

"So at what time is the viso?" I asked.

"Uhh, at 7 pm, I think," she replied.

I had been visiting Veronica in jail for almost two years. I knew exactly when the viso times were, and there is no viso at 7 pm.

Nicole was still frantically texting. Then she said: "Jeanie is already done shopping at Walmart. Now she wants me to meet her at the Racetrac gas station on Colonial."

"For what?" I asked. This was all complete bullshit. Even a blind person could see that.

"She still wants to buy my food stamps, so we'll buy stuff at the little Racetrac store," Nicole replied.

Once we got to the gas station, she jumped out of the car without even saying good bye. I knew what that meant. Her mind was totally preoccupied with what she was about to do next. She wasn't just meeting her friend Jeanie to babysit her kids.

She told me she would only be gone for an hour or so. The jail visitations are only an hour max. I dropped her off at the Racetrac at 6 pm. By 9:30 pm I still didn't hear from her. I figured she just disappeared on me again. I was right. She disappeared all night. I didn't hear from her until the afternoon of the next day. She claimed she had fallen asleep and her phone had died. That's every drug addict's favorite excuse when they disappear to fuck someone for drugs.

Later I found out that she had started posting escort ads on Backpage, and that's really where she was going. She had told me a dozen times she wasn't fucking anybody else, and then she got out of the car and fucked somebody else.

It reminded me of how Veronica lied straight to my face, shaking with anxiety and battling her diarrhea, during our viso at the Salvation Army. She swore she'd never talk to Dee again, and as soon as the viso was over, she talked to Dee again. Or when she used to tell me over and over on the phone that she wasn't dating Wendy. And as soon as she hung up the phone, she went right back to dating Wendy.

Or when Lucy said she wasn't talking to anyone else but me, and that I was the only person on her viso list, and then scheduled visos for 2 other people who were on her list.

Or when Alice swore she wouldn't run away from rehab, and then she ran away from rehab. It was the same shit over and over. Patty was right.

Anyway, later that night, Cassidy called me. She was whispering: "Please come and get me! I'm in Lehigh Acres. When I got out of jail early this morning, my baby daddy was sitting in the lobby, waiting for me. I had no choice but to go with him. He's really violent. I'm seriously afraid for my life. Please please come and get me!"

This was another job for James Bond. I packed my gun, just in case her baby daddy was gonna try to kill her or me. Around midnight, I arrived in front of the address, where she wanted me to pick her up. When she saw me, she quickly ran over to my car, got in and told me to take off.

She gave me Veronica's letter to Wendy. The letter contained the same retarded drivel she had written me and dozens of other people in the past. The funny thing was that Wendy's birthday was right after Thanksgiving, and mine was right before. Veronica wrote both of us almost exactly the same thing, that she was sorry she couldn't be with us on our birthday, and that she would make it up to us, once she got out of jail. And that she was looking forward to a life together with us. Comparing the two letters was like looking inside the mind of a deranged basket case.

Cassidy stayed with me for the next few days, and was clean. We went out to eat with George, watched movies and I took her to the Coconut Point Mall, so she could fill out some job applications. She was doing good.

Lucy had left some of her stuff at my house when I kicked her and Jasmine out, after I caught them in bed together. A book fell out of her bag. I noticed there were a bunch of her jail postcards in the front of the book. They were love letters to and from a bunch of different people.

Once again she mimicked Veronica. She too had left a

bunch of love letters from other people at my house, when I kicked her and Kim out, after I found them in bed together.

The most ironic thing was that among Lucy's left behind letters, there was a reply from Snickers. The same girl who had written all those replies to Veronica.

A few days later, I saw on the Sheriff's website, that Lucy, Jasmine and Wigger all got arrested on the same day. Jasmine bonded out later that day, so I called her and asked her what happened.

She told me Wigger got arrested while selling drugs at some club, and Lucy and Jasmine got arrested at a hotel room. Apparently the two incidents were unrelated. Lucy and Jasmine had been staying in hotel rooms together, ever since I kicked them out.

Lucy was tricking on Backpage, and the security guy at the hotel noticed that a bunch of guys were coming and going all night long, so he called the cops. When they checked the room, they found drugs. Jasmine admitted that the Suboxone was hers, but Lucy wouldn't take credit for her drugs. Jasmine said Lucy threw her under the bus. She was pissed at her.

A day or two later, Lucy bonded herself out of jail, and called me to pick her up. I told her Cassidy was staying with me, and she was sober, so I asked Lucy to promise that she wouldn't do any drugs in front of Cassidy: "Can you not do drugs? At least for a few hours?"

"Yeah, don't worry. Just come get me," she replied.

I picked her up at the jail and we were going to head home, when Lucy asked me to make a stop at the Howard Johnson.

"For what?" I asked. Of course I knew the answer.

"I just wanna get a D," Lucy replied.

"But you just promised on the phone that you would not do any drugs while you're staying with me. I don't want you to make Cassidy relapse," I said.

"Come on, you know I lied. I just wanna do a pill now, and then I'll be straight."

Then she started asking me questions about Cassidy. I could tell she was jealous that some other girl was staying with me: "Where am I going to sleep? Does Cassidy think I'm just some whore to you, or does she know I'm your girlfriend? You better tell her that I'm going to be sleeping in your bed with you."

I told her that wasn't necessary. Cassidy had a boyfriend, who was in the Salvation Army rehab program, and I didn't need to announce ahead of time that Lucy would be sleeping in bed with me.

When we got to the hotel, she disappeared in some dope boy's room for 20 minutes. I figured she was fucking him to get some drugs. I was totally disgusted and left.

She called me back after I had already driven half way

home.

"Why did you leave me stranded like this?" she asked.

"I'm not gonna sit in the parking lot while you fuck someone else. Sorry." I hated that she really didn't get, or didn't care, how much it hurt me when she did this shit.

"I wasn't fucking him. I just smoked some crack in his bathroom. I swear! Please come back and get me. I don't want to stay here. I want to stay with you."

So I turned around and picked her up.

Then she said now she needed to go to Liberty Bailbonds on Fowler Street, and drop off some money, or she'd get sent back to jail.

She had a jail check for $100, but Liberty wouldn't accept it. They told her to cash it first. So I drove her to a gas station, she got the money, and we headed back to Liberty.

Afterwards she told me she needed to pick up her clothes from Jasmine. For some strange reason, Jasmine was now sharing a room with Nicole, even though they didn't even know each other.

As it turned out, Lucy's sugar daddy Cho had been buying his crack from Wigger, so Jasmine had run into Cho a few times, when she was riding around with Wigger. When she had nowhere to go, she called Cho, and he told her to stay with Nicole. He knew that she was Lucy's aunt and also an addict, who was staying at a room at the Days Inn in North Fort Myers.

When Lucy and I arrived at the Days Inn, she disappeared in another hotel room. I texted her that I wasn't going to wait yet another 20 minutes.

Cassidy had asked me if it was ok if her cousin Claudia came to visit her today, and now they were both at my place together, without me, because I was driving around aimlessly with Lucy. I had briefly met Claudia, but I really didn't know her from a hole in the head. I didn't want to come home and find out that Claudia robbed me. So I was only going to quickly pick up Lucy from jail and take her straight home with me. I wasn't going to chauffeur her around on a bunch of drug errands all day. We hadn't even been talking to each other anymore since I had kicked her and Jasmine out. I really only picked her up from jail, because I didn't want her to be stranded.

I texted Lucy: "If u don't come out of room in 5 minutes, I'll leave." After 10 minutes I texted her: "That's it. I'm leaving. Bye."

Suddenly Nicole texted me back: "Can u give me a ride across the bridge?"

"Sure," I texted back. "But u gotta come out RIGHT NOW. I'm just about to pull out of the parking lot."

Nicole came running out of the room and down the stairs. Lucy followed her. I hadn't seen Nicole in a few days, because she had disappeared all night when she said she was only going to do a tattoo for an hour. I had been hanging out with Cassidy since then, and we ended up getting pretty close.

Anyway, Nicole was quicker than Lucy. When Nicole got in, she had a really sad, guilty look on her face. She knew I was mad at her, because she had been ditching me so much lately. She hugged me, gave me a kiss, and told me that she loved me and that she was sorry for the way she had been acting lately. I knew it was the drugs that made her act so grimey and unreliable, so I didn't say anything. Then Lucy got into the backseat.

I thought Nicole wanted a ride across the bridge to go home to Lucy's grandfather's house. But instead, now she and Lucy were arguing about where to get the biggest bags of heroin for their money. Lucy convinced Nicole they should go back to the Howard Johnson.

As we approached the Howard Johnson, I realized that Nicole would ask me to drive her back to the Days Inn, and Lucy said she wanted me to take her to yet another place, to get her clothes, because Jasmine wasn't at the Days Inn anymore when we got there earlier. This was getting ridiculous. I wasn't a fucking drug cab. I just wanted to go home. I had been driving Lucy around for hours now.

When she and Nicole got out of the car and disappeared in the dope boy's hotel room, I just left.

Lucy and Nicole both called and texted me, asking me to come back, but I was sick of this shit. I just went home.

The next day, Cassidy was meeting up with her boyfriend at the Salvation Army, and Lucy asked me to come get her at the Days Inn. When I walked into the hotel room, Nicole and Lucy were in the middle of shooting up. I had seen Lucy do it so many times, but she was still shy about it. She felt dirty and disgusting when she shot up, and she didn't want me to see her with a needle in her arm, because she was ashamed. She tried to hide in the bathroom.

Nicole used to be very shy about it, too. But she had slept over at my place so many times by now, and we were so comfortable around each other, she was not shy in front of me at all anymore, about anything. She walked around my house naked, pretended to be talking with her butt cheeks, danced her funny little dance while singing along to her favorite rock songs, let me see her without make-up, and shot up in bed right next to me.

While Lucy was walking into the bathroom to shoot up where I wouldn't see her, she noticed that Nicole was sitting on the bed across from me, and sticking the needle in her arm.

She was surprised, and said: "You're gonna do that in front of Oliver?"

"Yeah," is all Nicole said. She was busy.

They were texting and answering their phones, introducing themselves by their hooker names. They were obviously both tricking on Backpage together now. They offered guys two girl specials.

Abby and her sister Tabby used to fuck guys together. And apparently now Lucy and her aunt Nicole were doing the same thing. I didn't want either one of them to trick on Backpage. I couldn't stand the thought of them fucking some guy together. I know, I sound like a hypocrite, because I was having sex with both of them. But that was different, because I really cared about both of them. And it's not like I was in bed with both of them at the same time.

Then I started getting pissed at Lucy. It was bad enough that she was tricking on Backpage. But now she had dragged down Nicole to her level, and she was now doing it too, even though a few weeks ago she had told me she could never bring herself to have sex with random guys for money, because she wasn't the kind of girl who sleeps around. She said she wasn't like Lucy. But after spending a few weeks with Lucy, now she was exactly that kind of girl.

Lucy had said she wanted to talk to me, about us, about rehab, about the future. But once I got to the hotel, she and Nicole were busy getting high, and answering their phones to fuck other guys. I couldn't take it anymore. I needed to get out of there.

Then Nicole told me she had a call in Bonita Springs, and asked me if I would give her a ride there on my way home. I didn't think she was seriously asking me to drive her to go fuck someone else. I thought she was trying to find an excuse to come home with me, without Lucy getting suspicious. I agreed to drive her.

Lucy didn't want Nicole and me to leave without her. She said she wanted to come with us, because she wanted to stay with me, while her aunt was going to fuck some guy in Bonita Springs. But when we walked out the door, there was some weasely guy with black, greasy hair waiting in front of the door. Hey nodded at me with a grin and said "aayyy," like he was The Fonz from Happy Days. I just wanted to punch that douchebag in his stupid face. He was here to fuck my sweet little Lucy. I couldn't take it. She told him to hold on for a second, and closed the door again.

"I don't want to fuck him," Lucy whispered to me. "I'll tell Nicole to do him, and I'll come home with you."

But Nicole didn't want to fuck him either. She had already run down to my car.

"Just tell that guy he got the wrong room, and come with us," I told Lucy. But I guess she didn't want to lose out on the money, so she stayed and fucked him. I hated her so much.

While Nicole and I were driving back to Bonita Springs, she kissed me. Then she leaned her head against my shoulder, held my hand, and told me she loved me. Then she gave me the address of the guy she was going to fuck.

"What?!?! You're really going to fuck someone else? You are seriously asking me to drive you to some other guy's house, and you're going to fuck him? Are you fucking KIDDING me?"

She broke down crying. She was so ashamed of herself: "This is not me! I don't do this kind of stuff. I'm not like Lucy. I'm just doing it for a day or two, to take care of some bills. I'm not a whore!"

"That's what every girl says, who starts doing this."

"Don't compare me to those dirty whores on Backpage! I don't like doing this! I hate it! And I'm not gonna keep doing it! I'm just doing it for a day or two, to pay some bills!" she repeated. She was sobbing so hard. She was really upset at the thought that I would think of her as a dirty whore.

I replied: "Sweetie, I'm not trying to make you feel like shit about yourself. But I'm really hurt that you are seriously going to do this. I can't stand it. Don't you understand that? After meeting Alice, and Veronica, and Lucy, and all their drug addicted friends, I know that no girl likes tricking. They may pretend they like it, because of the fast money, or they may pretend that doing it doesn't bother them, but I know they all hate it."

I gave her a hug to calm her down, because she was still crying. Then I continued: "I've read enough interviews with drug addicted girls. You're not the only one who hates doing it. But just like you, they all told themselves they'd only do it for a little while, but then they get trapped in a vicious cycle of drugs and sex, and they end up doing it day after day. It becomes their life. Just look at Lucy. Do you really think she enjoys living like this?"

"I'm never gonna be like Lucy," Nicole objected. "I'm not gonna keep doing this every day!"

"Yes, you will," I replied. "You hate it so much, you have to get high before you walk into a room with some guy, right? And afterwards you have to get high, to forget what you just did. And you end up spending all the money you just made, to buy drugs. And then you gotta do another call, but you waste all that money on drugs, too. And that will be your life from then on. You'll need to get more and more drugs, so you'll need more and more money, so you'll fuck more and more guys."

"NO I WON'T!" she screamed with tears in her eyes. "STOP making me feel like SHIT!"

When we arrived at the guy's address, she gave me a sad, teary-eyed look and said: "I'll hurry. Will you please wait for me? I want to come home with you."

We kissed and she left. I killed some time at a nearby CVS. Half an hour later, she texted me: "Good news! I didn't have to have sex with him! He couldn't get hard!"

I don't know if she was telling me the truth, or if she was just trying to make both of us feel better. But I chose to believe it, so I wouldn't spend the rest of the night thinking about some other guy being inside of her. It was bad enough that I kept thinking about The Fonz fucking Lucy.

Nicole and I went home, cuddled up in bed and made

love. Lucy kept calling Nicole's phone. Obviously Lucy was getting suspicious that there was something going on between me and Nicole. Then she started calling my phone a bunch of times. Then she texted Nicole: "I hope ur having fun! I can't believe ur doing a date with Oliver! How could u do this to me?"

After I came, Nicole cleaned herself up and called Lucy back: "You're crazy! Oliver and I didn't do anything. He just gave me a lift to do a date with that guy in Bonita, and then we stopped at Oliver's place to get some of my clothes and make-up. I left them here, when I cleaned his house."

That made absolutely no sense. Why would she bring her clothes and make-up to my house while she was cleaning?

"I'm tired of hiding," I said. "We should just tell her. She had sex with your boyfriend Antonio when she was 17, so it's not like you're doing anything to her that she hasn't already done to you first. And if she really loved me, she wouldn't fuck all these other guys. She'd be here with me. But she'd rather fuck The Fonz at the Days Inn."

"I'm afraid to tell her," Nicole replied. "I think she really does have feelings for you. And I know how much it would hurt her, if we tell her. I don't want her to kill herself or something."

We headed back to the Days Inn. Lucy texted me that she bought me some Taco Bell, and that she wanted to finally have that talk we had planned for a while. But when we arrived, she met us in the parking lot. She already had the next guy in her room, waiting to fuck her. We didn't talk. She was too busy. She just handed me the tacos, gave me a hug, told me she loved me and went back to her room with Nicole. I wouldn't be surprised if they were gonna do a double. I was so miserable.

Another one of the LCJ girls had contacted me on Facebook after she was released from jail. She had heard about me from Veronica and Lucy, while she was in jail with them. Her name was Sonya. She was 21. Another beautiful blonde. She looked like a model. She kept telling me that she would like to meet me, but I kept blowing her off. I didn't mean to be rude, but there was just so much crazy drama going on every day.

Now I finally decided to meet her. If Lucy and Nicole were going to keep fucking other people, I might as well, too. I wanted to make them jealous.

Sonya was really nice. But of course she was addicted as well. To Ds. She told me she had her addiction under control and that she didn't need drugs all the time. She just did it recreationally, here and there. I had heard that story so many times before, and I knew the end result was always the same: a massive, uncontrollable addiction, and tricking on Backpage.

I hung out with her a couple of times. We had sex and she slept over. We went out to eat, hung out by the pool, fed the ducks by the lake behind my condo, and she cooked for me. At some point Cassidy stopped by. She had moved into a hotel room with her cousin, and she just wanted to pick up the rest of her stuff. She and Sonya knew each other from jail. They hugged and told each other how great they looked without their red LCJ uniforms.

When Cassidy went through her things, she started to cry: "She stole my stuff! Why would she do that? I just got out of jail! I have nothing!"

Cassidy and Nicole had both slept at my house on the same night, a few days after Lucy and Jasmine had slept here. Nicole in bed with me, and Cassidy in the guest room. When Cassidy was hanging out with her boyfriend at the Salvation Army, Nicole had gone through Cassidy's things, and said that she had taken some of Nicole's clothes, and she was taking them back.

Now Cassidy was telling me that Nicole had stolen things from her. She was really upset about it, so I don't think she was lying when she said a bunch of her new shirts were missing.

I texted Nicole and told her what Cassidy said. "I would never steal," Nicole replied. "You should know me better than that! But I think Lucy took some of Cassidy's stuff."

Lucy had a reputation for robbing her "clients." She really hated having sex with all these guys, and whenever possible, she took their money and ran, instead of actually letting them touch her. A lot of girls on Backpage do that.

And she kept stealing little things from me all the time.

Never anything big. Never anything that I wouldn't have given her anyway, if she had simply asked: a pink ceramic hair straightener that I had bought for Veronica, a notebook, pens, envelopes, a handcrafted Indian silk photo album, etc. So it wouldn't surprise me, if she really did take some of Cassidy's clothes. But I wasn't sure who took what.

THE END

"You want to believe that there's one relationship in life that's beyond betrayal. A relationship that's beyond that kind of hurt. And there isn't."
Caleb Carr

"There are only really a few stories to tell in the end, and betrayal and the failure of love is one of those good stories to tell."
Sean Lennon

"People are always fascinated by infidelity because, in the end - whether we've had direct experience or not - there's part of you that knows there's absolutely no more piercing betrayal. People are undone by it."
Junot Diaz

The next day, Nicole texted me late at night and told me she wanted to sleep over again.

She knew that I was about to fly to Europe in a few days, to spend the holidays with my parents in Gemany.

George was at my house, and we were watching God Bless America, a dark, cynical satire about a man who is so fed up with how fucked up life in America is, he decides to become a serial killer. Great movie. I could relate.

I told George I would go pick up Nicole after the movie, but he told me not to keep her waiting, and he'd go along for the ride.

She was at the same house where she had done some tattoos in the last few days. At least that's what she said she did there. I asked her if it was ok, if George was going to come along. I didn't want her to ask me to go on some sort of drug run before we headed home. She said it was alright.

When we picked her up, George introduced himself. Nicole was very quiet. She was dope sick. She told me she needed to go pick up all her clothes at some shitty little motel in North Fort Myers. On our way there, Lucy texted her. She was at the same motel, and the owner was about to call the cops on her if she didn't leave.

Now Lucy was hiding behind a tall white fence at a neighboring trailer park. Nicole said Lucy was stranded, and we would have to give her a lift. George introduced himself again, when Lucy got into the car.

Lucy and I hadn't talked to each other in a few days again, because the last time we saw each other, we were supposed to have a talk to figure out what was going on between us, but she just handed me some tacos and she and Nicole disappeared into a hotel room where some guy was waiting to fuck them.

"Where do you want me to drop you off?" I asked Lucy.

"I have nowhere to go," she said quietly. She hadn't slept in days again.

Nicole and I gave each other a look. We both knew we couldn't just leave Lucy stranded in the hood.

"You want to come to my house?" I asked.

"Yeah, I do," she replied.

Then Lucy asked Nicole: "What are you gonna do at Oliver's house?"

"Hang out," Nicole replied.

George probably felt like he was still watching God Bless America.

By now Lucy knew that Nicole and I were hanging out together more often than she had previously known about, but she still didn't know the full extent of it. But George did.

On the way home, we had to make a few stops, so Nicole and Lucy could get some drugs, and then do their drugs in the restroom of a gas station. I was embarrassed. I didn't want George to see this. I didn't want him to look down on them, or think I'm crazy for hanging out with them. But it was probably too late for that already. I had told him so many crazy stories over the past year, he probably thought I was nuts.

He often laughed and said: "If I didn't know you, I would think you made this stuff up. But I know it's true. Your stories are just too crazy and complicated to be made up. If you ever write a book about this stuff, nobody is going to believe you."

George and I were waiting in the car, while Nicole and Lucy were in a restroom. I said: "Well, at least now you know Nicole and Lucy are real, and I didn't make them up."

He laughed. He knew how much I cared about both of them, and that they were aunt and niece, and that this night had just taken a bizarre turn.

"Looks like you're finally gonna have your first threesome tonight," he joked.

We had planned to finish watching God Bless America, but it was much later than expected when we arrived at my condo, so George went home.

Lucy said she finally wanted to see Beautiful Creatures. We had tried to watch the movie at least five times by now. Most recently with Jasmine. But once she smoked crack, Lucy could not concentrate on a movie. And she hated being around any kind of noise or music.

Nicole knew that since we were trying not to let Lucy know what was going on between us, of course Lucy would sleep in bed with me, like she was used to, and Nicole would have to sleep in the guest room. She really didn't like that idea. She didn't want me to be alone in bed with Lucy.

While Lucy was smoking crack in the bathroom, Nicole suggested: "Let's watch the movie in the bedroom. That way we can all lie in bed together, and when we fall asleep during the movie, it won't look weird that we're both sleeping in the same bed with you."

That sounded like a good plan. I figured Lucy could lie in the middle and she could cuddle up with me, and Nicole could cuddle up with her.

Every time Lucy wasn't looking, Nicole gave me a hug or a kiss and told me she loved me. We were sitting on the bed, waiting for Lucy to get out of the bathroom. We left a gap in the middle for her.

When she finally came into the bedroom, she gave Nicole a weird look and said: "What are you doing in Oliver's bed? That's my spot."

"I thought we could watch the movie in the bedroom," Nicole said.

"No, I want to watch the movie in the living room," Lucy replied. She was annoyed.

So we all went into the living room. We brought a bunch of blankets and pillows. Nicole and I sat down on the couch, but Lucy went back in the bathroom. Then she went to smoke a cigarette on the porch. Then she went into the bathroom again.

"This is never gonna happen," I said. "We have tried to watch this movie five times now. She just can't sit still long enough. She can't concentrate on anything other than drugs for even 5 minutes.

We ended up staying up all night. Lucy told me she hated her life and she wanted to get clean and come live with me. I felt bad talking about this stuff in front of Nicole. She didn't want Lucy to know anything, but at the same time she didn't want me and Lucy to get too close again.

It was 7 am, and now Lucy didn't want to go to sleep anymore, because she wanted to call detox at 9 am. So she decided to cook breakfast. Nicole felt that was her place. So they both ended up making a great breakfast together.

While I ran to Publix, to get some milk and bread, Nicole texted me: "Lucy just told me that she wants to be in a real relationship with you. She really has feelings for you." Nicole was getting irritated by how affectionate Lucy was acting towards me.

When I got back to the house, we had breakfast. Then they both called detox, because they had both promised me they would go to rehab. They planned on going together. Finally they were ready to get some sleep. It was about time. I hadn't slept all night, and I was dead tired. Unlike them, I didn't have any crack to keep me awake for days.

But instead of going to sleep, Lucy suddenly told me that she had run out of drugs, and now she wanted me to drive her all the way to the Howard Johnson, to get some more. Then Nicole said she wanted to pick up the rest of her clothes at the Knights Inn in North Fort Myers. This was gonna turn into one of those days again, where we drive around aimlessly for hours. I really couldn't deal with that right now. I was way too tired. But I drove them anyway.

Finally we were on the way back to my house, and we were gonna get some sleep. But now Lucy wanted to smoke her crack and shoot up before going to bed. Then she told me she wanted to have sex. I didn't know how to respond to that. On one hand I really wanted to have sex with her, but on the other hand I didn't want to hurt Nicole by sleeping with Lucy while they're both at my house.

Nicole was in the guest room, while Lucy and I were in my bedroom. I was in bed, and Lucy was standing by the sink in the bathroom that connects to my bedroom, doing drugs.

It must have driven Nicole crazy, that Lucy and I were in the bedroom together, with the door locked. I really felt bad.

Then Nicole texted Lucy, that she wanted me to drop her off at Lucy's grandfather's house.

Lucy said Nicole was lying. She really wanted to go on a Backpage date with some guy. I was really pissed. I texted Nicole: "I can't believe you're gonna go fuck someone else!"

Nicole yelled through the house: "What are you talking about? I'm not going on any calls! It's Lucy's call. It's her ad. She wanted me to do the call for her and give her part of the money, but I don't want to. So then Lucy said she's gonna do the call."

I looked at Lucy and said: "What the fuck? You're

408

gonna go fuck someone else? Lovely. Just grab your stuff, and I'll drive you to your fucking call. I'm so done with you."

She got upset that things between us were falling apart again already and screamed at Nicole: "THANKS A FUCKING LOT FOR RUINING EVERYTHING! Now I have to LEAVE again because of YOU!"

They were screaming at each other for a few minutes. Then Lucy came back in the bedroom and locked the door. She told me again that the reason why Nicole wanted me to drive her to North Fort Myers was to go do a Backpage date. Lucy told me to ignore Nicole: "If we lock the door, and pretend to be sleeping, she'll call someone else for a ride eventually."

Now that I knew Nicole was about to go fuck someone else, I figured I might as well have sex with Lucy. Why not?

Lucy stood in front of the bathroom sink naked. I was lying on the bed, rubbing my dick, watching her beautiful breasts while she smoked crack. I was probably gonna end up having to masturbate for an hour again, because she just couldn't stop smoking crack. I was getting really frustrated. She saw how hard I was, so she came out of the bathroom, gently grabbed my dick and sucked the head for a little while, to tease me. Then she smiled her little mischievous smile and went back in the bathroom to smoke more crack.

Nicole wouldn't stop calling our names. She wanted to go to North Fort Myers as soon as possible. She kept texting Lucy that she wanted to leave, and texted me: "Really?" As if to say: "I can't believe you're fucking her!"

That made me feel really guilty. I got dressed.

"What are you doing?" Lucy asked. She hadn't slept in days, and it was finally catching up with her. Her speech was slurred, and her eyes were rolling in the back of her head.

"Nicole isn't gonna stop, so why don't you get some sleep, and I'll drop her off at your grandpa's house. I'll be back as soon as possible."

"No! I don't want you to drive anywhere alone with her. I want to come with you," Lucy replied. She was probably afraid I'd have sex with Nicole.

I told her that she really needed some sleep, and that I was afraid if she'd take a ride, she'd just end up disappearing in some dope boy's dirty motel room again, and then I'd end up driving home without her.

"No," Lucy promised, "I won't do that. I'll just take a ride and after we drop Nicole off, we'll finally make love and get some sleep."

On the way to North Fort Myers, our destination suddenly changed. They were both frantically texting. Then Nicole said she wanted me to drop her off at the Knights Inn. So obviously Lucy had told me the truth about Nicole going to do a call instead of going to her grandpa's house.

Meanwhile they were both answering their phones with their hooker names. Later I found out that both had posted fresh escort ads on Backpage that morning. Now they were both going to do calls.

They answered their phones right in front of me, talking to guys about fucking them, and how much it costs for half an hour or an hour, and that they do full service. They told guys they were available for doubles.

They didn't even realize I was there. Their mind was on their next fix, and what they would have to do to get it. It did not register in their brains at all, how upsetting it was to me to listen to them make plans to fuck other guys. The part of their brains that felt empathy was turned off.

"You two are like braindead zombies," I said angrily.

They didn't care. They were busy making plans. Nothing else mattered.

When we arrived at the Knights Inn, Nicole got out of the car without saying good bye or thank you. She knew I was going to Germany the day after tomorrow, and she wouldn't see me again for a while, but none of that mattered right now. She had drugs on her mind. She disappeared in some dope boy's room. For a fee, he was letting girls like Lucy and Nicole use the room to have sex with guys, and he gave them drugs and took all their money. It was heartbreaking to watch Nicole walk off into that room.

Then Lucy said, "I just gotta grab something out of the room."

"What?" I asked.

"Hold on, I'll be right back," she said and jumped out of the car to follow Nicole.

"You're not coming back, are you?" I asked.

"Of course I am! It'll only take a minute. I'll be right back! Don't leave without me," Lucy said.

I waited 10 minutes. Then I texted Lucy: "Ur not gonna come out, r u?"

"No," was all she texted back.

I fucking knew it. I was so sick of this shit. I had enough. At first Lucy had seemed so different from Veronica, but then she turned out to be just like her. And Nicole seemed so different from girls like Veronica and Lucy, but then she became just like them, as her addiction got worse.

I couldn't take it anymore.

I texted Lucy: "I can't believe u did this to me again. I hope ur proud of urself. It breaks my heart to see u like this. Good luck with everything. Have a nice life."

As I slowly drove out of the parking lot at the Knights Inn, I also texted Nicole: "I'm sorry, but I can't be with a girl who tricks on Backpage. I can't handle when a girl I care about has sex with other people."

I really, really couldn't take it anymore. I felt like I was stuck in some sort of crazy loop, reliving the same painful moments over and over and over. This nightmare had to end.

I know, I've said that about a dozen times throughout this book. So many times, the rational part of me screamed that enough was enough, that I had to quit, that I didn't want to be hurt anymore, but then that other side of me ran right back to one of these drug addicted girls. To start the cycle of pain all over again.

The truth of the matter was, I was an addict every bit as much as they were. They were addicted to crack and heroin. I was addicted to addicts. Have you ever noticed that it's a lot easier to deal with someone else's problems than your own?

They took drugs to forget their shitty life for a little while. And I spent all my time with addicts, worrying about their problems instead of my own, to forget about my own shitty, lonely life.

And the more drugs they took, the shittier their life got. And the more time I spent around drug addicts, the shittier my own life got. I was so busy distracting myself from my own life and my own problems, I completely stopped caring about even the most basic things. I didn't even pay my bills anymore. I didn't open my mail for months. I had a pile of unopened mail about 10 inches high on the kitchen counter. Everything I did was all about some addict girl in my life. I did

413

nothing that was not somehow related to whoever I was "dating" at the time. I was severely codependent.

You might wonder: "If you were so unhappy, why the hell didn't you just stop doing what you were doing? Stay away from crackheads!"

Easier said than done. Ask an obese person why they don't just eat less if being fat makes them miserable. Or ask a smoker why they don't just quit. Or ask a heroin addict why they keep doing heroin if everything about the heroin-lifestyle makes them miserable.

Anyway, so I slowly pulled out of the parking lot. Once I got home, I took a bath for hours. That's what I do to hide from my life when I'm not busy running around with a drug addict. I did a lot of thinking in the tub that night. I decided to write a book about my experiences with addiction and addicts.

Mainly to process everything that had happened. I read that when you write stuff down, you don't think about it all the time anymore. And hopefully reading in black and white how badly my life was going would help me find the strength to end this chapter of my life.

And maybe my book could serve as a warning to others. Maybe someone will read this and learn from my mistakes. Maybe it will help someone else realize that they're stuck in the same self-destructive spiral and get out before it's too late. I like to think that I'm a fairly smart and rational guy. I never would have dreamed of ending up in this crazy situation. And yet, here I was, soaking in the tub for hours, hiding from the world, after not one but two crackheads had broken my heart. Again.

If everything you've read in this book so far sounds absolutely nuts to you, count your blessings. Because that means you have no experience with addiction. But if you or one of your loved ones has struggled with addiction, you recognize all these bizarre scenes I chronicled in this book, because chaos and insanity is normal, typical life for an addict. If you have never experienced this world yourself, you probably think I just made up a bunch of crazy shit to fill a book. But if you have struggled with addiction yourself, you know it's all true.

The next morning, while I was packing my bags for my Christmas trip to Germany, George called: "So what happened last night? Did you have a threesome with Lucy and Nicole?"

"No, actually I didn't have sex with either one of them," I replied.

He thought that was hilarious: "You had two beautiful girls spend the night at your house, you love both of them, and they both love you, and you didn't have sex with either one? You FAILED! I'm gonna have to revoke your man card."

"We were up all night, because they were doing drugs. And the next day they ditched me at the Knights Inn. It hurt so bad to see them walk into that motel room," I said.

In the afternoon, I got a text from Lucy: "I'm so sorry. I can't believe I did that to u. I don't even know what to say. Just... I'M SO SORRY."

I knew that whenever she had a lucid moment, she really did feel terrible about all the things she had done to me and other people. That's why she couldn't bear to be sober for even a minute. Her head was filled with painful thoughts and traumatic memories. The only way she could get through a day was by completely numbing her emotions with drugs, so she didn't have to think about anything.

Have you ever seen The Notebook? It's a movie about these two old people in a nursing home. A man reads an old lady a story from a handwritten notebook. It's a love story about a young couple. The old lady seems to remember the story, but isn't sure. It turns out she has Alzheimer's, and she was the one who wrote the story of how she and the old man had met. Her disease had progressed to the point where she didn't remember their life together, or even who he was. He was a complete stranger to her now. But every night, when he finished the story, she remembered him for a few minutes. For a few minutes each night, she came back to him, and she remembered how much she loved him. And then the fog took her away again.

That's how I feel about Lucy and Nicole. I love them. They're sweet, beautiful, lovable girls, who deserve all the love, kindness and affection in the world. And sometimes, for just a few minutes, they remember who they used to be. But then the drugs cloud their minds, and the fog takes them away again.

I really hoped they'd get help some day, before it's too late for them.

But I finally began to realize that I didn't have the power to help them. All this time, I was the victim of my savior complex. I thought if I could be someone else's knight in shining armor, I'd feel better about myself, and wouldn't think about how shitty my own life was.

I decided that my trip Germany, to spend Christmas with my parents, was going to be the end of my adventures in Fort Myers' underworld. Getting on the plane would be like me riding into the sunset, while the words THE END slowly scroll across the screen.

And it was perfect timing. It was the end of 2013, so my New Year's resolution for 2014 would be: NO MO HO! No more whores. I decided that I was never going to see them again, I wouldn't contact them, and I wouldn't even think about them anymore. This trip was going to be a clean break, I thought. The beginning of the next chapter of my life.

But the whole time I was in Germany, I kept thinking about Lucy and Nicole. Finally, after about a week, I checked Backpage. It was Christmas Morning. And there they were, posing semi-nude in a whole bunch of their escort ads, day after day, offering to have sex with any random stranger.

I messaged Nicole on Facebook: "Remember our conversation in the car a few weeks ago, when I told you, you wouldn't just fuck guys for a day or two to pay bills, but soon you would be doing it all day every day, and it would become your new life? See, I was right. It always starts like that. And are you happy with your life now? Are you happy living like this? Are you proud of yourself? I know you're not, sweetie. This isn't really you. Please stop. You're slowly killing yourself with this shit. And you're killing me, because I care about you, and I can't stand the thought of you doing this. You told me you are not the kind of girl who sleeps around. But now you spent Christmas Eve and Christmas morning letting pervs fuck you and sucking their dick. Did you ever think it would come to this?"

I think I wrote that more for me than for her.

Then I opened Microsoft Word and started typing. I didn't plan out the book. I just started typing, and it all came pouring out of me.

NO MO HO

*"Being a nice guy doesn't mean you are a push over.
It also doesn't mean you are easy to manipulate or
take advantage of. No, being a nice guy simply means
you care, have no time to get mad at the small stuff,
and you think of the world in larger terms than self.
And despite living in the shadow of the bad guys and
paying for mistakes you didn't make, you hold on
sometimes more than you should, but when you can
no longer, you move on because it's the right thing to
do."*
Eugene Nathaniel Butler

*"Letting go doesn't mean that you don't care about
someone anymore. It's just realizing that the only
person you really have control over is yourself."*
Deborah Reber

*"Some people believe holding on and hanging in
there are signs of great strength. However, there are
times when it takes much more strength to know when
to let go and then do it."*
Ann Landers

*"The truth is, unless you let go, unless you forgive
yourself, unless you forgive the situation, unless you
realize that the situation is over, you cannot move
forward."*
Steve Maraboli

"Pain will leave you, when you let go."
Jeremy Aldana

"The beautiful journey of today can only begin when we learn to let go of yesterday."
Steve Maraboli

*If you liked this book,
please remember to
rate it on Amazon.*

*Questions? Comments?
You can contact me at:
oliver.m.malloy@mail.com*

Find out how the story ends in the third and final book:

<u>Bad Choices Make Good Stories 3</u>
<u>Finding Happiness in Los Angeles</u>

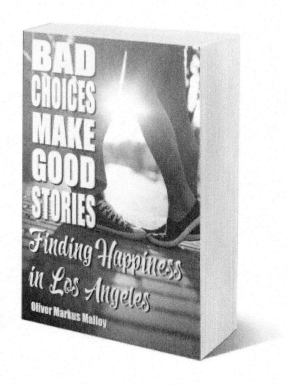

Now available at
<u>www.BadChoices.us</u>

CPSIA information can be obtained
at www.ICGtesting.com
Printed in the USA
LVOW13s1333160718
583919LV00020B/518/P